ALL-AMERICAN
COWBOY
COOKBOOK

ALL-AMERICAN
COWBOY
COOKBOOK

Home Cooking on the Range

Ken Beck & Jim Clark

Rutledge Hill Press®
Nashville, Tennessee

A Thomas Nelson Company

Published by Rutledge Hill Press, a Thomas Nelson Company, P.O. Box 141000, Nashville, Tennessee 37214.

Typography by D&T/Bailey Typesetting, Inc., Nashville, Tennessee
Design by Harriette Bateman

Library of Congress Cataloging-in-Publication Data

Beck, Ken, 1951–
    The all-American cowboy cookbook : home cooking on the range /
Ken Beck & Jim Clark.
      p. cm.
    Includes index.
    ISBN 1-55853-365-6
    1. Cookery. American—Western style. 2. Western films—United
States—Miscellanea. 3. Motion picture actors and actresses—United
States—Miscellanea. I. Clark, Jim, 1960–   . II. Title.
TX715.2.W47B43 1995
641.5978—dc20   95-24938
                                                                          CIP

Printed in the United States of America

8 9 10 11 12 13 14 15—05 04 03 02 01 00

To
the great American cowboy.
May he long ride the range.

BROCK TRUCKING
Rt. 1 Box 35
Littlefield, TX 79339

BROCK TRUCKING
Rt. 1 Box 35
Littlefield, TX 79339

BROCK TRUCKING
Rt. 1 Box 35
Littlefield, TX 79339

CONTENTS

COWBOY'S GRACE

Baxter Black

Dear Lord,

Yer lookin' at a man who never learned to cook,
*   unless you count pork and beans.*
And a flowery grace like you'd read in a book,
*   is really beyond my means.*

But you can believe I'm a thankful man
*   though it might be undeserved.*
And I'll eat whatever comes out of the pan,
*   no matter what's bein' served.*

I don't take it lightly if it's real good,
*   'cause I'd eat it anyway.*
See I know there's people, in all likelihood,
*   that might not eat today.*

So count me in if yer needin' grace said,
*   and bless those who provide it.*
The farmers and ranchers, the bakers of bread,
*   the loving hands that fried it.*

But most of all, Lord, we give thanks to You,
*   'cause we who work on the land,*
Know how much our harvest and bounty is due
*   to the gainful touch of Yer hand.*

So bless this food and the life we embrace,
*   and please forgive us our pride.*
When others with tables a-plenty say grace,
*   for what we've helped You provide.*

Copyright 1994, Baxter Black

A ROUND-UP OF APPLAUSE

Compiling this cookbook was a lot like trying to lasso a stray longhorn in the midst of a stampede along the Chisholm Trail. There were so many great cowboys and cowgirls we wanted to include. Just tracking down them or their families called for some experienced scouting.

Fortunately, we received a great deal of support from some mighty fine folks. First of all, we thank cowboy poet Baxter Black for his "Cowboy's Grace." Likewise, we're grateful to cowboy, actor, and western gentleman Ben Johnson for allowing this cookbook to be a part of his network of support for his Helping Hand program for children.

We of course thank all of the people who sent us recipes. Attributions accompany each recipe. (You'll also find a list of participating ranches and their addresses and phone numbers toward the back of the book. Try out their hospitality firsthand sometime!)

We simply couldn't have done this cookbook without the tremendous advice and help of Fred Goodwin, Steve Cox, Jesse Wayne, Linda Dotson and Sheb Wooley, Ray Nielsen, Rusty and Amy Richards, Hugh Waddell, Betty Hofer, and Buster Brown.

Others we would like to thank for providing suggestions and help in gathering recipes, photos, or other material are Mae Axton, George Lindsey, Dana Schneider, Kay West, Mary Sharp, Monty Hitchcock, Amanda Posey, Mary H. Moore, Karla Buhlman, Mary Ellis, Jenny Alford, Jane Hansen, Albert Culbreath, Penny Parsons, Sue Fawver, Ed Shipman, Anita Craighead, Milo Holt, Dale Warren, Stephanie Beck, Carroll Fisher, Suzanne Armistead, Steven Stevens, Brenda McClain, Les Leverett, Gigi Garner, Tim Ormond, Fred LaBour, Ms. Rory Calhoun, Evelyn Shriver, Judy Roberts, Peter McCrea, Mary Haines, Dana Sullivant, Robert K. Oermann, Melissa Roker, Lenore Haff, Ruth Ann Rowland, Chris Scott and Vicki Watson, Mrs. Marilyn Tucker, Marilyn Carey, Pilar Wayne, Mickey Willing, Dolphia Blocker, Justin Tubb, Mrs. Walter Brennan, Florence and Mike Brennan, Lydia King, Myrtis Butler, Kit McNear, Joanna Hale, Linda Layne Stone, Susan Sizemore, Ruth Dennett, Velma Spencer, Gretchen Carson, Jean De Rita, Peter Nash, Jim McBride, Mary Murphey, Marla Riggan, Rose Mary Grumley, Torrie Curtis, Mrs. Dale Robertson, Joni Hartman, Paula Szeigis, Wayne Perryman, Nikki Mitchell, Beverly Keel, Reno Cling, Jenny Bohler, Sally Blair, Frank Curry, Mrs. Elsie Frost, Cindy Lou Black, Mrs. Mel Blanc, Myrna Swenson, Ronnie Robbins, Shannon Waggoner, Laura Bates, Dusty Rogers, Gail Steagall, Amy Schweitzer, Shirley Brinegar, Alex Chachere, Esme Chamblee, Jane Stone, Tom Corrigan, Max Harrison, Ronnie Robbins, Lee Pfeiffer, Tim Lilley, Scott Whitfield, Alice Maltin, Packy Smith, Mary Scoggins, Stephanie Green, Becky Gilbert, Pamela Cooper, Terry Miller, Johanna Mitchell, Jessie Schmidt, Ray Kreutziger, Cecil Wrye, Kathy L'Amour, Melissa Mathews, Diane Malone Wills, Marilyn Tuttle, Karl Farr Jr., Lynn Farr, Lindalee Wakely, Bobbie Mileusnich, Tom Ritter, Rex Perry, Glenda Washam, Frank Sutherland, Drew White, Kathy Helms, Rhonda Revercomb, Neile Toffle, Terry McQueen, Vivian Gilley, Kate Haggerty, T. J. McFarland, and Berdee Holt.

And as always, we are most grateful for the patience and support of our families. The Texas/Oklahoma Kid (Ken) learned to eat like a cowboy by enjoying Mama Hazel Beck's home cooking. (And today, when he makes trips back home to visit his parents in North Little Rock, it would be a stretch to say he feels like "Arkansas Slim" when he leaves.) Ken's wife, Wendy, daughter, Kylie, and son, Cole, help Ken continue his hearty eatin' ways in Tennessee. Ken thanks all three for being his steady saddle pals during the long drive back to the ranch with this cookbook.

Jim was no stranger to plenty of good food while growing up in North Carolina and eating Okie Mom (Nancy) Clark's and Gramma (Tonya) Hamel's cooking. But it took moving to the Tennessee frontier for him to develop a heartfelt devotion to the splendors of the West. That's where he met Albuquerque native, wife Mary, who always seems to know just the right spice. All of the Albuquerque Ellises (Mary, Jim, Jane, and Robert) continue to further Jim's appreciation for the region's wonderful flavors.

Finally, we thank everyone at Rutledge Hill Press who has worked with us from the beginning of the drive out on the wide open range until we closed the gate on the corral. We tip our ten-gallons to high sheriff Larry Stone, trail boss Amy Lyles Wilson, wagonmaster Jennifer B. Greenstein, medicine man Bryan Curtis, designer Harriette Bateman, head cook Teri Mitchell, and all of the folks back at the Rutledge Hill ranch.

To all of these people who helped make this book happen, thanks from the rims of our cowboy hats to the spurs on our boots.

Now come and git it!

Gazing at the stars in this collage from *How the West Was Won,* see if you can spot Carroll Baker, Lee J. Cobb, Henry Fonda, Carolyn Jones, Karl Malden, Raymond Massey, Gregory Peck, George Peppard, Robert Preston, Debbie Reynolds, Thelma Ritter, James Stewart, Eli Wallach, John Wayne, and Richard Widmark.

INTRODUCTION

If all the world's a stage, the American cowboy is perhaps its most legendary rider. The image of the cowboy has been revered and romanticized for generations by people all over the world.

The American cowboy is admired for his rugged self-reliance, his commonsense approach to justice and fair play, his agile roping and horsemanship, and his skillful use of firearms—all of which make for a mighty hearty appetite!

And, boy howdy, that's where this book comes in. We've set out to round up some of the most delicious recipes from some of the best western cooks and best-known cowboys in the land.

This is a complete cookbook, from appetizers to desserts and everything in between. These are the favorite foods of all your favorite cowboys—from Silver Screen idols like Gene Autry, Roy Rogers, and Randolph Scott, to TV legends like James Garner, Chuck Connors, and Dale Robertson (not to mention Yosemite Sam!), to singing cowboys like Bob Wills, Tex Ritter, and George Strait, and even the "Cowboy's Sweetheart," Patsy Montana.

We've also lassoed recipes from world champion rodeo cowboys like Jim Shoulders, Larry Mahan, Roy Cooper, and Ty Murray, plus Miss Rodeo USA for 1994, Lucynda Hendricks. In addition, more than two dozen working and guest ranches across the West contributed some of their favorite dishes.

And that's not all. You'll find a few more surprises as we stretch the boundaries to recognize the cowboy spirit in folks like Gen. Chuck Yeager and stock car legend Richard Petty. And what would a cowboy cookbook be without a Dallas Cowboy or two? (Look for terrific recipes from Troy Aikman and Jay Novacek.)

All in all, we've rounded up well over three hundred recipes from more than two hundred folks who represent what it means to be a cowboy. We've included most all of the cowboy foods you might expect—lots of meat and potatoes and cornbread, plus an entire section of nothing but chilis. Then again, don't say we didn't warn you when your taste buds are pleasantly ambushed by some delicious surprises like amaretto cheesecake.

In addition to all of the great recipes in *The All-American Cowboy Cookbook*, we wanted the book to have the look and feel of the Old West. So, we've corralled the spirit of the West through photographs of beloved cowboy legends of today and yesteryear. We've included a variety of lists, quizzes, and other tidbits of cowboy information throughout the book in hopes that they'll make this cookbook as tempting for reading as it is for cooking.

Finally, we're pleased to say that a portion of royalties from the sale *of The All-American Cowboy Cookbook* is supporting Ben Johnson's Helping Hand program in its various projects working with children. (The program's current efforts are assisting the Sunshine Home for children in Mesa, Arizona.) We're happy that this book is able to contribute to this project because, well, it just seems like the Cowboy Way.

Anyway, pardners, the table's all set and the coffee's brewing, so get ready to help yourself to some hearty all-American cowboy fare.

Happy meals to you!

Hungry Hombres—Jack Elam, Ernest Borgnine, and Strother Martin (left-right) look hungry enough to eat a horse as they play bank robbers in the 1972 western *Hannie Caulder.*

MENUS

These sample menus use some of the recipes in this cookbook. These menus are intended to be a starting point for developing your own combinations of meals from the favorite cowboy fixin's featured throughout this book.

Ranch Favorites

Recipes from ranches

Susan's Broccoli Salad, p. 37
Sheepherder's Bread, p. 201
Gallopin' Scallopin' Potatoes, p. 51
Diana's Spiced Roast Beef, p. 125
Corral Caramel Dumplings, p. 240
Cowboy Spurs, p. 229
Coffee

Sing for Your Supper

Recipes from cowboy singers

Red's Eight-Layer Dip, p. 21
Boomtown Broccoli and Rice Casserole, p. 53
Ranch Biscuits, p. 201, or San Antonio Rose Cornbread, p. 193
Shalom's Pork Chops, p. 145
Cowgirl's Lemon Poppy Seed Pound Cake, p. 211
Coffee or tea

Tex-Mex Feast

Tortilla chips
Mickey's Pico de Gallo, p. 183
Wind River Chili Con Queso, p. 183
Red's Eight-Layer Dip, p. 21
Pancho Villa's Corn Soup with Cheese and Chilies, p. 70
Great Southwest Beef Enchiladas, p. 136
Gilley's Fajitas, p. 136
Santa Fe Trail Quesadillas, p. 153
Subrosa Chilies Rellenos, p. 162
Mother's Lemon Pie , p. 223
Pancho's Margarita Villa Punch, p. 31

Slim Pickens

Vegetarian meal

Dep'ty Dawg's Sweet and Sour Tofu with Vegetables, p. 59
Jackpot Grilled Vegetables, p. 62
Montana Cream Cheese Patties, p. 161
King Richard's Angel Food Cake, p. 212
Gold Rushin' Tea, p. 30

Fourth of July Picnic

Amos Tucker's Chicory and Kidney Bean Salad, p. 38
Sky Blue Cornbread, p. 191
Papa Roy's Baked Beans, p. 44
Rusty Old Halos, p. 51
Ranch Burgers, p. 135, or Big Timber Sloppy Joes, p. 139
Bull's-Eye Creamy Banana Pudding, p. 233
Billy the Kid's Brownies, p. 227
Frost's Best Homemade Ice Cream, p. 233
Fresh watermelon slices
Long, Tall Drink of Lemonade, p. 33

Spaghetti Western Dinner

Clint Eastwood's Spaghetti Western, p. 128
Tossed salad
Pony Express Poppy Seed Bread , p. 209
Cattle Call Coconut Cream Pie, p. 226
Iced tea

On the Trail

Wyoming Jerky, p. 22
Grandmother's 1880 Cornbread, p. 195
Strait-Shootin' Spanish Rice, p. 53, or Papa Roy's Baked Beans, p. 44
Campfire Cob Corn and Taters, p. 47
Campfire Quail, p. 149
Wind and the Wire Oatmeal Cookies, p. 228
Coffee

High Noon Chili Duel

Ernie's Tex Chili, p. 87   vs.   Johnny Cash's "Old Iron Pot" Family-Style Chili, p. 96

Tossed salad		Tossed salad
Cody Sweet Cornbread, p. 191		Oklahoma Cornbread, p. 194
Appaloosa Applesauce Cake, p. 210		Shoot 'Em Up 7-Up Cake, p. 215
Coffee		Iced tea

Gary Cooper and Grace Kelly in the timeless western classic *High Noon*

Wishful thinking:

"I'm not trying to be a hero. If you think I like this, you're crazy. Look, Amy, this is my town and I've got friends here. I'll swear in a bunch of special deputies and with a posse behind me, maybe there won't even be any trouble."—Gary Cooper to Grace Kelly in *High Noon*

Fantastic Fish Fiesta

Hoss's Cajun Gumbo, p. 64
South Dakota Sourdough Fry-Bread, p. 205
Johnny Western Green Bean Casserole, p. 48
Big Reward Green Rice, p. 56
Smiley's Corn and Salmon Loaf, p. 107, or Tracy Byrd's Beer-Battered Bass, p. 157
T Cross Mile-High Pie, p. 223
Iced tea

Cowboy Barbecue

Tortilla Pinwheels, p. 28
Humpty-Dumpty Heart Mexican Cornbread, p. 196
Cowboy Corn Salad, p. 49
Okie Dokie Sliced Baked Potatoes, p. 51
Boston Baked Beans Brennan, p. 43
Long X Ranch Prime Rib, p. 126
Bunkhouse Buttermilk Pie, p. 223
Coffee or tea

Wild Brunch for a Bunch

Rustlers Raspberry Gelatin Salad, p. 41
Haywire Hash Brown Potato Casserole, p. 59
Scone, Scone on the Range, p. 202, or Cowboy Biscuits, p. 202
Bar H Bar Hot Chicken Salad, p. 48
Rise 'N' Shine Breakfast Burrito, p. 170
Country Breakfast Pie, p. 172, or Easy Overnight Breakfast, p. 175
Horse Wranglers Scrambled Breakfast, p. 177
Miss Rodeo USA's Chocolate Amaretto Cheesecake, p. 238
Fruit juices
Gold Rushin' Tea, p. 30
Coffee

Chow Wagon Dinner

Pee Wee's Rounded Cheese Tee Pee, p. 24
Leon's Easy Fried Cabbage, p. 44
Cheyenne Chicken Fried Steak, p. 120
Charlie's Great Chocolate Cake, p. 213
Coffee or tea

Holiday Bonanza

Holiday Bonanza—The Cartwrights (left to right), Adam (Pernell Roberts), Ben (Lorne Greene), Hoss (Dan Blocker), and Little Joe (Michael Landon) share a song for the Yuletide season before pitching into a Christmas feast prepared by Hop Sing.

Clint Eastwood and Sheb Wooley—*Rawhide* partners

APPETIZERS

THE FRONTIER

RED'S EIGHT-LAYER DIP

1   16-ounce can jalapeño re-fried beans
1   teaspoon cumin, divided
1   teaspoon garlic powder, divided
6   avocados
    Juice of ½ lemon
½   cup picante sauce
    Salt
1   cup sour cream
1   cup real mayonnaise
1   1¼-ounce package taco seasoning
1   bunch green onions, chopped
1   tomato, chopped
1   4.5-ounce can chopped green chilies
2   cups shredded colby cheese
1   2.25-ounce can chopped black olives

Layer 1: In a small mixing bowl, blend beans with ½ teaspoon cumin and ½ teaspoon garlic powder (add a little picante sauce if needed to make it spreadable).

Layer 2: Peel and seed avocados into a separate bowl. Mash well. Add lemon juice, ½ teaspoon cumin, ½ teaspoon garlic powder, picante sauce, and salt to taste. Blend thoroughly.

Layer 3: Mix sour cream, mayonnaise, and taco seasoning in a separate bowl.
Layer 4: Chopped onions
Layer 5: Chopped tomato
Layer 6: Chilies
Layer 7: Cheese
Layer 8: Black olives
Using a 9x3-inch glass dish or a large plate, spread layer 1 evenly to form base.

Next spread avocado mixture over entire surface of beans, then add sour cream mixture. Sprinkle layers 4, 5, and 6 in any order, using as little or as much as your taste dictates. Generously cover with layer 7, cheese, finishing with layer 8, the black olives, for garnish.

Note: This could be a 5-, 6-, 7-, 8-, or 9-layer dip depending on your own taste and imagination. Play with it and listen to the raves from your party guests.

Makes 15 to 20 servings.

Red Steagall, singer

The first train robbery in the United States was committed on October 6, 1866, by the Reno Brothers (John, Frank, Simeon, and William) near Seymour, Indiana. Three of the brothers were lynched by vigilantes in New Albany, Indiana, in 1868.

WYOMING JERKY

Rawhide!

1   large roast (elk, deer, moose, or any red meat)
4   tablespoons Colgin liquid smoke
3   tablespoons soy sauce
⅓   cup packed brown sugar
2   teaspoons Lawry's seasoned salt
    Pepper to taste
½   cup water, or more, to cover meat

Slice meat evenly and thinly (it's easier to slice when partially frozen). Cutting across the grain will make the meat easier to chew. Combine all ingredients and mix well. Marinate for 24 hours or more, stirring occasionally. Well-marinated meat will lose all pink color. Dry in a dehydrator or dry in the oven for approximately 6 hours on lowest setting, with the door slightly ajar. Turn once after a couple of hours.

Mary Allen, Allen's Diamond Four Ranch Lander, Wyoming

EIGHT SECONDS LAYERED NACHO DIP

Everyone will eat seconds!

1   16-ounce can re-fried beans
½   a 1¼-ounce package taco seasoning mix
1   6-ounce carton avocado dip (or make your own by mixing mashed avocado, mayonnaise, and lemon juice)
1   8-ounce carton sour cream
1   4½-ounce can chopped ripe olives (optional)
2   large tomatoes, diced
1   small onion, finely chopped
1½ cups shredded Monterey Jack cheese
    Corn chips

Combine beans and seasoning mix; spread bean mixture evenly into a 12x8x2-inch dish. Layer remaining ingredients in order. Serve with large corn chips.
    Makes 10 servings.

Jim Shoulders, rodeo champion

During the 1950s and 1960s, Jim Shoulders was one of pro rodeo's top stars. He earned sixteen world champion titles, more than any other rodeo cowboy—including seven bull riding and five all-around cowboy titles.

DOC HOLLIDAY'S SPINACH AND ARTICHOKE DIP

You'll fall for this one.

2   1½-pound round loaves sourdough bread (cut up 1, leave 1 whole)
1   16-ounce carton light sour cream
1   1-ounce envelope Hidden Valley Ranch party dip mix
1   14-ounce can artichoke hearts, rinsed, drained, and chopped
1   10-ounce package frozen chopped spinach, drained
1   2-ounce jar diced pimientos, rinsed and drained
    Assorted vegetables, cut up (optional)

Combine sour cream and dip mix in a medium bowl. Add the artichoke hearts, spinach, and pimientos. Cut slice off top of 1 loaf of bread. Hollow out center of bread, leaving a 1-inch shell. Reserve bread pieces for dipping. Spoon dip into bread shell. Serve warm or cold. To serve warm, bake in preheated 400° oven for 20 to 25 minutes. Cover loaf with foil if it browns too quickly. Serve with bread cubes or assorted vegetables for dipping.

Makes about 12 servings.

Donna Hall, stuntwoman

GO WEST GUACAMOLE

1   cup mashed ripe avocado
1   tablespoon lemon juice
1   teaspoon salt
¼   teaspoon chili powder
⅓   cup mayonnaise
    Corn chips

Combine avocado, lemon juice, salt, and chili powder. Blend in mayonnaise. Serve with corn chips.

Makes 1⅓ cups.

Foy Willing, Riders of the Purple Sage

HOMER'S VENISON JERKY

3   pounds venison, cut into ¼-inch-thick strips
1   teaspoon Lawry's seasoned salt
1   teaspoon black pepper
1   teaspoon cracked red pepper
½   cup soy sauce
4   tablespoons liquid smoke (optional)
2   tablespoons monosodium glutamate (can use saltpeter)
1   teaspoon garlic powder
1   teaspoon onion powder
½   cup Worcestershire sauce

Mix all ingredients well. Marinate the meat for 24 hours, turning over at least once. Remove the meat and allow to drain. Place in a dehydrator for approximately 24 hours or until the jerky is suitably dry. Or, use the oven on lowest setting with the door ajar and the meat placed on a rack for approximately 8 hours.

Makes 12 to 16 servings.

Carol and Bob Steinruck, Lazy Hills Ranch Ingram, Texas

Back in the 1950s, Hollywood folks in the know considered the four fastest draws of the cowboy actors to be Ben Cooper, Dale Robertson, Rory Calhoun, and World War II hero-turned-screen cowboy Audie Murphy. In fact, Murphy may well have been Hollywood's top fast-draw expert, and actor Hugh O'Brian was always wanting to test him out one on one. Murphy always refused. Finally, Murphy agreed to a contest but only by his rules. "I'll tell you what. You get real bullets in your gun and I'll get real bullets in mine, and we'll have a go at it. What'ya say?" And that was the end of that.

Pee Wee King and his Golden West Cowboys joined the Grand Ole Opry in 1937. They specialized in western swing and cowboy ballads. Pee Wee co-wrote the classic "Tennessee Waltz," and he appeared in several films starring Gene Autry and Charles Starrett.

WYOMING SPREAD HOT SPINACH DIP

- 2 tablespoons pure olive oil
- ½ teaspoon dried basil leaves
- ½ teaspoon dried thyme leaves
   Salt and pepper to taste
- ½ cup minced shallots
- 2 tablespoons minced garlic
- 2 bunches fresh spinach, chopped
- 1 8-ounce package light cream cheese, softened to room temperature
- ¾ cup low-fat ricotta cheese
- 1 cup tomatoes, peeled, seeded, and chopped
   Parmesan cheese
   Toast wedges or crackers

Preheat the oven to 350°. Heat oil in a skillet. Add basil, thyme, salt, and pepper and stir to infuse these flavors in the oil. Sauté shallots and garlic for 30 seconds. Add spinach and cook until leaves are wilted, about 5 minutes. Remove from heat. Beat cream cheese and ricotta together and then fold into the spinach mixture. Adjust seasoning if needed. Spread into a 9-inch ovenproof dish and bake for 20 minutes. Top with tomatoes and Parmesan. Bake for 5 more minutes. Serve with toast wedges or crackers.

Makes 20 servings.

Breteche Creek Ranch
Cody, Wyoming

PEE WEE'S ROUNDED CHEESE TEE PEE

- 8 ounces bleu cheese, softened to room temperature
- 3 8-ounce packages cream cheese, softened to room temperature
- 1 jar Old English cheese, softened to room temperature
- 2 tablespoons Worcestershire sauce
- 1 cup ground pecans
- 1 small onion, grated
- 1 cup diced dried parsley or fresh parsley

Mix the first six ingredients well. Divide and shape into balls and roll in parsley. May be frozen.

Makes 2 large or 4 small cheese balls.

Pee Wee King, singer/songwriter

Clark McEntire was the Pro Rodeo Cowboy Association's world steer-roping champion in 1957, 1958, and 1961. He and wife Jackie are the parents of Alice Foran and of country singers Susie Luchsinger, Pake McEntire, and Reba McEntire.

McENTIRE RANCH MOUNTAIN OYSTERS

½ cup cornmeal
½ cup flour
  Light beer
  Salt
  Pepper
  Garlic powder
  Mountain Oysters (fresh, not frozen, are best)
  Vegetable oil

Make the batter by combining the cornmeal, flour, and beer. Season with salt, pepper, and garlic powder to taste. Slice the oysters about ¼ inch thick. Dip in the batter. Cook in hot oil until medium crisp. Best to serve while hot. Enjoy!

Jackie and Clark McEntire, rodeo cowboy

MARSHAL'S MARINATED MUSHROOMS

1 hard-boiled egg yolk, mashed
½ cup malt vinegar
⅛ cup vegetable oil
1 teaspoon salt
½ teaspoon pepper
2 teaspoons chopped parsley
2 teaspoons prepared mustard
1 teaspoon garlic powder
1 teaspoon onion powder
1 tablespoon plus 2 teaspoons brown sugar
1 pound fresh mushrooms (small or medium)

Combine all ingredients except mushrooms in a saucepan. Bring to a boil. Add mushrooms. Cover and let boil for exactly 5 minutes, stirring occasionally. Remove from heat immediately and put in a quart jar. When cool, refrigerate overnight.
  Makes 1 quart.

Torrie and Ken Curtis, actor and singer

Sons of the Pioneers in 1951—(clockwise from top) Tommy Doss, Karl Farr, Lloyd Perryman, Shug Fisher, Hugh Farr, and Ken Curtis

WILD 'N' WOOLEY ARMADILLO EGGS

Breading mix (can use ready-made type for onion rings, etc.)
1 teaspoon garlic powder
1 tablespoon sugar (optional)
¼ teaspoon black pepper
¼ teaspoon cayenne pepper
¼ cup minced onion
1 cup shredded sharp Cheddar cheese
1 cup shredded Monterey Jack cheese
¼ cup minced parsley
1 egg
1 dozen fat, small jalapeño peppers (for hot version) or 1 dozen fat, small banana peppers (for milder version)
Vegetable oil

Mix your preferred breading mix with the garlic powder, sugar, and pepper (black and cayenne). In a separate bowl, mix minced onion, cheeses, and parsley. Beat the egg in a separate bowl. Wash, core, and seed the peppers, leaving them whole (open only the very tops for seeding). Dip the peppers in the beaten egg, then stuff with the cheese mixture. Pack firmly. Dip stuffed peppers again in egg and roll in the breading. Deep fry in vegetable oil until golden brown. Serve while hot. You may want to prepare more than one dozen initially—they're good! Great snack with a nice picante sauce or honey mustard dip. Enjoy!
Makes 6 servings (2 peppers each).

Sheb Wooley, actor and singer/songwriter

GUNSMOKE STUFFED MUSHROOMS

Cap guns.

1 pound large mushrooms
1 stick margarine
¼ cup chopped onions
1 garlic clove, minced
½ teaspoon dried oregano
1 tablespoon chopped parsley
½ teaspoon salt
1 egg, beaten
2 tablespoons Parmesan cheese
Fresh ground pepper
½ cup crushed, seasoned croutons
1 4½-ounce can deviled ham
1 8-ounce can water chestnuts, chopped

Remove stems from mushrooms and chop. Melt the margarine in a skillet. Add mushroom caps and stir to coat. Remove. Add chopped mushrooms, onions, and garlic. Cook over low heat until pulpy, about 10 minutes. Preheat the oven to 325°. Mix all the remaining ingredients, then add the chopped stems. Mix well. Stuff the caps with mixture. Bake for 30 minutes. Enjoy this with a green salad.
Makes 8 to 10 servings.

Torrie and Ken Curtis, actor and singer

SAWTOOTH BAKED BRIE WITH RASPBERRY CHUTNEY

6 cups frozen raspberries
1 tablespoon lemon zest
1 cup raisins
2 to 3 cinnamon sticks
1 cup water
1 cup vinegar
¾ cup honey
1 teaspoon soy sauce
1 tablespoon cracked pepper
1 cup chopped celery
½ cup minced green onions
2 to 4 wedges Brie cheese
2 eggs
2 tablespoons milk
2 cups ground walnuts or hazelnuts
Vegetable cooking spray

Combine all ingredients except nuts, eggs, milk, and Brie in a small stockpot or pan. Cook over low to medium-low heat for 2 to 4 hours or until thickened (should be the consistency of preserves). Watch carefully and stir occasionally to prevent scorching. Whisk eggs with milk until blended, and pour into a wide, shallow dish into which the Brie wedges can be dipped easily. Spread ground nuts on a plate. Dip each wedge of Brie into egg and cover evenly. Dredge Brie in the ground nuts, being sure to pat sides and top with nuts. Set each piece aside. If you are preparing more than one wedge of Brie it is best to wrap each piece of nut-covered Brie in plastic wrap and chill until needed. Chutney and Brie can be refrigerated for a week or so.

To serve, preheat the oven to 375°. Place Brie on a pie plate sprayed with vegetable cooking spray and bake for 10 to 15 minutes or just until sides start to melt. Remove from the oven and place on a warm plate spread with heated chutney. Serve with assorted crackers or crusty French bread.

Makes 8 servings.

Jeana Leavell, Idaho Rocky Mountain Ranch
Stanley, Idaho

SOUTHWEST SPICY DRUMSTICKS

12 chicken drumsticks
2 tablespoons chili powder (chavmo)
2 tablespoons cumin powder
1 tablespoon vegetable oil
1 medium onion, quartered and separated
4 ounces chipotle in adobe chili pepper
3 serrano chili peppers
3 garlic cloves
6 ounces fresh orange juice
    Chopped cilantro to taste
1 cup plain yogurt
    Hot, cooked rice

Preheat the oven to 400°. Coat drumsticks with chili powder and cumin. Place in skillet with oil and onion. Brown lightly, being careful not to burn spices. Add chipotle, serrano, garlic, and orange juice. Place in ovenproof dish and bake until tender, about 45 minutes. Remove drumsticks to platter. Strain sauce remaining in dish and place in saucepan. Heat until warm. Remove from heat and add cilantro and yogurt, off heat to avoid yogurt separating. Pour over drumsticks. Serve with rice and lots of sauce.

Makes 6 servings (2 drumsticks each).

Mike Pawlick, Cibolo Creek Ranch
Shafter, Texas

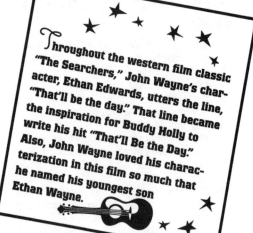

Throughout the western film classic "The Searchers," John Wayne's character, Ethan Edwards, utters the line, "That'll be the day." That line became the inspiration for Buddy Holly to write his hit "That'll Be the Day." Also, John Wayne loved his characterization in this film so much that he named his youngest son Ethan Wayne.

TORTILLA PINWHEELS

8 ounces cream cheese, softened to room temperature
8 ounces sour cream
4 ounces mild green chilies, chopped
4 ounces black olives, chopped
1 cup shredded Cheddar cheese
½ cup chopped onions
½ teaspoon garlic salt
5 10-inch flour tortillas
    Mild salsa

Mix all ingredients except tortillas and salsa. Chill slightly. Spread on tortillas (do not spread to one edge of each tortilla). Roll up and cover with a damp towel. Chill until ready to serve. Cut into 1-inch pieces. Serve with mild salsa.

Makes 50 pinwheels.

Dorothy and Lavon Shearer, Western Dakota Ranch Vacations
Wall, South Dakota

CARSON'S CITY HERB COCKTAIL CRACKERS

1 cup vegetable oil
1 teaspoon dried dill weed
½ teaspoon garlic
1 package ranch salad dressing mix
24 ounces oyster crackers

Mix oil, dill, garlic, and dressing in a small bowl. Pour over oyster crackers. Mix well and let sit for 1 hour. Store in a sealed bowl to keep fresh. Shake well before serving.

Makes approximately 10 to 12 servings.

Ken Carson, Sons of the Pioneers

WILD WEST WALLA WALLA ONION TART

- ¾   cup warm water
- 1   ¼-ounce package active dry yeast
- 2   cups all-purpose flour, divided
- 1¼ teaspoons salt
- 1   large egg
- ⅛   cup pure olive oil, divided
- 4   large Walla Walla onions (Vidalia work well, too)
- ⅛   cup chopped fresh herbs (rosemary, thyme, and oregano)
     Fresh ground black pepper
- ¼   cup minced garlic

Dough:

Put warm water in a measuring cup and add yeast. Set aside for 5 minutes. While yeast is proofing, sift 1⅔ cups flour and ¼ teaspoon salt together and stir. Make a well in the center, then pour in the proofed yeast. Crack the egg into the center of the well. With a fork, start slowly stirring wet ingredients in the middle, gradually incorporating the dry ingredients into the wet ingredients. Turn onto a floured surface, knead in last ⅓ cup flour, and continue kneading for about 5 minutes to get a smooth, satiny finish. Coat the dough with ⅛ cup oil and rub dough around the bowl to coat. Drape a clean, wet dishtowel over the bowl and put in a warm place to rise until doubled in bulk, about 45 minutes for quick-rising yeast, 1½ hours for regular yeast.

Caramelized Onion Topping:

Peel onions and cut in half, then slice thinly into half-rounds. Heat a 12-inch sauté pan, then add ¼ cup oil. Add herbs and salt and cook over low heat for about 5 minutes. Add onions and pepper and stir to coat. Cover with a circle of wax paper, cut to fit inside the pan and with a hole cut in the center. (This will allow the onions to "sweat" while trapping the moisture; the onions will become soft and limp without browning.) Cook over low heat for about 15 minutes. Add minced garlic and cook for another 15 minutes, stirring every 10 minutes or so.

Assembling the Tart:

Turn risen dough onto an ungreased cookie sheet and press out with fingertips until the dough meets the edges of the pan. Turn onions onto dough and distribute evenly, leaving a quarter-inch border. Set aside to rest and rise for 30 minutes if using quick-rising yeast, 1 hour for regular yeast. Preheat the oven to 350°. Bake for about 40 minutes or until brown on edges. Let rest for 5 minutes. Cut into squares and serve warm as an appetizer, or with a green salad as a luncheon dish.

Makes 6 to 8 servings.

Breteche Creek Ranch
Cody, Wyoming

WATERING HOLE

TEX MALTIN'S CANTALOUPE PUNCH

A reel cool drink.

1   cantaloupe
2½ cups water
3   tablespoons sugar

Cut the cantaloupe in half and spoon out the seeds. Scoop out cantaloupe into a blender. Place 1½ cups water in the blender, then add sugar. Blend on HIGH for 20 seconds. Pour 1 cup water into a pitcher. Pour blended cantaloupe into the pitcher and mix, adding 9 ice cubes.

Makes 40 ounces (not including volume of ice cubes).

Leonard Maltin, film critic and western movie fan

GOLD RUSHIN' TEA

1   cup lemon-flavored iced tea mix
3   tablespoons Tang orange-flavored drink
    mix
1   tablespoon allspice
1   teaspoon cinnamon
1   teaspoon nutmeg
1   ½-ounce package lemonade mix

Mix and store in an airtight container. Use 1¼ teaspoons per cup of hot water.

Leonard Maltin's FAVORITE WESTERNS

The first westerns I saw and loved, as a boy, were the TV episodes of *The Roy Rogers/Dale Evans Show.* My interest in westerns—and the American West—was only rekindled in recent years; now I'm hooked for life. I regret that I couldn't include some of those TV episodes here. I still love 'em, along with so many of the Saturday matinee films of Hopalong Cassidy and Gene Autry. Here are my favorite "adult" westerns.

Hell's Wings (1916), with Williarm S. Hart
Three Bad Men (1926) directed by John Ford
The Big Trail (1930) directed by Raoul
    Walsh, with John Wayne
Stagecoach (1939) directed by John Ford,
    with John Wayne
Destry Rides Again (1939) directed by
    George Marshall, with James Stewart
    and Marlene Dietrich
My Darling Clementine (1946) directed by
    John Ford, with Henry Fonda
High Noon (1952) directed by Fred
    Zinneman, with Gary Cooper
The Searchers (1956) directed by John Ford,
    with John Wayne
Ride the High Country (1962) directed by
    Sam Peckinpah, with Joel McCrea and
    Randolph Scott
High Plains Drifter (1973) directed by and
    starring Clint Eastwood

Happy Smiles to You—Leonard "Tex" Maltin enjoys a visit with cowboy idol Roy Rogers. (Courtesy of Leonard Maltin)

PANCHO'S MARGARITA VILLA PUNCH

1 12-ounce can frozen lemonade concentrate, thawed
1 12-ounce can frozen limeade concentrate, thawed
1 cup confectioners' sugar
5 egg whites
6 cups crushed ice
4 cups club soda
   Lime slices
   Coarse salt

In a 1-gallon, nonmetal container, combine juice concentrates, sugar, egg whites, and crushed ice. Mix well. Cover and freeze. Stir periodically. Remove from freezer about 30 minutes before serving. Spoon 2 cups of mixture into a blender and add 1 cup club soda. Blend until frothy. To serve, rub rim of glass with a lime slice and twist rim gently in the salt. Fill glass and garnish with lime slices.

Makes 24 servings.

MEXICALI HOT CHOCOLATE

Loco cocoa.

¼ cup cocoa
¼ cup sugar
½ teaspoon cinnamon
   Pinch of salt
3 cups milk, divided
1 cup half and half
1 teaspoon vanilla extract
   Whipped cream
   Cinnamon sticks
   Dash of nutmeg

In a large saucepan, over low heat, combine cocoa, sugar, cinnamon, salt, and 1 cup milk. Mix until smooth. Bring to a light simmer and add remaining milk, half and half, and vanilla. Heat through. Remove from heat and beat until frothy. Serve in mugs. Top with whipped cream and nutmeg; add cinnamon sticks for stirring.

Makes 6 servings.

REAL COWBOY COFFEE

Recycle your gallon coffee cans, punch holes in the tops, and thread stout wires for your handles. Bring fresh, not cow track vintage, water to boil, and add three ladles, or two man-size handfuls of grounds, to water. When she boils up again, settle the grounds with a cup of cold water or a couple of cackleberry shells. When we're lying with our heads on our saddles contemplating the Big Dipper, we've made this brew with fresh ground beans carried from home. Think you deserve the best, too?

Hargrave Cattle and Guest Ranch
Marion, Montana

The Ponderosa's Favorite Cook—Hop Sing (Victor Sen Yung). (Courtesy of Steve Cox Collection)

MAUI MONTANA DRINK MIX

Cranberry juice
Multi-fruit juice
Lemonade
Powdered fruit drink, mixed according to package directions
Orange juice
Apple juice

Take your pick and combine and chill any of the juices. Just before serving add any of the following: sparkling wines, ginger ale, carbonated soft drink, or orange or lime sherbet. Serve in your best washtub. Freeze any of the juices, adding such edible flowers as rose buds or violets (add as a chunk to keep brew chilled over time). For special wingdings, a chunk of dry ice will keep the children staring at the mystery smoke until Uncle Joe comes over and gives a plausible explanation, sort of.

Hargrave Cattle and Guest Ranch
Marion, Montana

Here's a recipe for cowboy coffee: Take a pound of coffee, add water, boil for half an hour. Throw in a horseshoe; if it sinks add more coffee.

ED BRUCE'S BLOODY MARY

Longbranch brunch favorite.

1   cup Clamato juice
1   shot vodka (or 2, depending on the size of your headache)
½   teaspoon horseradish
½   teaspoon Worcestershire sauce
3   dashes of celery salt
⅛   teaspoon black pepper
⅛   teaspoon lemon juice
⅛   teaspoon Tabasco sauce

Combine all ingredients well.
   Makes 1 serving.

Ed Bruce, singer/songwriter and actor

TEN-GALLON TEA PUNCH

¾   cup instant tea powder
1   quart cranberry juice cocktail, chilled
2   6-ounce cans frozen orange juice concentrate
1   6-ounce can frozen lemonade concentrate
1   quart water, preferably chilled
1   32-ounce bottle ginger ale, chilled
1   cup (½ pint) lime sherbet
1   cup (½ pint) lemon sherbet
    Orange and lime slices

In a punch bowl combine tea, cranberry juice cocktail, juice concentrates, and water. Just prior to serving, add the ginger ale and top with scoops of sherbet. Serve with ice and garnish with orange and lime slices.
   Makes approximately 20 five-ounce servings.

LONG, TALL DRINK OF LEMONADE

2½   cups sugar
1   cup water
2   cups lemon juice
1   gallon water

Boil the sugar and 1 cup water for 2 minutes. Cool. Add the lemon juice and 1 gallon water. Chill and serve in tall glasses over ice.
   Makes enough for about 6 cowboys, or 1 very thirsty cowboy.

Breteche Creek Ranch
Cody, Wyoming

Roy Cooper is known as the "World's Ropingest Cowboy." He has captured eleven Pro Rodeo Cowboy Association titles, including one all-around cowboy title, six world champion calf-roping titles, and one steer-roping title.

STINGY DRINK

This drink is so good that you only offer it to your best buddies—and then only half a glass.

4   quarts tomatoes, quartered
½   package celery, sliced
2   large green bell peppers, seeded and sliced
1   large onion, quartered
1   to 2 jalapeño peppers
1   tablespoon salt
½   cup sugar
1   teaspoon Worcestershire sauce

Cook tomatoes, celery, green peppers, onion, and jalapeños in a large pot for 30 minutes over medium heat. Stir constantly. Crush mixture through a colander and put juice back in the pan. Bring juice to a boil. Add remaining ingredients. Pour into quart jars.

Makes approximately 5 to 6 quarts.

Roy Cooper, rodeo champion

BEVERAGES

TEMPLE BUT NOT SHIRLEY

"If you've got a recipe from Jack Elam, take my advice: Don't eat it!"
—Gene Evans

3   parts Cutty Sark
1   part water
    Ice cubes

Mix. If not satisfied, repeat the same, again and again. Add a few salted peanuts for food value.
   Makes 1 serving.

Jack Elam, actor

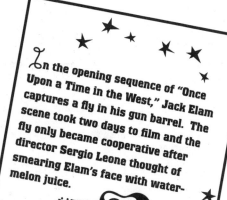

In the opening sequence of "Once Upon a Time in the West," Jack Elam captures a fly in his gun barrel. The scene took two days to film and the fly only became cooperative after director Sergio Leone thought of smearing Elam's face with watermelon juice.

One of the all-time greatest of the western character actors, Jack Elam is a fanatical poker player. Among his many western films are *Gunfight at the O.K. Corral*, *Firecreek*, *The Man from Laramie*, *Once Upon a Time in the West*, *Support Your Local Sheriff*, and *Support Your Local Gunfighter*. He also starred in several TV westerns: *The Dakotas*, *Temple Houston*, and *The Texas Wheelers*.

COWBOY COFFEE—YUPPIE STYLE

Giddy-up cups.

- 1 **pound ground regular or decaffeinated coffee**
- 1 **pound ground French vanilla (or any other flavor) coffee**

Mix thoroughly and brew according to manufacturer's directions.

Makes 80 servings, so invite your neighbors.

Karen S. May, North Fork Ranch
Shawnee, Colorado

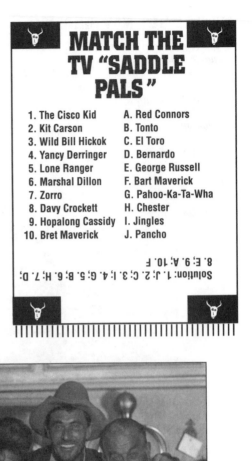

MATCH THE TV "SADDLE PALS"

1. The Cisco Kid	A. Red Connors
2. Kit Carson	B. Tonto
3. Wild Bill Hickok	C. El Toro
4. Yancy Derringer	D. Bernardo
5. Lone Ranger	E. George Russell
6. Marshal Dillon	F. Bart Maverick
7. Zorro	G. Pahoo-Ka-Ta-Wha
8. Davy Crockett	H. Chester
9. Hopalong Cassidy	I. Jingles
10. Bret Maverick	J. Pancho

Solution: 1. J.; 2. C.; 3. I.; 4. G.; 5. B.; 6. H.; 7. D.; 8. E.; 9. A.; 10. F.

The 1965 cast of *Gunsmoke* celebrated the tenth anniversary of the long-running western series with a cake in Miss Kitty's Longbranch Saloon. From left are James Arness, Burt Reynolds, Amanda Blake, Ken Curtis, and Milburn Stone.

CRANBERRY SALAD CLARENCE

1 6-ounce package strawberry-flavored gelatin
1 cup boiling water
1 cup cold water
Juice of 1 orange
1 cup sugar
1 cup small marshmallows
1 cup chopped nuts
1 pound cranberries, ground

Dissolve the gelatin in the boiling water. Add the cold water and the orange juice. Stir. Add the remaining ingredients. Stir well. Pour the mixture into a mold and chill to set.
Makes 8 servings.

Clarence Swensen, actor

MAMA'S CRANBERRY SALAD

My dear, sweet Mama was the best cook on earth,
And all who knew her will attest to her worth.
I can't cook good but like good cookin',
So I'm sending a salad Mama made and
I'll bet my boots and ole blue jeans,
You'll love it and lick the platter clean.

2 3-ounce packages cherry-flavored gelatin
1¼ cups sugar
3 cups boiling water

1 cup diced celery, with strings scraped and removed
2 cups fresh cranberries, washed and ground
2 large oranges, membranes removed from the section pieces
1 cup chopped pecans
Frozen nondairy topping

Mix the gelatin and sugar, and pour the boiling water over the top. Let sit until it reaches the consistency of egg whites. When cool, add remaining ingredients, stir, and chill overnight. Serve with frozen nondairy topping. Bueno Appetito!

Cindy Walker, songwriter

SUSAN'S BROCCOLI SALAD

1 cup mayonnaise
½ cup sugar
3 tablespoons red wine vinegar
2 bunches broccoli (or 1 bunch broccoli and 1 bunch cauliflower), cut into small florets
½ cup crumbled bacon
½ cup Cheddar cheese, cut into squares

At least 4 hours before mealtime, combine the first three ingredients to make dressing. Combine the remaining ingredients. Pour the dressing over the salad 30 minutes before serving.
Makes 8 servings.

Shepp Ranch
Boise, Idaho

Pop music lovers of the 1970s remember David Gates as the lead singer for Bread. Today he's a country music singer and runs a ranch of his own.

In 1967, long before he got in cahoots with the Apple Dumpling Gang, Tim Conway was all tied up as a Texas Ranger stationed in Gopher Gulch, Texas, in the western comedy series *Rango*.

WIDE OPEN FROZEN FRUIT SALAD

No fences, just Gates.

This salad is always served at Thanksgiving and Christmas dinners. David's mother gave us the recipe as it was always served at their family holiday dinners. David's mother grew up on a ranch in Wyoming, as did my parents in Missouri (but there it's a farm). We try to keep family traditions strong. That's the cowboy way for us.

1   8-ounce package cream cheese, softened to room temperature
2   tablespoons mayonnaise
½   pound small marshmallows
1   small can crushed pineapple
½   pint whipping cream

Blend the first four ingredients. Whip the cream and fold it into the other ingredients. Freeze and cut into squares to serve.
    Makes 4 to 6 servings.

Mr. and Mrs. David Gates, singer and rancher

AMOS TUCKER'S CHICORY AND KIDNEY BEAN SALAD

Greens 'n' beans.

2   heads chicory or escarole
1   16-ounce can red kidney beans
1   medium onion, sliced
3   tablespoons olive oil
2   tablespoons red wine vinegar
     Salt and pepper to taste

Wash the chicory or escarole, discarding the tougher outer leaves (unless you're an antelope). If you have a lettuce spinner, give the greens a few whirls. Pour the kidney beans and liquid into a bowl and mash lovingly with a potato masher. Put the chicory in a bowl and pour the kidney beans and liquid on top. Add the onion, olive oil, vinegar, salt and pepper, and then toss. Serve this salad with a pita, or Italian or French bread. Try it. I think you'll like it.
    Makes 4 to 6 servings.

Tim Conway, actor

Ladies Love Outlaws—Jessi Colter and Waylon Jennings

LEATHER AND LACE GRILLED CHICKEN SALAD

A favorite of the cowboy and the lady.

6   boneless, skinless chicken breasts
2   tablespoons olive oil
    Cajun-style seasoning
2   bunches romaine lettuce
8   green onions, sliced thinly
1   purple onion, sliced diagonally
1   cucumber, diced
2   tomatoes, diced
1   red bell pepper, cut into 1½-inch x 1¼-inch
    matchstick-size pieces
2   6.2-ounce boxes long grain and wild rice
    (5-minute cooking recipe)
1   cup low-fat honey mustard dressing
    Fresh ground pepper

Baste chicken breasts in olive oil and sprinkle generously with Cajun-style seasoning. Refrigerate for 2 to 8 hours.

To make the salad, discard outer leaves of lettuce and chop up or tear into bite-size pieces. To this, add green onions, purple onion, cucumber, tomatoes, and bell pepper.

Grill the chicken until done and slice in long thin strips, approximately ¼ inch thick. Cook the rice according to the package directions, but omit the butter.

To assemble the salad, put the greens in a big circle on the plate, leaving a little hole in the center. It should look like a doughnut or a tire. In the center hole, place 1 cup of rice. Divide the chicken evenly and place on top of the salad greens. Spoon the honey mustard dressing over the entire salad and rice. Grind fresh pepper over the top and serve.

Makes 6 servings.

Waylon Jennings, singer/songwriter
Courtesy of Twenty-Five Years with Waylon and Still Cooking *by Jessi Colter and Maureen Raffety*

From 1959 until 1973, Dan Blocker starred as one of TV's most beloved characters, gentle giant Hoss Cartwright of *Bonanza*. Before he became Hoss, Blocker co-starred in the 1958 TV western *Cimarron City* as Tiny Budinger.

NEVADA NUTTY SLAW SALAD

- 1 package slivered almonds
- 2 tablespoons sesame seeds
  Butter
- 1 16-ounce package coleslaw mix (or grated white and red cabbage)
- 8 green onions, chopped
- 2 teaspoons salt
- 1 cup vegetable oil
- 1 teaspoon pepper
- 4 tablespoons sugar
- 6 tablespoons rice vinegar
- 2 packages Oriental ramen-style noodles

Brown almonds and sesame seeds with butter. Mix slaw and onions in a large bowl. Cool nuts and sesame seeds. Mix with slaw. For dressing, mix oil, salt, pepper, sugar, and vinegar. When ready to serve, break noodles over slaw and pour on dressing as desired.

Note: Poached chicken can be added to create a luncheon salad.

Makes 6 servings.

Dan Blocker, actor

SALADS, VEGETABLES, AND SIDE DISHES

RUSTLERS RASPBERRY GELATIN SALAD

2   3-ounce packages raspberry-flavored gelatin
2   cups hot water
1   8-ounce package cream cheese, softened to room temperature
1   cup chopped walnuts
2   10-ounce packages frozen raspberries
½   cup cold water
    Cream cheese, softened to room temperature
    Sour cream

Dissolve the gelatin in the hot water. Combine the cream cheese and walnuts and form into tiny balls. Add the raspberries and cold water to the gelatin mixture. Add the cheese balls. Pour into mold. Set. Unmold onto a pretty plate. Pipe with cream cheese mixed with a little sour cream.

Makes 6 to 8 servings.

*Dorothy and Lavon Shearer, Western Dakota Ranch Vacations
Wall, South Dakota*

CRUNCHY CABBAGE SALAD

Dressing:
    Flavor packet from noodle mix (see below)
2   tablespoons sugar
3   tablespoons vinegar
⅓   to ½ cup vegetable oil
½   teaspoon pepper

Salad:
2   tablespoons sesame seeds
½   cup slivered almonds
½   large head cabbage, shredded (5 cups)
4   green onions, chopped
1   3-ounce package Oriental ramen-style noodles

Make dressing early in the day. Mix well and refrigerate. Toast sesame seeds and almonds in a 350° oven for 15 minutes. Combine shredded cabbage, onions, and uncooked noodles (which have been broken into pieces by hand). Mix lightly. Before serving, add dressing, seeds, and nuts. Toss lightly. Serve immediately.

Makes 10 servings.

*Gail Lander, Kedesh Ranch
Shell, Wyoming*

Born on a Colorado ranch, Wesley Tuttle was a member of various western cowboy groups in the 1930s and 1940s, recorded country and western songs for Capitol Records in the 1940s and early 1950s, and made several films with Tex Ritter, Jimmy Wakely, and Charles Starrett. (Courtesy of Fred Goodwin Collection)

ZIPPY BEAN SALAD ZANE GREY

1   16-ounce can red kidney beans, drained
6   slices bacon, fried crisp and crumbled
1   cup diced celery
½   cup diced pickles
2   hard-boiled eggs, diced
⅓   cup mayonnaise
2   tablespoons lemon juice
1   tablespoon minced onion
    Salt and pepper to taste

Mix all ingredients together, cover, and chill thoroughly. Serve in a lettuce-lined bowl.

Makes 6 servings.

Marilyn and Wesley Tuttle, singer and actor

BEANS BONANZA

This is an intuitively spicy dish. The bonanza is yours as it requires your taste test and daring when preparing. It may be served as an appetizer (alone or with corn chips), a side dish, or over rice as the main meal. Eat, be happy, and sleep with the windows open!

1 pound black-eyed peas, sorted and rinsed
1 pound black beans, sorted, rinsed, and soaked overnight (⅓ part beans to ⅔ parts water)
1 pound pinto beans, sorted, rinsed, and soaked overnight (⅓ part beans to ⅔ parts water)
2 large onions, diced
2 carrots, finely shredded
4 ribs celery, diced
6 to 8 garlic cloves, chopped
   Dash of black pepper, as needed
   Dash of salt, as needed
   Dash of cilantro, as needed
   Dash of cumin, as needed
   Tabasco sauce to taste (don't be timid but don't go crazy yet)
   Jalapeño peppers (as many as you want, whole or chopped, depending on your daring)
3 cups grated cheese (aged sharp Cheddar, Romano or Parmesan, or Monterey Jack)
1 bunch washed, shredded mustard (or collard) greens without stems
3 to 4 large, ripe, but firm, tomatoes, diced

Sort and soak beans overnight in separate pots to avoid discoloring the pinto beans with black bean juice. (A quick method for soaking beans is to boil beans for 2 minutes, reduce heat, and leave to soak for 1 to 2 hours.) Do not soak the black-eyed peas. Drain in the morning and add 1½ quarts water to each pot and bring to a boil. Cook for 20 to 30 minutes or until nearly tender (black-eyed peas may take longer). Drain, but save some water and put beans aside.

In a skillet, sauté onions, carrots, and celery in olive oil. When tender, add the garlic and generous dashes of pepper, salt, cumin, and cilantro. Don't be too particular; I guarantee you'll add more before it's over! Add 4 cups pinto bean or black-eyed pea juice mixed with several dashes of Tabasco sauce and jalapeño peppers; simmer lightly and keep tasting.

Preheat the oven to 300°. Transfer beans to a large, covered casserole dish, Dutch oven, or any other oven-worthy covered cooker. Gently fold in sautéed vegetables with remaining liquid (add more bean juice if the beans appear dry), grated cheeses, and mustard greens. Give the mixture the taste test and add anything that is missing, more Tabasco sauce, more pepper, etc. Bake for 30 to 40 minutes or until beans are tender. Add more bean juice as needed, just enough to keep them moist. Do not let the beans dry out! Gently fold in diced tomatoes so that when the beans are served hot, the tomatoes are just right (cannot be accomplished with leftovers.)

Note: Try boiling the beans with a little beer. The alcohol burns off, leaving a wonderful aroma and flavor to die for. For more protein, add some spicy chopped pork sausage, diced smoked ham, or sautéed beef, venison, or elk tips. Re-bake, re-fry, and serve the beans with scrambled eggs and salsa (green or red). Give or take a little from the recipe itself. Who, in her or his right mind, can follow directions verbatim?

Makes 12 to 24 servings, depending on the course, of course.

Tricia Regan, 7 D Ranch
Cody, Wyoming

MATCH THE "SADDLE PALS" OF THE SILVER SCREEN

(a letter can be used more than once)

1. Roy Rogers
2. Gene Autry
3. Lash LaRue
4. Red Ryder
5. Tex Ritter
6. Jimmy Wakely
7. Monte Hale
8. Rex Allen
9. Buster Crabbe

A. Arkansas Slim Andrews, Al Fuzzy St. John
B. Al Fuzzy St. John
C. Little Beaver
D. Smiley Burnette, Sterling Holloway, Pat Buttram
E. Smiley Burnette, Raymond Hatton, Gabby Hayes, Pat Brady, Gordon Jones
F. Dub "Cannonball" Taylor, Lee Lasses White
G. Paul Hurst
H. Slim Pickens and Buddy Ebsen

Solution: 1. E; 2. D; 3. B; 4. C; 5. A; 6. F; 7. G; 8. H; 9. B

BOSTON BAKED BEANS BRENNAN

This recipe is similar to the way my mother made baked beans. My parents moved to California from Lynn, Massachusetts, where they both grew up.
    —Mike Brennan, son of Walter Brennan

    2   pounds white beans, soaked overnight
    1   teaspoon baking soda
    1   large yellow onion, sliced
    ½   pound salt pork or bacon pieces
    ⅔   cup molasses
    2   teaspoons dry mustard
    3   teaspoons salt
    ½   teaspoon pepper

Cook beans in ample water with baking soda for 10 minutes. Drain and rinse. Place onion in the bottom of a 3-quart casserole dish. Layer half the meat, then half the beans, then the rest of the meat, and finally, the remaining beans. Mix molasses, mustard, salt, and pepper. Pour over beans. Add enough water to barely cover. Do not stir. Bake at 300° for 6 hours. After a couple of hours, stir and check beans. You may need to add more water, but do not make the beans too wet.

Walter Brennan, actor

Before he was an island professor, Russell Johnson was Marshal Gib Scott in the 1959 TV western *Black Saddle.*

COWBOY BEANS

On a cattle drive, vegetables mean beans. They are cheap, easy to store, and filling. The basic recipe for beans at the Allen Ranch doesn't include meat seasoning because we sometimes serve to people with special dietary requirements, such as vegetarian or kosher. You can use this recipe as is to make good tastin' Cowboy Beans or add a ham hock or some fatback to give 'em a little extra kick.

    1   pound dry pinto beans
    1   teaspoon garlic powder
    1   teaspoon onion powder
    1   teaspoon salt

Wash beans, making sure to check for little stones. Put in a large pot and cover with 2½ to 3 inches water. Bring to a boil, then add the dry ingredients. Cover and simmer for 5 to 6 hours. These are especially good with Allen Ranch Barbecue Sauce (p. 184).
    Makes 10 to 12 servings.

Allen Ranch
Bixby, Oklahoma

BLACK SADDLE COLCANNON

    6   potatoes
        Butter
        Milk
    1   bunch green onions, chopped (including tops)
    4   cups cooked, chopped cabbage
    1   pound bacon
        Salt and pepper to taste
    ¼   pound butter
        Paprika

Peel and boil the potatoes, then mash them, adding butter and a bit of milk to make potatoes smooth. Steam or boil the cabbage for 5 minutes, chop into ½-inch pieces, and mix with potatoes. Add onions to the cabbage mixture. Preheat the oven to 375°. Fry the bacon, crumble, and add to cabbage mixture. Add salt and pepper to taste. Place all in a buttered baking dish. Bake for 30 minutes or until lightly browned on top. Top with bits of butter; sprinkle paprika on top.
    Makes about 8 to 10 servings.

Russell Johnson, actor

Leon Rausch was the featured vocalist for Bob Wills and his Texas Playboys from 1958 through 1961.

PAPA ROY'S BAKED BEANS

The old-fashioned western flavor—quick and easy. Happy trails!

5   to 6 slices Canadian bacon, cut into 1-inch pieces
½   green bell pepper, chopped
1   medium onion, chopped
¼   cup packed brown sugar
1   tablespoon prepared mustard
½   cup ketchup
2   19-ounce cans pork and beans

Preheat the oven to 325°. Sauté the bacon until partly done. Add bell pepper and onion. Cook until onion is clear and bacon is nearly done. Combine with remaining ingredients in a casserole dish. Bake for 1 hour.
    Makes 10 to 12 servings.

Roy Warhurst, Sons of the Pioneers

LEON'S EASY FRIED CABBAGE

Delectable cowtown fare!

1   onion, chopped
3   tablespoons vegetable oil or bacon drippings
4   cups coarsely shredded or chopped cabbage
    Salt, pepper, sugar, nutmeg, and dash of vinegar to taste

Sauté onion in oil for 3 minutes. Add cabbage and sauté for 5 minutes, stirring frequently. Add seasonings. Cover and allow to steam for 5 more minutes.
    Makes 4 servings.

Leon Rausch, singer

TUCSON CORN BAKE

This is a vegetable dish from the Southwest.

- 2 16- to 17-ounce cans cream-style corn
- 2 eggs, beaten
- ¾ cup yellow cornmeal
- 1 teaspoon garlic salt
- 6 tablespoons vegetable oil
- 1 4-ounce can green chilies, finely chopped
- 2 cups grated Cheddar cheese

Preheat the oven to 350°. Mix all ingredients except chilies and cheese. Divide the mixture in half. Place half of the mixture in a greased 8-inch-square baking dish. Mix chilies and cheese; place on top of the corn mixture in the dish. Cover with remaining corn mixture. Bake for 35 minutes.

Makes 8 servings.

Margie and Dale Warren, Sons of the Pioneers

BLUE-EYED ELAINE'S CORNBREAD CASSEROLE

- 3 tablespoons low-fat margarine
- 1 8-ounce package egg substitute
- 1 box cornbread mix
- 1 8-ounce carton low-fat sour cream
- 1 15-ounce can sweet kernel corn
- 1 15-ounce can cream-style corn
    Vegetable cooking spray

Preheat the oven to 350°. Mix all ingredients together in a large bowl. Spray a 9x12-inch ovenproof glass casserole dish with vegetable cooking spray. Pour ingredients into the dish. Bake for 1 hour.

Makes 6 to 8 servings.

Ernest Tubb, troubadour

Sons of the Pioneers in 1964—(clockwise from top left) Rusty Richards, Roy Lanham, Pat Brady, Lloyd Perryman, and Dale Warren

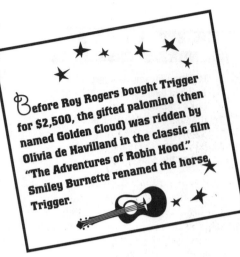

Before Roy Rogers bought Trigger for $2,500, the gifted palomino (then named Golden Cloud) was ridden by Olivia de Havilland in the classic film "The Adventures of Robin Hood." Smiley Burnette renamed the horse Trigger.

CORPORAL AGARN'S CORN PUDDING F TROOP

1 14-ounce can cream-style corn
1 cup cornmeal
¾ cup milk
⅓ cup vegetable oil
2 eggs
1 teaspoon salt
1 teaspoon baking soda
   Chopped parsley to taste
1 4-ounce small can hot chilies, slivered
1 cup grated sharp Cheddar cheese
   Paprika

Preheat the oven to 400°. Mix all ingredients except chilies, cheese, and paprika. Put half the batter into a greased baking dish; layer the chilies and half the cheese. Pour remaining batter over top. Cover with remaining cheese and sprinkle with paprika. Bake for 30 minutes.
   Makes 4 to 6 servings.

Larry Storch, actor

COWBOY LOGIC CORN PUDDING

2 tablespoons all-purpose flour
2 cups cream-style corn
1 tablespoon sugar
1 cup milk
2 teaspoons salt
3 tablespoons butter or margarine, melted
3 eggs or equivalent egg substitute, beaten

Preheat the oven to 325°. Grease a 1-quart casserole dish. Mix the flour and corn. Add the sugar, milk, salt, and butter. Stir in the eggs. Pour into the prepared dish. Place the dish in a pan of hot water. Bake for about 1½ hours or until firm.
   Makes 4 to 6 servings.

Michael Martin Murphey, singer/song-writer

NUGGETS OF GOLD CARROTS

Eureka!

2 cups thinly sliced carrots
¼ cup water
2 tablespoons margarine
2 tablespoons sugar
   Dash of salt

Combine all ingredients in a pan and cover. Simmer until the water is absorbed.
   Makes 4 servings.

The Masked Singer

Singer, songwriter, and actor Sheb Wooley starred as trail scout Pete Nolan from 1959 to 1965 on *Rawhide,* and played part of the Frank Miller gang that menaced Gary Cooper in the western film classic *High Noon.*

CAMPFIRE COB CORN AND TATERS

Do not eat this dish if you have a date or are eager to kiss someone!

6   large baking potatoes
6   ears corn, shucked
1   tablespoon fresh, pressed garlic
    Butter
    Salt to taste
6   green onions
    Parsley

Clean all vegetables well. Cut foil into large sections big enough to cover the veggies for steaming. Use a fork to pierce the potatoes. Coat the potatoes with a mixture of garlic, butter, and salt. Place each potato in foil and add 1 green onion (whole or chopped) and a sprinkling of parsley before sealing and twisting the ends of the foil to seal. Place in a hot bed of ashes from your campfire or on a well-heated grill rack and close the cover of the grill to steam-cook the potato. Prepare corn on the cob in the same manner (onion and parsley are optional). Place under campfire ashes alongside the "taters," or on the grill. Cook corn only for approximately 30 minutes so it will remain crisp and juicy. . . cook "taters" until you can easily pierce them with a fork. Serve immediately with lots of garlic butter.

Makes 6 servings.

Sheb Wooley, actor and singer/songwriter

JOHNNY WESTERN GREEN BEAN CASSEROLE

Have beans, will travel.

2	10-ounce packages frozen French-cut green beans
1	teaspoon salt
¾	cup milk
1	10 ¾-ounce can cream of mushroom soup
⅛	teaspoon black pepper
2	tablespoons diced pimiento
1	3-ounce can Durkee O&C French fried onions, divided

Cook frozen beans in salted water according to package directions; drain. Preheat the oven to 350°. Combine salt, milk, soup, and pepper; pour over beans. Add ½ can onions; pour into a 1½-quart casserole dish. Bake for 20 minutes. Garnish with remaining onions and pimiento and bake for 5 more minutes.

Makes 6 servings.

Johnny Western, singer/songwriter

BAR H BAR HOT CHICKEN SALAD

The best, bar none.

2½	cups diced, cooked chicken
4	hard-boiled eggs
1¼	cups cooked rice
1	10¾-ounce can cream of chicken soup
1¼	cups mayonnaise
1¼	cups diced celery
¾	cup sliced almonds
4	tablespoons chopped green onions
1	teaspoon salt
1¾	tablespoons lemon juice
¼	cup chopped green bell pepper

Preheat the oven to 350°. Mix all ingredients well. Place in a buttered casserole dish. Bake for about 30 minutes.

Makes 4 to 6 servings.

Bar H Bar Ranch
Soda Springs, Idaho

Johnny Western (center), who wrote and performed the theme song to *Have Gun, Will Travel*, takes a break on the set with his friend Paladin (Richard Boone, right) in 1958. Western is one of the world's greatest singers of TV and feature film cowboy theme songs.

RED RIVER GNOCCHI DI PATATE (POTATO GNOCCHI)

Buenos gnocchi.

1½   pounds boiling potatoes (not new potatoes)
1¾   cups all-purpose flour
       Salt to taste
½   tablespoon olive oil (extra virgin, preferably)
       Rango-Lobo Marinara Sauce (p. 187)

Boil potatoes in their skins until done, yet firm. Peel while hot (do not run under cold water). Spread flour on a pasta board. Mash the potatoes. Place on the flour and sprinkle with salt. Start mixing the flour into potatoes a little at a time until the dough is well blended and firm. Knead gently for 6 to 8 minutes. Sprinkle dough with sifted flour. Cut into several pieces. Roll each piece into a long, sausage-like shape, ½ inch in diameter. Then cut into 1-inch pieces. Dust again with sifted flour. Let rest for 5 minutes.

To form gnocchi: Using your thumb, gently roll pieces down the inside of a table fork so that they curl and are imprinted with the tines. Bring a large pot of salted water to a boil; add oil. Quickly drop gnocchi, one by one, into the pot. Stir water with a wooden spoon so that gnocchi will not stick together. In a few seconds gnocchi will come to the surface of the water. Let them cook for 1 more minute. Strain by using a strainer-skimmer. Lay gnocchi on a serving platter on which you may pour sauce of your choice or place directly on serving plates. Gnocchi is best if served immediately after cooking.

Makes 6 servings.

Frankie Laine, singer

COWBOY CORN SALAD

2   16-ounce cans whole kernel corn, drained
1   cucumber, peeled and chopped
2   stalks celery, chopped
1   onion, diced
1   green bell pepper, diced
1   tomato, diced
½   cup Miracle Whip salad dressing
       Garlic to taste
       Salt to taste

Combine all ingredients. Keep in the refrigerator. This is not only tasty, but also festive looking.

Makes about 6 cups.

Dorothy and Lavon Shearer, Western Dakota Ranch Vacations Wall, South Dakota

Head 'Em Up, Move 'Em Out—Certainly one of the greatest western balladeers of all time is Frankie Laine. TV fans know him best as the singer of the *Rawhide* theme. Among his other hits are "Mule Train" and the theme to the film *Gunfight at the O.K. Corral.*

SIDEKICKS

49

Character actor Gene Evans (left) has guest starred on dozens of TV western episodes from *Gunsmoke* to *The Big Valley*, and he starred in *My Friend Flicka* from 1956 to 1958, as seen here with Johnny Washbrook and Anita Louise. He also co-starred in such films as *The Ballad of Cable Hogue, Nevada Smith, The Bravados, War Wagon,* and *Pat Garrett and Billy the Kid.*

MEAN GREEN BEANS

- 1 pound fresh green beans
- 3 onions, chopped
- 2 green bell peppers, chopped
  Salt and pepper to taste
- 2 tablespoons butter

String and break beans. Preheat the oven to 350°. Grease a dish and layer the vegetables, starting and ending with beans. On each layer sprinkle salt and pepper and drizzle melted butter. Bake, covered, for about 1 hour or until tender.

Makes 4 to 6 servings.

Gene Evans, actor

COWBOY SPUDS

Eatin' speaks louder than words.

- ½ pound thick-sliced bacon
- 1½ cups sliced onions
- 6 medium potatoes, unpeeled and cut into ¼-inch slices
- ¼ teaspoon salt
- ¼ teaspoon black pepper, divided
- 1½ cups milk
- ¼ cup chopped parsley

Cut bacon cross-wise into ½-inch pieces and sauté in a skillet until crisp. Remove, drain on paper towels, and set aside. Sauté onions in bacon drippings until tender. Remove half of the onions. Arrange half of the potatoes over onions in a skillet. Sprinkle with ⅛ teaspoon pepper. Add remaining onions. Top with remaining potatoes and sprinkle with remaining salt and pepper. Pour milk over potatoes. Add half of the reserved bacon and heat to boiling. Reduce heat and simmer, covered, for about 25 minutes or until potatoes are tender. Sprinkle with parsley.

Makes 4 servings.

Clint Howard, actor

BRAVADOS BAKED SWEET POTATOES WITH HONEY BUTTER

Bravo!

- Sweet potatoes
  Cinnamon
- 3 tablespoons butter
- ¼ cup honey

Preheat the oven to 400°. Wash and scrub 1 potato for each serving. Prick each with a fork several times. Bake for about 45 minutes to 1 hour or until done. Cut each potato open, sprinkle with cinnamon, and serve with honey butter (blend butter with honey).

Gene Evans, actor

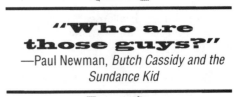

"Who are those guys?"
—Paul Newman, *Butch Cassidy and the Sundance Kid*

GALLOPIN' SCALLOPIN' POTATOES

It behooves you to try them!

10 potatoes, peeled
5 tablespoons butter
1 cup milk
5 slices Velveeta cheese

Preheat the oven to 350°. Slice potatoes and place in an oblong dish; dot with butter. Pour milk over all. Bake for 1 hour and 15 minutes. Top with cheese after the potatoes are done; let melt and serve.
Makes 8 to 10 servings.

Chris LeDoux, rodeo cowboy and singer/songwriter

POOHAWK COUCH POTATOES

How good!

22 Idaho potatoes, unscalped (skins intact)
¼ cup garlic butter
2 tablespoons grated parsley
Poohawk Pemmicanburgers (p. 135)

Place potatoes in the microwave on a couch, divan, or settee, and plug in. Cook the potatoes for 8 minutes on HIGH. Remove potatoes from oven and open them with tomahawk or (if no one's watching) a knife. Warm garlic butter and brush it liberally on open potatoes, then sprinkle heavily with parsley (the grated parsley represents mohair, to enhance the couch ambiance. Also in tribute to the Mohawk Tribe, which the Poohawks have always wished they were). Serve hot with Poohawk Pemmicanburgers (p. 135).
Makes 20 servings.

Tom K. Ryan, artist

RUSTY OLD HALOS (POTATO CHIPS)

2 medium potatoes
1 stick butter
Pepper to taste

Slice potatoes thin; lay on a flat tray. Dot with butter; sprinkle with pepper. Broil until crisp.
Makes 2 servings.

Hoyt Axton, singer/songwriter and actor

OKIE DOKIE SLICED BAKED POTATOES

4 medium potatoes
1 teaspoon salt
2 to 3 tablespoons melted butter
2 to 3 tablespoons chopped fresh herbs, such as parsley, chives, thyme, or sage
4 tablespoons grated Cheddar cheese
1¼ tablespoons Parmesan cheese

Preheat the oven to 425°. Peel the potatoes if the skin is tough, otherwise just scrub and rinse them. Cut the potatoes into thin slices but not all the way through. Use a handle of a spoon instead of a knife to avoid cutting all the way through. Put the potatoes in a baking dish and fan out slightly. Sprinkle with salt and drizzle with butter. Sprinkle with herbs. Bake for about 50 minutes. Remove from the oven and sprinkle with cheeses. Bake for another 10 to 15 minutes until lightly browned, cheeses are melted, and potatoes are soft inside. Check with a fork.
Makes 4 servings.

Lucynda Hendricks, Miss Rodeo USA, 1994

The Peanut Butter Kid—Clint Howard let his outfit do his talking as sandwich-packing cowboy Leon on *The Andy Griffith Show*.

Asleep at the Wheel—Modern-day cowboy swingers

RAY'S RED BEANS

- 1   1-pound package red beans
- 2   medium onions, chopped
- 2   ribs celery with leaves, chopped
- ½   green bell pepper, chopped
- 2   garlic cloves, minced
    Ham bone or ¼ cup bacon drippings (optional)
    Oregano to taste
    Thyme to taste
    Salt to taste
    Cayenne pepper to taste
    Garlic powder to taste
    Bay leaves to taste
- 1   pound large-link smoked sausage, cut into ½-inch slices
    Hot, cooked rice
    Shredded Cheddar cheese (optional)
    Chopped green onions (optional)

Wash and drain the beans in a 4-quart saucepan; add 2 quarts water and beans. Soak overnight. (Or, in a 4-quart saucepan, add 2 quarts water and red beans; bring to a boil. Cover, reduce heat, and simmer for 2 minutes. Remove from heat and let stand for 1 hour before continuing.) Do not drain off water. Two hours before serving, add onions, celery, bell pepper, garlic, and ham bone to beans and bring to a boil. Cover, reduce heat, and simmer for about 1½ hours or until beans are soft and begin to thicken. Do not stir beans more than necessary or they will get mushy. Gently stir in oregano, thyme, salt, cayenne pepper, garlic powder, bay leaves, and sausage. Simmer for 30 more minutes or until beans are tender. Serve over hot, cooked rice and top with cheese and onions, if desired.

Makes 6 servings.

Ray Benson, bandleader of Asleep at the Wheel

STRAIT-SHOOTIN' SPANISH RICE

Si how you like it, by George!

1   cup rice, uncooked
2   tablespoons vegetable shortening
1   small onion, chopped
½   green bell pepper, chopped
1½ teaspoons salt
2   teaspoons chili powder
1   10-ounce can tomatoes, chopped
2   cups water

In a skillet, brown rice in shortening. Add the onion and bell pepper. Stir. Add salt, chili powder, and tomatoes, including juice. Add water. Cover and simmer for 30 minutes or until rice is tender and liquid is absorbed.
   Makes 6 servings.

George Strait, singer, actor, and rancher

BOOMTOWN BROCCOLI AND RICE CASSEROLE

2¼ cups instant rice, cooked
1   10-ounce package broccoli cuts, cooked
1   10¾-ounce can cream of mushroom soup
1   16-ounce jar Cheese Whiz (can use jalapeño flavored)
3   to 4 slices soft bacon, chopped
¾   cup chopped onions

In a casserole dish, combine cooked rice, broccoli, soup, and Cheese Whiz. Set aside. Preheat the oven to 375°. In a skillet, sauté bacon and onions until bacon is crisp and onions are soft. Blend with the rice mixture. Bake for about 30 minutes or until heated thoroughly.
   Note: Before baking you can place slices of bacon on top of casserole and bake until heated.
   Makes approximately 6 servings.

Toby Keith, singer/songwriter

Country singer George Strait is a member of the Pro Rodeo Cowboy Association and competes in team roping. He hosts the George Strait Team Roping in Kingsville, Texas, each June.

RED'S GREEN CHILIES AND RICE CASSEROLE

1   cup rice, cooked
2   cups sour cream
1   8-ounce can chopped green chilies
½ pound Jack cheese, grated
    Salt and pepper to taste
    Paprika for garnish

Preheat the oven to 350°. In a large bowl, mix all ingredients. Pour mixture into a greased 8x12-inch dish. Bake for 30 minutes. Serve this tasty dish instead of potatoes. It is not hot, just pleasantly spicy.

Makes 4 servings.

Red Steagall, singer

Cowboy, singer, and songwriter Red Steagall has hosted numerous nationally televised rodeos and is the official Cowboy Poet of Texas. He also hosts his own "Cowboy Corner" radio show, which is broadcast to forty-three states and celebrates the lifestyle of the American West through poems, songs, and stories of the cowboy. (Photo by Peter Nash)

SALADS, VEGETABLES, AND SIDE DISHES

It's just another day at the office for Ty Murray as he does a bit of bronc busting.

RODEO BAKED RICE DRESSING

½   pound ground lean pork
½   cup ground chicken gizzards
1   cup rice, uncooked
⅓   cup finely chopped onions
⅓   cup chopped green bell pepper
⅓   cup finely chopped celery
1   cup chopped green onion tops (scallions)
1   cup minced parsley
1   10¾-ounce can cream of mushroom soup
1   10¾-ounce can French onion soup
    Red and black pepper to taste

Preheat the oven to 325°. Mix meats with uncooked rice. Add onions, bell pepper, celery, onion tops, and parsley. Mix in the soups and season with red and black pepper. Put in a heavy casserole dish and cover with close-fitting cover or foil to retain all juices. Bake for 2 hours.

Makes 4 servings.

Ty Murray, rodeo champion
Courtesy of Cajun Country Cookbook *by Tony Chachere*

SAN ANTONIO SPANISH RICE AND BEEF

¾   pound ground beef
1   10-ounce package frozen corn
1   cup water
1   14½-ounce can stewed tomatoes
½   teaspoon oregano
½   teaspoon chili powder
½   teaspoon salt
¼   teaspoon garlic powder
⅛   teaspoon black pepper
1½ cups Minute Rice

Brown meat, breaking it into pieces and stirring for about 5 minutes. Drain off excess drippings. Add corn, water, tomatoes, and seasonings and bring to a boil. Stir in rice. Cover and remove from heat. Let stand for 5 minutes.

Makes 4 servings.

Bill Cody, disc jockey

BIG REWARD GREEN RICE

Most wanted.

- 2 cups rice
- 2 cups milk
- 1 cup chopped green onions
- 1 cup chopped parsley
- 1 pound grated cheese, divided
- ½ cup vegetable oil
- 1 cup chopped green bell pepper
- ½ garlic clove

Preheat the oven to 350°. Cook rice according to package directions. Drain off excess liquid. Add remaining ingredients (use half the cheese, save the rest for the top) and mix well. Place in a greased 9x13-inch pan. Top with reserved cheese. Bake for 1 hour.

Makes 8 to 10 servings.

Mabel Boehm, Peaceful Valley Lodge
Lyons, Colorado

ROOTINEST, TOOTINEST RICE CASSEROLE IN THE WEST

- 2 cups instant rice, uncooked
- 2½ cups bouillon
- 1 cup chopped celery
- 1 cup grated carrots
- ½ cup chopped green onions
- ½ cup chopped parsley
- ½ cup slivered blanched almonds

Preheat the oven to 350°. Combine rice and bouillon in a casserole dish. Bake, covered, for 30 minutes. Add vegetables and nuts to rice. Continue baking at the same temperature for 10 more minutes. This goes well with Yosemite Sam's Cranberry Chicken (p. 151.)

Makes 6 to 8 servings.

Estelle and Mel Blanc, voice actor

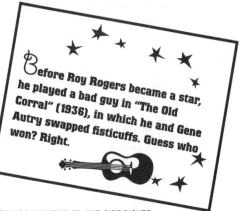

Before Roy Rogers became a star, he played a bad guy in "The Old Corral" (1936), in which he and Gene Autry swapped fisticuffs. Guess who won? Right.

THE DITTY DOZEN: Famous songs from westerns

1. "High Noon (Do Not Forsake Me, Oh My Darlin')" from *High Noon;* sung by Tex Ritter
2. "Don't Fence Me In" from *Hollywood Canteen;* sung by Roy Rogers
3. "Dust" from *Under Western Stars;* sung by Sons of the Pioneers
4. "The Theme from The Man Who Shot Liberty Valance"; sung by Gene Pitney
5. "The Theme from Gunfight at the O.K. Corral"; sung by Frankie Laine
6. "The Theme from The Searchers"; sung by Sons of the Pioneers
7. "The Green Leaves of Summer" from *The Alamo*
8. "The Theme from True Grit"; a hit by Glen Campbell, but not on the film soundtrack
9. "The Sons of Katie Elder"; sung by Johnny Cash, but not on the film soundtrack
10. "They Call the Wind Mariah" from *Paint Your Wagon*
11. "Raindrops Keep Falling on My Head" from *Butch Cassidy and the Sundance Kid;* sung by B.J. Thomas
12. "The Theme from The Hanging Tree"; sung by Marty Robbins

ROPINGEST COWBOY SPINACH SOUFFLÉ

- 4 tablespoons all-purpose flour
- 3 eggs
- 1 10-ounce package frozen spinach, thawed
- 1 8-ounce carton cottage cheese
- 8 ounces Cheddar cheese, grated
- ½ teaspoon salt
- ½ teaspoon pepper

Preheat the oven to 350°. Beat the flour and eggs until smooth. Squeeze the spinach dry and add to eggs. Add remaining ingredients. Blend well. Place in a greased 8x8-inch baking dish. Bake for 1 hour.

Makes 4 to 6 servings.

Roy Cooper, rodeo champion

Together with Brooks & Dunn partner Ronnie Dunn, Louisiana native Kix Brooks (right) has created one of country music's hottest duos with such hits as "You're Gonna Miss Me When I'm Gone," "Neon Moon," and "Rock My World (Little Country Girl)."

BRAND NEW MAN'S RED BEANS AND RICE

You're gonna miss 'em when they're gone.

- 2 pounds dried red kidney beans
- ½ pound salt pork
- 6 fist-size ham hocks (or more)
- 1 15-inch long pepperoni, sliced and quartered into ¾-inch chunks
  Hot Italian sausage links (remove casing)
  Kielbasa, 3- to 10-inch lengths
- 3 to 4 3-inch onions, diced (2 cups or more)
- 4 stalks celery, sliced diagonally
- 1½ to 2 cups diced green peppers
- 1½ to 2 cups diced red bell peppers
- 2 or 3 fresh tomatoes, sliced
- 2 large cans whole peeled tomatoes (put in the juice from 1 can only)
- 1 bunch green onions, chopped
- 1 large can tomato sauce
- 4 to 6 pods garlic (if you use powder, cover the top with a layer)
- 3 tablespoons Tabasco sauce (or more)
- ½ teaspoon thyme
- 3 tablespoons Worcestershire sauce
- 1 teaspoon crushed red pepper
- 3 tablespoons cumin
- ½ tablespoon oregano (or more)
- 1 teaspoon pepper
- 1 tablespoon salt

Soak beans overnight in a large saucepan. (For a quicker method, boil beans and simmer for 2 to 3 minutes. Let set for 1 hour.)

In a skillet, brown the hot Italian sausage. (These will break up in the long cooking process, but the flavor is terrific!) In a large saucepan or Dutch oven, sauté the remaining meats, onion, green pepper, red bell peppers, green onions, and garlic. Add the Italian red sausage and the remaining ingredients to the saucepan and simmer for 25 to 35 minutes. Serve with rice.

Makes about 6 servings.

Kix Brooks of Brooks & Dunn, singer/songwriter

AUDRA BARKLEY'S CHILI CHEESE TOMATOES

1 cup sour cream
½ teaspoon salt
¼ teaspoon pepper
1 tablespoon all-purpose flour
2 tablespoons chopped green onions
2 tablespoons chopped green chilies
3 tomatoes, peeled (drop in boiling water for 1 minute and slice thick)
2 cups Cheddar cheese, shredded

Combine sour cream, salt, pepper, flour, onions, and chilies. Place tomato slices on a cookie sheet. Cover them with sour cream mixture and then cheese. Broil 4 inches from heat for 4 minutes or until cheese is melted.

Makes 4 servings.

Linda Evans, actress

Linda Evans, who starred as Audra Barkley on *The Big Valley* from 1965 to 1969, celebrates a birthday on the set as her TV brothers Charles Briles and Richard Long offer her a bite of cake.

SALADS, VEGETABLES, AND SIDE DISHES

Dayton Allen was the voice behind that southern sleuthhound Dep'ty Dawg, as well as such rascals as Muskie the Muskrat and Heckle and Jeckle, dagnabbit.

HAYWIRE HASH BROWN POTATO CASSEROLE

1   32-ounce package shredded frozen pota-
    toes, thawed
1   stick butter, melted
1   10¾-ounce can cream of chicken soup,
    undiluted
12 ounces grated American cheese
1   8-ounce carton sour cream
1   teaspoon salt
½   small onion, chopped
2   cups crushed cornflakes
1   stick butter, melted

Preheat the oven to 350°. Place potatoes in a 9x13-inch baking dish. Mix next 6 ingredients together and pour over potatoes. Top with crushed cornflakes; drizzle melted butter over all. Bake, uncovered, for 45 minutes.
    Makes 12 servings.

Carol and Bob Steinruck, Lazy Hills Ranch Ingram, Texas

DEP'TY DAWG'S SWEET AND SOUR TOFU WITH VEGETABLES

Well, I finally got to talk with Dep'ty Dawg. He consented to allow the world to learn what a strong digestive system can tolerate. When I put the blocks to him, he opened up. "In a way, I'm glad you asked me for my favorite recipe," Dep'ty Dawg began. "In another way, I'm a little slightly embarrassed. It was on last Groundhog Day (a very, very touching day for us). I had some friends over for dinner. They were Muskie, Vincent Van Gopher, and those nutty boys, Heckle and Jeckle. I served catfish, hot dawgs, rabbit stew, and barbecued spare ribs. Well, when they arrived and I told them what I had prepared, you should have heard them. Muskie leaned over to me and said, 'Dep, are you still chasin' and bitin' hubcaps? You must be ready for a balloon and fireman's hat. I wouldn't serve that meal to a dawg. OOPS! I beg your pardon, Dep'ty. I guess I meant a vulture.' Vince looked at me like I just cooked his mother and said, 'It's like eatin' a swell relative. We ain't no cannibals. How could you?' Heckle and Jeckle piped in something touching, 'Yeah, and on such a solemn holiday.' Well, I never felt so ashamed in my entire life. I felt like crawling under the hen house. But I told them I'd make it up to them on the Fourth of July, and that they'd get a bang out of my new No Animal, Fish, or Fowl Stew."

1 tablespoon cornstarch
¾ cup vegetable broth or water, divided
3 tablespoons white wine vinegar
3 tablespoons sugar
1 tablespoon ketchup
2 tablespoons soy sauce or tamari sauce
½ teaspoon ground ginger
¼ teaspoon cayenne pepper (optional)
2 tablespoons vegetable oil
2 garlic cloves, crushed
1 medium onion, thinly sliced
2 medium carrots, cut into matchstick-size pieces
1 green bell pepper, sliced into strips
1 rib celery, sliced into strips
½ cup sliced mushrooms
1 cup snow peas
1 pound firm tofu, cut into strips
   Hot, cooked rice

Mix cornstarch with 3 tablespoons broth or water in a small cup until well blended. Add the rest of the stock, vinegar, sugar, ketchup, soy sauce, ginger, and cayenne pepper and set aside. Heat oil in a wok or large frying pan over high heat. Stir fry garlic, onion, and carrots until the carrots begin to soften, about 5 minutes. Add pepper, celery, mushrooms, and snow peas, and stir fry for 2 or 3 more minutes. Stir the sauce well and add to the vegetables. Cook until the mixture thickens. Add tofu and cook until tofu is heated thoroughly. Serve immediately over rice.
   Makes 4 to 6 servings.

Dayton Allen, voice actor

"It ain't news. This is the West. When the legend becomes a fact, print the legend."— *The Man Who Shot Liberty Valance*

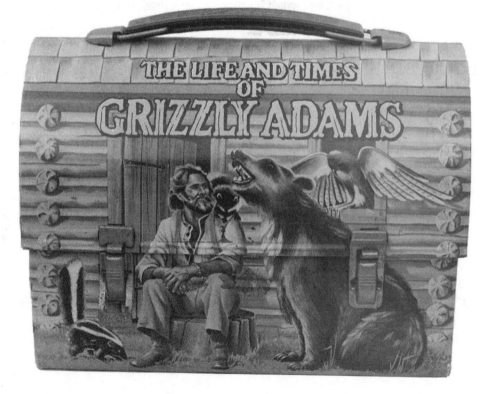

One of the most popular leading ladies in B-westerns of the 1940s, Peggy Stewart played opposite legends like Lash LaRue, Jim Bannon, Whip Wilson, Bill Elliott, Allan Lane, Sunset Carson, and Bob Livingston.

SILVER SCREEN QUEEN GREEN BEANS

- 2 pounds fresh green beans
- 3 tablespoons unrefined canola or safflower oil
- 2 garlic cloves, minced
- ½ teaspoon thyme
  Herbs or spices to taste
- 4 to 6 vegetable bouillon cubes
- 1½ cups water
- 2 tablespoons butter, optional

Trim and break ends off the beans and snap or cut. Heat your oil in a big, heavy saucepan. Add garlic to the oil. Sauté garlic briefly; don't let it brown. Add green beans and stir well over high heat so beans are coated with oil and beginning to sear. Add thyme, herbs or spices, and bouillon. Mix together. Add water and bring to a boil. Stir until bouillon dissolves. Cover pan tightly and reduce heat to medium-low. Simmer beans for about 20 minutes or until tender. You can save the juice and drink it cold or hot. It's delicious.

Makes 4 large servings.

Peggy Stewart, actress

*P*onderosa Quartet—In the very first episode of "Bonanza," the four Cartwright men ride up singing the words to the theme song. Once was enough.

CALAMITY JANE'S SICILIAN CHEESE CASSEROLE

No secret anymore.

Here is a no-meat dish that I really love.

1   cup tiny shell macaroni
1   medium eggplant
1   small onion, chopped
3   tablespoons olive oil
3   ounces tomato sauce
¼   cup parsley
2   tablespoons lemon juice
½   cup halved olives
½   teaspoon basil
½   teaspoon marjoram
    Salt, pepper, and garlic salt to taste
½   pound sliced Monterey Jack cheese
1½ cups Parmesan cheese

Preheat the oven to 375°. Cook macaroni and drain. Pare eggplant and cut into ½-inch cubes. Sauté eggplant and onion in oil. Combine with macaroni, tomato sauce, parsley, lemon juice, olives, basil, marjoram, salt, pepper, and garlic salt. Put in a 2-quart baking dish and top with cheeses. Bake, uncovered, for 30 minutes.

Makes 6 to 8 servings.

Doris Day, actress

JACKPOT GRILLED VEGETABLES

Successful grilling is achieved via a hot, clean surface (not always possible on pack trips, we know, but hey, when you're camping everything tastes great!) Remember to start your fire approximately 30 to 45 minutes prior to cooking. Glowing coals are best, because they minimize flare-ups and provide maximum heat. If cooking indoors, follow the same rules: clean, hot pan under a hot broiler. Try any—or all—of your favorites, such as beets, peppers, carrots, potatoes, carrots, corn, scallions, eggplant, sweet potatoes, fennel, summer squash, leeks, tomatoes, mushrooms, turnips, or onions.

Clean vegetables and cut into thick slices, ⅓ to ½ inch. Toss with vegetable oil to coat, sprinkle with salt and pepper to taste, and fresh or dried herbs, such as herbes de Provence. Grill over hot coals for approximately 2 minutes per side, or until well browned and grill marks have appeared.

Serve either hot or cold with an entrée (we often pair them with marinated flank steak), or on their own as an entrée. Leftovers make great sandwiches that are ideal for the trail because they don't spoil in the hot Wyoming sun.

Breteche Creek Ranch
Cody, Wyoming

COWBOY CORN

Put three tablespoons of hogback or bacon fat in a pan. Heat up until it comes to a real smoke. Dump in a can of cream-style corn. Add a handful of black pepper, a little bit of salt, and a bunch of sugar. Cook until most of the juice is out. There you have it. It will get your attention. Quite a dish, it gets you really on your feet.

L.Q. Jones, actor

L.Q. Jones has appeared in countless westerns. Among his best-known films are *Ride the High Country, The Wild Bunch, The Ballad of Cable Hogue, Major Dundee, Pat Garrett and Billy the Kid* (all by director Sam Peckinpah), and *Lightning Jack.* He also has appeared in dozens of TV westerns, including many episodes of *Gunsmoke.* In addition, he was a regular as Smitty in TV's *Cheyenne* during the 1950s and as Belden in *The Virginian* during the mid-1960s.

Doris Day proved she could ride, shoot, and sing with the best of 'em when she starred as *Calamity Jane*.

SOUPS AND STEWS

STIR-UPS

O.K. CORRAL MEATBALL SOUP

1 pound ground beef
2 cups beef stock
1 can condensed tomato soup
1 teaspoon salt
1 can water
1 tablespoon oliveoil

Combine soup, water, beef stock, and salt. Allow to boil gently. Heat olive oil and brown the beef, which has been shaped into small meatballs. Drain and add to soup. Boil for 1 hour.
   Makes 4 servings.

Hugh O'Brian, actor

HOSS'S CAJUN GUMBO

Yah-eee!
   As a kid growing up in my mama's Cajun kitchen (in Port Arthur, Texas, near the Louisiana border), I was told there were no written-down gumbo recipes. Only a natural-born feel, and generations of practice. As I have grown older, I have tried to put into print a gumbo recipe to let you experience this wonderful spicy Cajun dish the way I have for years, so maybe you could pass it on and help preserve a dwindling Cajun heritage. There are several types of gumbo: seafood, chicken and sausage, okra and tomato, duck and oyster (my favorite), crawfish, etc. Do you like muskrat? Me either. So today, let's make chicken and sausage gumbo.
   The word gumbo originates in Africa and means "mud." If you have ever seen roux, then you know why. Roux is flour and oil, browned

in a cast-iron skillet. Some Cajuns fry their chicken first, then use the drippings for roux. I prefer either to make my roux, or buy it. Roux is added to a stock of chicken or seafood, depending on what kind of gumbo you're making. Today, we begin with this list of ingredients:

   Stock (canned or your own boiled chicken stock)
   Roux
   Salt
   Chicken (whole if boiling, breasts for me)
2 medium onions
1 stalk celery
2 to 3 bunches green onions
1 red bell pepper
   Pepper
1 small bottle soy sauce
   Fresh garlic (or powder)
   Beef sausage
   Fresh parsley

Bring stock to boil in a large pot. Add roux, mix well, and add salt to taste. (Approximately 1 jar roux to 1 gallon stock.) Add chicken, chopped vegetables, pepper, soy sauce, any other seasonings you may discover, and garlic. Let boil until chicken is tender, about 30 minutes, and season again to taste. Add sausage and parsley near the end. Let boil gently for 30 minutes to 1 hour longer, stirring, tasting, and seasoning until done. Eat over rice, with crackers and ice tea with sugar and lemon, and you are an honorary Cajun!
   Makes 6 servings.

Hoss Burns, disc jockey

From 1955 to 1961, Hugh O'Brian starred in one of television's most popular series, *The Life and Legend of Wyatt Earp*. He also appeared in a number of western films, including *The Man from the Alamo, Saskatchewan, Drums across the River, Broken Lance,* and *The Shootist.*

WAYLON'S CORN CHOWDER

- ½ pound bacon
- 1 large onion, diced
- 1 cup diced celery
- ½ cup all-purpose flour
- 2 quarts chicken stock
- 2 cups diced potatoes
- ½ teaspoon thyme
- 1 bay leaf
- 4 sprigs parsley, chopped
- 6 peppercorns, crushed
- 1 garlic clove
- 6 ears sweet corn or 2 cups corn
- 2 tablespoons butter
- 2 cups half and half
  Salt and pepper to taste

In a 4-quart stock pot, sauté bacon until the fat is rendered. With a slotted spoon remove the bacon and discard, leaving the fat in the stock pot.

Add the onion and celery to the stock pot and sauté until transparent, but do not brown. Add the flour and continue cooking over low heat for 10 minutes, but do not brown. Add the chicken stock and bring to a boil, stirring until no lumps remain. Reduce to a simmer and add the potatoes, thyme, bay leaf, parsley, peppercorns, and garlic. Cut corn off the cob with a sharp knife, being careful not to cut the cob. Add the corn to the soup. Continue simmering until the potatoes are tender. Add butter and half and half and return to a simmer. Season with salt and pepper. Ladle into soup bowls and garnish with parsley, if desired.

Makes 8 to 10 servings.

Waylon Jennings, singer/songwriter
Courtesy of Twenty-Five Years with Waylon and Still Cooking *by Jessi Colter and Maureen Raffety*

TEXAS TWO-STEP CORN SOUP

Put your best foot forward with this one.

- 2 tablespoons cornstarch
- 6 to 8 cups whole milk, divided
- 1 medium onion, peeled and chopped
- 1 garlic clove, minced
- 1½ sticks unsalted butter (do not use margarine)
- 2 teaspoons chili powder
- 2 teaspoons ground cumin
- 1 teaspoon garlic powder
- ½ teaspoon black pepper
- 1½ teaspoons salt or to taste
- 4 cups fresh or frozen corn
- ½ cup masa harina
- 3 to 4 green chilies, chopped
  Salt
  Grated cheese
  Picante or pico de gallo sauce

Dissolve cornstarch in 1 cup milk and set aside. In a large saucepan or soup pot, sauté the onion and garlic in butter until soft and translucent, about 8 to 10 minutes. Add spices and stir to dissolve them. Add the corn and then transfer to a blender or food processor. Turn the machine on and, while it is running, add the reserved cup of cornstarch and milk. Return to medium heat and add masa harina and the remaining milk, stirring occasionally. (The thickness of this soup will vary. Thin with milk or water according to your preference.) Add the green chilies and cook for 10 to 15 minutes. Salt to taste. To serve, pour the hot soup into ovenproof serving bowls. Top with grated cheese and heat in the oven just long enough to melt the cheese. Do not brown. Top with picante or pico de gallo and serve with chips.

Makes about 1½ gallons.

Ray Benson, bandleader of Asleep at the Wheel

From 1957 to 1962, Oklahoman Dale Robertson starred as troubleshooter Jim Hardie in TV's *Tales of Wells Fargo.*

WELLS FARGO CHICKEN LENTIL SOUP

Hardie eatin'!

  4   boneless chicken breasts
  ½   cup lentils
  ¼   cup olive oil
  4   15-ounce cans chicken broth
  2   16-ounce cans whole tomatoes
  2   cups grated cabbage
  2   cups chopped celery
  2   cups diced zucchini
  2   cups chopped onions or leeks
  2   tablespoons lemon juice
  ¼   cup cooking sherry
       Seasoning: Tabasco sauce, curry powder, salt, pepper, and herbs to taste

Slowly cook chicken breasts in boiling water for 45 minutes. In a separate pan, cook lentils in olive oil and chicken stock and juice from canned tomatoes for 30 minutes. When lentils are done, pour in all the vegetables. Cut chicken into bite-size pieces and add to vegetables. Cook until vegetables are tender. Add lemon juice and sherry. Heat and stir to blend.

Makes 4 to 6 servings.

Mr. and Mrs. Dale Robertson, actor

Those purveyors of the Cowboy Way, Riders in the Sky—(l-r) Woody Paul, Ranger Doug, and Too Slim

MAMA MEAT'S BEAN SOUP

This'll make the cowboy weigh.

Sidemeat asked me to write this out for him "on account of I ain't so handy at writing. Looks like a lot of chicken scratchin' to me. Meeyah whew!

"This here recipe are fer what I call the 'culinary challenged,' them that likes to eat but can't rattle the pots and pans worth a hoot. I myself don't bother with no dad-blamed sissified recipes. I just throw in what's handy, be it thirty weight, number nine Portland, a big D can of pintos, whatever. My specialty is 'Snake 'N' Beans' but it ain't appropriate fer mixed company so instead here's 'Mama Meat's Bean Soup and Goulash.' I know it ain't real goulash but it's what Mama Meat always called it so ask her. Except you can't. She's passed on. And it weren't my cooking either so wipe that wisecrack off yer brain. Open the gate and let'er rip! Meeyah whew!"

1	1-pound bag navy beans
1	ham bone
1	16-ounce can tomatoes, cut up
1	onion, diced
	Celery, diced
	Salt
	Pepper
	Bay leaves
	Oregano

Soak navy beans overnight in 8 cups of water. Remember to get the water upstream from the herd. Add a meaty ham bone, cut-up tomatoes, diced onion, and some diced celery. Add some salt, pepper, bay leaves, oregano, or whatever. This here's your chance to be creative or else use up what's festering in back of the pantry. Simmer for 2 to 4 hours. Dice the meat, put it back in the soup, give the bone to your dog. Secret touch of greatness: Put about 2 cups of soup in a blender and rile it up 'till it's a cloudy liquid and pour it back in the soup. Let it cook 'till it's the way that suits you. Ummm boy, now that's good eatin'.

Makes 8 to 10 servings.

Sidemeat, trail cook for Riders in the Sky

THE BEST OF THE WEST

Scene Two

Match the actor to the lawman, western hero, or cowboy he portrayed.

1.	Fess Parker	A.	Wyatt Earp
2.	Henry Fonda	B.	Jason McCord
3.	Chuck Connors	C.	Hondo Lane
4.	Walter Brennan	D.	Davy Crockett
5.	James Arness	E.	Will Sonnett
6.	Richard Boone	F.	Judge Roy Bean
7.	Ralph Taeger	G.	Marshal Dan Troop
8.	Edgar Buchanan	H.	Paladin
9.	John Russell	I.	Marshal Simon Fry
10.	Hugh O'Brian	J.	Marshal Matt Dillon

Solution: 1. D; 2. I; 3. B; 4. E; 5. J; 6. H; 7. C; 8. F; 9. G; 10. A

CIMARRON CITY CHICKEN SOUP WITH CORN

4	cups frozen or canned corn
2	garlic cloves, chopped
½	stick butter
2	cups chicken broth
1	cup milk
½	teaspoon oregano
	Salt and pepper to taste
2	tablespoons chopped green chilies
1	whole chicken breast, cooked and diced
1	cup cubed Monterey Jack cheese
1	cup diced fresh tomato
2	tablespoons chopped fresh parsley
2	tablespoons chopped fresh cilantro
	Corn tortillas, fried crisp and dried

Sauté corn and garlic in butter until tender. Purée in blender or food processor. In a 3-quart pan, combine corn mixture, broth, milk, spices, chilies, and chicken. Heat until completely warmed (may be held or frozen at this point). To serve, heat, but do not boil, soup. Place cheese and tomato in bottom of each bowl. Add soup and stir gently. Top with parsley, cilantro, and crisp tortilla squares (if tortilla squares are not crisp, warm in oven a few minutes).

Makes 4 servings.

Dan Blocker, actor

WAYMORE'S TOMATO FLORENTINE SOUP

You'll always want way more.

1 large onion, chopped
1 garlic clove, minced
2 cups finely diced celery
1 tablespoon olive oil
2 14½-ounce cans diced tomatoes
2 14½-ounce cans stewed tomatoes
2 14½-ounce cans tomato wedges
2 10¾-ounce cans tomato soup
2 tablespoons sugar
1 tablespoon dried oregano
1½ teaspoons salt
8 cups chicken stock or canned chicken broth
2 cups finely chopped fresh spinach
8 ounces dry pasta shells or baby bow tie pasta, cooked al dente according to package directions
4 ounces Parmesan cheese
1 tablespoon cream or evaporated skim milk
¼ cup finely chopped fresh parsley
   Fresh ground black pepper

Sauté the onion, garlic, and celery in olive oil in a Dutch oven and cook until tender, but not brown. Add the next eight ingredients and simmer for 2 hours. Stir in the chopped spinach and cook for 10 more minutes. Add the cooked pasta. Do not cook the pasta in the soup or it will get overcooked and mushy. Stir in the Parmesan cheese, cream, parsley, and freshly ground black pepper. Serve immediately.

Makes 8 to 10 servings.

Waylon Jennings, singer/songwriter
Courtesy of Twenty-Five Years with Waylon and Still Cooking, *by Jessi Colter and Maureen Raffety*

"The Ballad of Davy Crockett" was a Top Twenty tune for four different singers, including Fess Parker, ol' Davy himself.

PANCHO VILLA'S CORN SOUP WITH CHEESE AND CHILIES

Croutons:
½ teaspoon cayenne pepper
1 teaspoon ground cumin
¼ teaspoon salt
½ stick butter, melted
1½ cups cubed French or Italian bread (½-inch cubes)

Soup:
5 large ears fresh corn or 3 cups kernels
1 cup water
½ stick butter
2 tablespoons minced onions
3⅓ cups half and half
1 teaspoon salt
1 teaspoon Tabasco sauce
¼ teaspoon pepper
½ pound Monterey Jack or Cheddar cheese, shredded
3 tablespoons diced roasted hot green chilies

Preheat the oven to 325°. Combine the crouton seasonings with the butter and toss with bread cubes until they are well coated. Spread the cubes in a single layer on a baking sheet and bake for 10 to 15 minutes, stirring once midway through, until golden brown.

Cut kernels off corn cobs. Whiz the kernels with water in a food processor or blender to make a coarse purée. Melt the butter in a large saucepan. Add the onions and sauté until soft and translucent. Add the corn purée and cook over medium heat for 5 minutes, stirring occasionally. Add the half and half, salt, Tabasco sauce, and pepper. Gently heat through, but do not allow to simmer. To serve, ladle the soup into 5 deep soup bowls. Sprinkle each serving with some cheese and chilies. Garnish with croutons.

Makes 4 to 6 servings.

The Home Ranch
Clark, Colorado

OLD-FASHIONED CHICKEN NOODLE SOUP

8 to 10 cups chicken broth (chicken soup base or canned broth may be used)
2 to 3 cups diced cooked chicken
2 cups diced potatoes (leftover mashed potatoes work great)
1 cup chopped carrots
   Salt and pepper to taste

Waylon Jennings—One of country music's greatest outlaws

Combine all ingredients and cook until vegetables are tender. Add Homemade Noodles to boiling soup. Cook for about 15 minutes, until noodles are tender.

Homemade Noodles:
2   cups all-purpose flour
1   teaspoon salt
3   eggs
1   tablespoon vegetable oil
2   to 4 tablespoons cold water

Place flour and salt in a large bowl. Make a depression in the center and add eggs and oil. Gradually stir in flour from edges adding water, 1 tablespoon at a time, until floor is moistened enough to form a ball. Divide dough into 4 equal parts. Roll 1 part at a time onto wax paper. Form into a rectangle on a well floured board. Cut into ¼-inch strips. Carefully drop noodles into chicken soup. Cook until tender.
   Makes 8 to 10 servings.

Bar H Bar Ranch
Soda Springs, Idaho

WRANGLER JANE'S RAINY DAY SOUP

My favorite recipe of all time is my grandmother's recipe for Rainy Day Soup. Believe me this soup is fantastic! I hope you enjoy this soup as much as I have since I was a very small child.

You need a large soup pot to make this in, and I must tell you that it even tastes better the second and third day. I usually freeze half of it because I like to have it later without all the fuss of making it. I must warn you though that the reason it is called Rainy Day Soup is because it takes all day to make it. We always had it on a rainy day when we couldn't go out.

2 to 3 pounds short ribs
4 to 6 onions, peeled and divided
1 16-ounce can tomato sauce
1 28-ounce can stewed tomatoes
   Small red potatoes (as many as you like), peeled
8 ounces elbow macaroni, cooked

Salt and pepper to taste
Parsley flakes

Place the short ribs in a large pan. Cover with water. Add 2 whole onions. Cook on medium heat for 4 hours, or until the meat falls off of the ribs. Remove the ribs from the meat and skim off the fat. Now you are ready to make the soup.

Add a little more water to fill at least half the pot. Add salt and pepper and a lot of parsley flakes. Add tomato sauce and stewed tomatoes. By this time the first onions have cooked down so add 3 or 4 more, along with the potatoes. Let the soup cook for at least 1 hour for flavor. Then add the precooked macaroni. The macaroni is the last thing to be added, and you don't want to overdo this because the macaroni swells up and could absorb too much juice.

This soup will feed a large crowd, or you can freeze half for another day.

Melody Patterson, actress

While just a teenager, Melody Patterson rode the wild and funny West as Wrangler Jane in *F Troop*.

HOT SHOT POTATO SOUP

5   pounds potatoes, peeled and diced
½   cup grated celery
½   cup grated carrots
    Salt and pepper to taste
    Margarine
¼   cup onion flakes
¼   cup parsley flakes
    Milk

Combine potatoes, celery, and carrots in a large pot. Add just enough water to keep it from sticking. Cook until tender. Add salt, pepper, margarine, onion flakes, and parsley flakes. Let sit for about 5 minutes (so onion flakes can soften). Mash potatoes in the water and add milk until it reaches the thickness you desire. Serve with salad and hot, hard bread.

Makes 10 to 12 servings.

Gail Davis, actress

NORTH FORK TOMATO CHEDDAR SOUP

It's from North Fork, but use a spoon anyway.

¼   of a #10 can whole tomatoes with juice
¼   of a #10 can tomato sauce
1   8-ounce can V-8 juice
⅜   cup Worcestershire sauce
½   teaspoon celery seed
    Dash of Tabasco sauce
1   tablespoon horseradish
2   cups grated sharp Cheddar cheese

Mash whole tomatoes and add all other ingredients, except the cheese. Heat thoroughly. Add cheese to soup just before serving.

Makes 4 to 6 servings.

Karen S. May, North Fork Guest Ranch
Shawnee, Colorado

WRANGLER SOUP

4   pounds ground beef
2   onions, peeled and chopped
4   28-ounce cans tomatoes
4   16-ounce cans tomato sauce
4   17-ounce cans whole kernel corn, drained
4   15½-ounce cans kidney beans
4   1¼-ounce packages taco seasoning mix
    Sour cream, chopped chives, and shredded sharp Cheddar cheese

In a large Dutch oven over medium heat, brown the beef. Drain excess drippings. Add the onion, tomatoes, tomato sauce, corn, kidney beans, and taco seasoning; cook until bubbling. Garnish with sour cream, chives, and cheese. Serve with tortilla chips.

Note: You can easily half or quarter the recipe for smaller crowds.

Makes 20 servings.

Gail Lander, Kedesh Ranch
Shell, Wyoming

STIR-UPS

73

EAGLE-EYE ANNIE OAKLEY'S ONION SOUP

A sure-fire favorite.

3   tablespoons butter
6   medium onions, sliced
3   tablespoons vegetable oil
1   teaspoon sugar
2   tablespoons flour
3   10½-ounce cans beef broth
3   soup cans water
½   teaspoon sage
1   cup pale dry sherry
1   bay leaf
     Sourdough muffins
     Swiss cheese
     Parmesan cheese

Simmer first three ingredients on medium heat, covered, for 20 minutes. Add sugar and cook for 20 minutes, until golden colored. Add flour and cook for 2 minutes, then add beef broth, water, sage, sherry, and bay leaf. Bring to a boil and simmer for 30 minutes. Serve with a floating toasted sourdough muffin, topped with melted Swiss cheese. Sprinkle with Parmesan cheese.

Gail Davis, actress

Pigtailed Gail Davis was probably the first actress to star in her own western series when she portrayed the sharpshooting Annie Oakley from 1953 to 1958. Brad Johnson co-starred as Deputy Lofty Craig. Davis also co-starred in a number of Gene Autry films.

Ken Curtis as deputy marshal Festus Haggen on *Gunsmoke*

WHATCHA GONNA DO STEW

5 to 7 potatoes, peeled and cubed
2 to 4 carrots, sliced
½ cup chopped onions
1 garlic clove, minced
2 to 4 stalks celery, sliced
1 16-ounce can tomatoes
1 T-bone or something good along with the fat, bone and all (cut the meat into chunks, but add the bone to stock, too)
Water (enough to boil the vegetables)
Salt and pepper to taste

Add the vegetables to boiling water. Cook until tender, then add all the other stuff and cook until it tastes good enough to eat.
    Makes 4 to 6 servings.

Chris LeDoux, rodeo cowboy and singer/songwriter

RUTH'S CABBAGE SOUP

Stubbornly good!

4 8-ounce cans tomato sauce
4 8-ounce cans water
2 16-ounce cans stewed tomatoes, blend in blender with 2 onions
1 bay leaf
½ teaspoon seasoning salt
½ teaspoon celery salt
2 to 3 pounds short ribs or neck bones
1 medium or 1/2 large cabbage
1 cup packed light or dark brown sugar
Juice of 2 lemons

Combine tomato sauce, water, tomatoes, and onions in large heavy pot. Add bay leaf, seasoning salt, celery salt, and ribs. Bring to a boil, lower heat and simmer for 2 hours. Shred cabbage and add to pot with brown sugar and lemon juice. Continue to cook for 2 more hours. Serve with warm black bread.
    Makes 8 to 10 servings.

Torrie and Ken Curtis, actor and singer

COW HAND STEW

If the boss don't allow whiskey on yer outfit then leave it out, but it shore adds something on those real cold days. Some folks think this recipe is too hot. I like to try it out on one of the hired hands first. If they say it's all right then I can always blame it on them.

2½ to 3 pounds beef, cubed
2 tablespoons all-purpose flour
1 teaspoon paprika
1 teaspoon chili powder
½ teaspoon salt
3 to 4 tablespoons vegetable oil
2 onions, sliced
¼ teaspoon dried minced garlic
¼ cup soy sauce
1 16-ounce can stewed tomatoes
1 11.5-ounce can Spicy Hot V-8 juice
2 tablespoons Worcestershire sauce
½ cup chunky-style mild salsa
1 tablespoon chili powder
½ teaspoon ground cloves
½ teaspoon cinnamon
½ cup Yukon Jack whiskey
¼ to ½ teaspoon crushed red pepper
2 cups chopped potatoes
2 cups chopped carrots
1 cup chopped celery

Coat the beef in a mixture of flour, paprika, 1 teaspoon chili powder, and salt. Brown in oil in a Dutch oven. Add, stirring in remaining ingredients. Stir a couple of times while cooking. Cook until vegetables are done, about 45 minutes. It can be served then, but I like to let it simmer awhile.

Makes 6 to 8 servings.

*Jack Bradt, Triple R Dude Ranch
Keystone, South Dakota*

HUNTER'S STEW

Doggone fixin's.

Depending on where you are, there are a lot of different ways to make this stew. First of all, a little camp meat helps a lot (deer, rabbits, squirrels, maybe a skinned snake or two, and a variety of walking birds—hopping birds ain't good). Throw in a spud or two and some carrots if you have any. Onions help a great deal.

Let cook until done, take off flame, and let cool. Feed it to your dog and open a can of pork and beans!

Rory Calhoun, actor

James Garner has a secret recipe for chili burgers, which he guards very closely. One of his dreams is to open a chain of chili burger stands. Make that a Maverick burger, hold the onions.

SANTA YNEZ VALLEY HARVEST STEW

This comfortable dish can be served with crusty French bread and a simple salad of mixed greens with a Dijon vinaigrette. For a refreshing finish, serve with slices of fresh mango drizzled with a light raspberry sauce.

Step One:
4 tablespoons olive oil, divided
¾ cup diced salt pork
1 stick butter, divided
2 carrots, coarsely chopped
1 leek, coarsely chopped
4 shallots, coarsely chopped
1 large onion, coarsely chopped
1 garlic clove, minced
1 homemade bouquet garni (thyme, bay leaf, celery)
   Salt and fresh ground black pepper to taste
3 pounds beef (top round or rump), cut in large cubes and floured
4 tablespoons Cognac, warmed
½ bottle (about 2 cups) good red wine
2 cups beef stock, heated, or hot water

Step Two:
18 small onions, coarsely chopped
2 tablespoons butter
1 tablespoon sugar
1 tablespoon lemon juice
   Fresh chopped parsley

Put 2 tablespoons olive oil in a skillet and sauté pork. Remove and set aside. In the same skillet, add 4 tablespoons butter to oil and sauté vegetables; season with salt and pepper. Remove and place with pork and bouquet garni. Add another 2 tablespoons olive oil and brown floured beef. Remove and add to sautéed mixture. Preheat the oven to 300°. In a hot skillet pour in warmed

Besides his frontiersmen roles, Fess Parker starred in such western films as *Old Yeller* and *The Jayhawkers*. He's pictured here with Robert Taylor and Tina Louise in *The Hangman*.

Cognac and light. After the flame dies, combine with sautéed mixture and transfer to a 4-quart casserole dish (I prefer earthenware). Pour all but 4 tablespoons red wine on ingredients and then add hot beef stock or water to cover. Cook slowly in a moderate oven (280°–300°) for 1½ to 2 hours. Stir and continue to cook for 2 more hours. Add more wine if necessary (I prefer a higher ratio of wine to broth for a richer flavor).

Brown and caramelize remaining onions in butter and sugar. Add 4 tablespoons red wine and cook in covered skillet until almost tender. Sauté mushrooms in butter and lemon juice. Keep warm. When meat is tender, add onions and mushrooms and sprinkle lavishly with parsley.

Makes 6 to 8 servings.

Marcy and Fess Parker, actor

CHUCKWAGON SON-OF-A-GUN STEW

Son-of-a-Gun Stew was first heard of on the early Texas cattle drives and in the cow camps. I've eaten it a number of times and each time the ingredients and preparation seem to be a little different. So, when you make it, you're the boss. This recipe is the one most likely used by the old time chuckwagon cook—or cocinero.

First, you should have a freshly killed, young beef. Cut about ½ of the liver, ⅛ of the heart. Take a piece of the tongue, peel it, the sweetbreads and the marrow gut, two syrup buckets full of the stew meat, and maybe some of the sirloin steak if the cowboys are not looking. All these ingredients should be cut up in bite-size pieces. Brown this in a heavy iron pot with a couple of handfuls of the paunch fat. Add salt and pepper, barely cover the ingredients with hot water, and cook over a very slow fire for 5 hours, maybe 6. Just let it simmer. After about 4 hours, add the brains and maybe ½ cup of chili powder, if you have some handy. If you like garlic, chop up a couple of cloves and throw 'em in. Some sliced onions would be fine. During the last hour of cooking, see what you have left from last night's meal. Any cold steak? Chop it up and use it. Any cans of tomatoes? Use a couple. Remember to stir often and keep adding a little hot water as needed, just enough to keep it from sticking to the pot. How many will it serve? First come, first served. "Come and git it . . . come and git it, or we'll throw it out."

Tex Ritter, singer and actor

BUFFALO STEW

- 1   **pound ground beef**
- 1   **large onion, chopped**
- 2   **10-ounce cans Rotel tomatoes (with green chilies, if desired)**
- 2   **15-ounce cans ranch style beans**
- 3   **10-ounce cans minestrone soup**
- 1   **15-ounce can cream-style or plain corn**

Brown the beef with the onion. Drain excess drippings. Combine all ingredients in a large pot. Simmer for 2 hours.
   Makes 6 to 8 servings.

Carol and Bob Steinruck, Lazy Hills Ranch Ingram, Texas

Tex Ritter, one of the Silver Screen's top singing cowboys, poses with his little buckaroos, sons Tommy and John in 1951. Tex was nicknamed "America's most beloved cowboy."

Forrest Tucker, who played a Cavalry officer in "F Troop," really was in the U.S. Cavalry during World War II.

TV buffs recall Walter Brennan in the title role of *The Guns of Will Sonnett* in the late 1960s, but the three-time Academy Award winner's western film credits are fabulous: *Three Godfathers, My Darling Clementine, Red River, Rio Bravo, How the West Was Won, The Cowboy and the Lady,* and *Support Your Local Sheriff,* among others.

MRS. BRENNAN'S CLAM CHOWDER

Buckaroo soup, so to speak.

- ½ pound bacon or salt pork, diced
- 2 medium onions, diced
- 2½ cups diced raw potatoes
- ½ teaspoon salt
- ¼ teaspoon pepper
- 2 cups boiling water
- 6 or more clams, chopped fine (reserve liquid), or 1 10-ounce can minced clams (drained and liquid reserved)
- 1 quart milk
- 2 tablespoons butter
  Cornstarch

Cook the bacon or pork until crisp; add onions, and sauté for about 5 minutes. Drain off excess drippings. Add potatoes, seasonings, and water. Cover pan and simmer for about 10 minutes or until potatoes are tender. Add clam liquid, milk, and butter. Heat and thicken with cornstarch mixed with a little of the hot liquid, if desired. Add clams (do not boil) and heat thoroughly. May use a little less milk, if desired. Season to taste.

Makes 4 to 6 servings.

Walter Brennan, actor

"I'm a cowboy. I don't know nothin' else."
—Charlton Heston in *Will Penny*

COWBOY EMMY WINNERS

1957 (presented in 1958)—Best Dramatic Series with Continuing Characters: *Gunsmoke*

1958 Best Supporting Actor in a Dramatic Series—Dennis Weaver *(Gunsmoke)*

1965 Outstanding Continued Performance by an Actress in a Leading Role—Barbara Stanwyck *(The Big Valley)*

1966 Outstanding Performance by an Actress in a Supporting Role in a Drama—Agnes Moorehead *(The Wild, Wild West)*

1967 Outstanding Performance by an Actor in a Supporting Role in a Drama—Milburn Stone *(Gunsmoke)*

1972 Outstanding Directorial Achievement in a Drama—Jerry Thorpe *(Kung Fu)*

1977 Outstanding Single Performance by a Supporting Actor in a Comedy or Drama Series—Ricardo Montalban *(How the West WasWon)*

POWDER KEGS

E. T.'S TEXAS TROUBADOUR CHILI

They'll waltz across Texas for this one.

- 2 pounds beef, chopped or ground
  Flour
- 1 cup water
- ½ cup shortening or lard
- ½ cup chopped onions
- 2 tablespoons minced garlic
- 4 tablespoons chili powder
- 2 tablespoons paprika
- ½ teaspoon cayenne pepper
- 1 teaspoon salt
  Juice of 1 lemon
- 3 ounces tomato sauce

Cook the beef in a pot of cold water until it boils and meat is brown. Skim off excess grease. In a small skillet, combine enough flour and 1 cup water to make a thin paste. Cook until browned. Add to beef. Add remaining ingredients and cook slowly for 1 hour.

Makes 6 to 8 servings.

Ernest Tubb, troubadour

The legendary Ernest Tubb's hits included "Slippin' Around," "Goodnight, Irene," and his signature "Walking the Floor Over You." He also appeared in several western films, including *Ridin' West* and *Fighting Buckaroos*.

"Dyin' ain't much of a livin', kid."—
Clint Eastwood to a bounty hunter in *The Outlaw Josey Wales*

Glen Campbell, the Rhinestone Cowboy, made his film debut in John Wayne's *True Grit* as a Texas Ranger.

RHINESTONE COWBOY CHILI

½	pound dry pinto beans
5	cups canned, peeled tomatoes
1	pound green bell peppers, seeded and coarsely chopped
1½	pounds onions, peeled and coarsely chopped
2	garlic cloves, crushed
1½	tablespoons olive oil
½	cup parsley, minced
2½	pounds hamburger meat
1	pound ground lean pork
⅓	cup chili powder
2	tablespoons salt
1½	teaspoons pepper
1½	teaspoons cumin seeds

Soak pinto beans overnight in cold water in a large chili pot. Cover beans with fresh cold water and simmer for 2 hours. (Pouring out water and rinsing beans reduces gaseous effects.) Sauté green bell peppers, onions, garlic, and parsley in olive oil. Add pork and hamburger; brown. Add spices and cook for 10 minutes. Combine with beans and cook, covered, for 1 hour. Uncover and cook for 30 more minutes (add water if needed).

Makes 4 quarts.

Glen Campbell, singer

HOSS'S BIG TEXAS CHILI

Not that Dan really measured the ingredients!

- 2 tablespoons vegetable oil
- 3 pounds boneless chuck, cut into 1-inch cubes
- 2 to 3 garlic cloves, chopped
- 4 to 6 tablespoons chili powder
- 2 teaspoons ground cinnamon
- 3 tablespoons all-purpose flour
- 1 tablespoon oregano
- 2 10½-ounce cans beef or chicken broth
- 1 teaspoon salt
- 1 teaspoon pepper
- 1 15-ounce can pinto beans (optional)
  Shredded Longhorn cheese
  Jalapeño peppers
  Sour cream
  Lime wedges

Heat oil in a 4-quart pan over medium heat. Add the beef and stir until meat changes color, but do not brown. Lower heat and stir in garlic. Combine chili powder, cinnamon, flour, and oregano, and stir into meat. Add broth, salt, and pepper. Stir and bring to a boil. Reduce heat to simmer and cook, partially covered, for 1½ hours. Stir occasionally. Add beans, if desired, and cook for 30 more minutes. May be prepared in advance and refrigerated. Re-heat before serving. Serve with "serve yourself" side dishes of shredded cheese, jalapeños, sour cream, and lime wedges.

Makes 10 to 12 servings.

Dan Blocker, actor

Tim Holt, the son of early film star Jack Holt, was a top-ten box office star of B-westerns in the 1940s. He also starred in the film classics *Stagecoach, My Darling Clementine,* and *The Treasure of the Sierra Madre.* (Courtesy of Berdee Holt)

"Like I say, pilgrim, you eat here till you get back on your feet."—John Wayne to Jimmy Stewart in *The Man Who Shot Liberty Valance*

"May I have your name?"—Jimmy Stewart in response

"Donithon, Tom Donithon. You can forget what I said about buying the gun. You're a tenderfoot. Liberty Valance, the toughest man south of the picket wire—next to me!"—John Wayne's response

COWBOY BEANS CHILI

- 1 pound hamburger meat
- 1 large onion
  Salt and pepper
- 2 cans pork and beans (discard the pork)
- 1 can chili
- 1 can tomato sauce
- 1 bay leaf (optional)
  Dash of oregano (optional)

Brown the meat with the onion. Add salt and pepper to taste. Drain off fat. Add pork and beans, chili, and tomato sauce. Add bay leaf and oregano if a spicier taste is desired. Heat to desired temperature.

Tim Holt, actor

Silver Screen Heroes— (l-r) Roy Rogers, Rex Allen, and Monte Hale

HALE AND HEARTY CHILI

3   pounds coarse lean ground beef
1   pound coarse lean ground pork
    Canola oil
3   garlic cloves, chopped
3   cups chopped onions
3   to 4 tablespoons chili powder
2   teaspoons salt
1   teaspoon pepper
2   teaspoons oregano
4   cups tomatoes
2   cups tomato sauce
    Chopped onions
    Grated cheese

Brown meat in canola oil. Drain off excess drippings. Stir in garlic, 3 cups onions, and spices. Add tomatoes and tomato sauce. Simmer, uncovered, over low heat for about 1½ hours. Serve with chopped onions and grated cheese.

Makes 12 to 16 servings.

Monte Hale, actor

REAL MAHAN CHILI

- 2 pounds bacon, cut into small bits
- 5 pounds boneless sirloin tip (lean coarse ground beef)
- 3 medium white onions, chopped
- 12 ounces beer
- 12 ounces tomato sauce
- 1 cup hot water
- 12 ounces beef bouillon
- 4 15-ounce cans pinto beans, drained (optional)
- 6 large garlic cloves, minced
- 1 pound tomatoes, diced
- 5 tablespoons paprika
- 2 teaspoons salt
- 1½ teaspoons black pepper
- 8 to 9 tablespoons chili powder
- 5½ tablespoons ground cumin
- 1 teaspoon oregano
- 3 tablespoons diced jalapeño peppers

In a frying pan, cook the bacon until crisp. Drain on paper towels. Brown the meat in the same pan. Sauté the onions in another pan with a small amount of bacon drippings. Add onions to meat, then add the bacon. Add remaining ingredients. Simmer over low heat, covered tightly, for 2 hours. Stir occasionally.

Makes 20 or more servings.

Robin and Larry Mahan, rodeo champion

Pro rodeo cowboy Larry Mahan won five consecutive all-around champion cowboy titles from 1966 to 1979 and qualified for twenty-six national finals during his illustrious career. He retired with six all-around world titles.

Western Stare—Denver Pyle is paying close attention in this shot from *The Rounders,* the 1965 film that also starred Glenn Ford, Henry Fonda, Chill Wills, and Sue Ann Langdon. Pyle has appeared in many classic westerns, including *The Man Who Shot Liberty Valance* and *Maverick* on the Silver Screen and as a regular on TV's *The Life and Legend of Wyatt Earp* and *The Life and Times of Grizzly Adams.* (Courtesy of Denver Pyle)

AUNT TIPPI'S QUICK CHILI

Now the secret of this recipe, and probably the most difficult part, is to get yourself a low-fat rabbit. The best place to acquire one is in East Texas because they've got to walk maybe a quarter of a mile between blades of grass, and this will skinny up a rabbit quicker than anything.

1 pound ground rabbit
1 package chili seasoning mix
1 cup diced tomatoes or 1 8-ounce can tomato sauce
1 cup water
1 14-ounce can chili beans
   Chili powder
   Chopped onions
   Grated Longhorn cheese

Take about a pound of meat off the low-fat rabbit and grind up the meat. Stir in the chili seasoning mix, tomatoes or tomato sauce, water, and chili beans. Add some chili powder for a little more heat, bring to a boil, and simmer for 15 minutes. That's right, 15 minutes. That's why I call this Aunt Tippi's Quick Chili. When you set this out put some chopped onions and grated Longhorn cheese with it. And remember, when you are trying something new, the fewer people who know about it, the better.

Makes 2 to 3 servings.

Denver Pyle, actor

ERNIE'S TEX CHILI

Great for the wild bunch!

- 3 pounds ground sirloin or ground round
- 1 stick butter
- 1 pound lean ground pork
- 3 green bell peppers, chopped
- 3 onions, chopped
- 3 garlic cloves, minced
- ¼ cup chili powder
- 2 tablespoons salt
- 1½ teaspoons pepper
- 3 teaspoons cumin
- ½ tablespoon cayenne pepper
- 3 1-pound cans tomatoes, chopped (include liquid)

In a large pot, brown the meat in butter. Pour off ⅓ cup liquid from meat. Use it to sauté peppers, onions, and garlic in a separate skillet until tender. Add to meat mixture and stir in chili powder, salt, pepper, cumin, and cayenne pepper. Add tomatoes. Simmer, covered, for 1 hour. Remove lid and simmer for at least 30 more minutes.

Makes 10 servings.

Ernest Borgnine, actor

Oscar-winner Ernest Borgnine made many a fine western film over the years, including *Bad Day at Black Rock, The Wild Bunch, Johnny Guitar, Jubal, Hannie Caulder,* and *The Badlanders.*

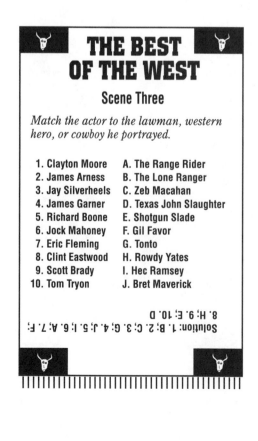

THE BEST OF THE WEST

Scene Three

Match the actor to the lawman, western hero, or cowboy he portrayed.

1. Clayton Moore	A. The Range Rider
2. James Arness	B. The Lone Ranger
3. Jay Silverheels	C. Zeb Macahan
4. James Garner	D. Texas John Slaughter
5. Richard Boone	E. Shotgun Slade
6. Jock Mahoney	F. Gil Favor
7. Eric Fleming	G. Tonto
8. Clint Eastwood	H. Rowdy Yates
9. Scott Brady	I. Hec Ramsey
10. Tom Tryon	J. Bret Maverick

Solution: 1. B; 2. C; 3. G; 4. J; 5. I; 6. A; 7. F; 8. H; 9. E; 10. D

SWEETHEARTS TURKEY CHILI

Vegetable cooking spray
1 medium onion, chopped
2 garlic cloves, minced
1 medium green bell pepper, chopped
1 pound ground turkey
3 14-ounce cans stewed tomatoes,
   undrained and chopped
2 15-ounce cans pinto beans, drained
⅔ cup salsa or picante sauce
1 tablespoon chili powder
1 tablespoon ground cumin
¼ teaspoon ground red pepper
1 tablespoon sugar

Chopped onions
Shredded cheese
Sour cream

Spray a pot with vegetable cooking spray. Sauté onion, garlic, and green pepper. Add turkey, and cook until crumbly. Add the next seven ingredients, and simmer for 30 minutes. Serve with chopped onions, shredded cheese, and sour cream.

Note: For spicier chili, turn up the heat by adding more red pepper, which supplies the "fire" in this recipe.

Makes 6 servings.

Sweethearts of the Rodeo

Sweethearts of the Rodeo, sisters Janis Gill (left) and Kristine Arnold. One of their recent releases on the Sugar Hill label was *Rodeo Waltz.*

ROADHOG CHILI

Aw right, mighty fine!

- 1 pound hamburger
- 1 cup minced onions
- 2 6-ounce cans tomato paste
- ½ small box chili powder
- 3 tablespoons red pepper

Brown hamburger and onions together. Drain excess grease. Stir in remaining ingredients one at a time. Simmer for at least 3 hours.

Makes 4 servings.

Brenda and Harold Reid, the Statler Brothers

Aw Right, Mighty Fine!—Lester "Roadhog" Moran and the Cadillac Cowboys: (l-r) "Wesley" W. Rexrode, Henry "Red" Vines, Raymond "Wichita" Ramsey Jr., and leader Lester are right at home in country music's basement (they always get good sound in there). Lester and the boys are pals with the Statler Brothers, whose many hit songs include "Whatever Happened to Randolph Scott?"

Gene Autry—The quintessential all-American cowboy

CHILIS

GENE AUTRY'S TEXAS CHILI

Legendary.

1½ pounds lean ground round
1   garlic clove, chopped
1   medium onion, chopped
1   medium green bell pepper, finely chopped
1   package chili sauce or 1 bottle Red Devil chile sauce
1   16-ounce can kidney beans
1   8-ounce can tomatoes, finely chopped
1   cup grated Jack cheese
    Chopped onions (optional)

Brown the first four ingredients in a large pan until tender. Add all remaining ingredients except cheese. Cook on a high simmer for 1 hour. Add cheese to thicken, just before serving. I like this best topped with chopped fresh onions.
   Makes 6 servings.

Gene Autry, singer and actor

CHARLIE'S DIET CHILI

Worth its weight in flavor!

1   pound lean ground beef
1   medium onion, chopped
2   cups sliced celery
½   cup chopped green bell peppers
½   teaspoon garlic salt
1¾   cups or 1 15-ounce can undrained kidney beans
4   cups or 2 16-ounce cans undrained tomatoes
½   to 1 teaspoon chili powder
1   bay leaf

Brown the ground beef and onion in a Dutch oven. Drain thoroughly. Add remaining ingredients. Simmer, covered, for 1 to 2 hours. Remove bay leaf. Serve hot. Freezes well.
   Makes 8 servings (1 cup = 156 calories).

Charlie Daniels, singer/songwriter

Charlie Daniels has idolized cowboys ever since he saw them as a boy on the Silver Screen. An annual rodeo in Murfreesboro, Tennessee, bears his name, and he owns the Twin Pines Ranch on the outskirts of Nashville.

Roy Rogers and Trigger—King of the Cowboys and the smartest horse in the movies

CHILI TEX

You'll sell your saddle for this stuff!

Chili (no beans)
Hominy
Chopped onions
Grated Cheddar cheese

Preheat the oven to 350°. In a casserole dish, layer the ingredients in desired quantities, to your taste. Bake for 40 minutes.

Dale Evans and Roy Rogers, Queen of the West and King of the Cowboys

HE-MAN CHILI

6	slices bacon
1	pound hot smoked sausage
1	pound lean ground beef
1	large onion, chopped
1	green bell pepper, chopped
2	garlic cloves, minced
1	hot green jalapeño pepper, diced
¼	cup Worcestershire sauce
1	teaspoon dry mustard
1	teaspoon celery seed
2	tablespoons chili powder
3	cups Italian pear tomatoes
1	tablespoon cayenne pepper
1	15-ounce can pinto beans
2	15-ounce cans kidney beans
1	cup burgundy wine

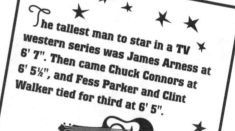

The tallest man to star in a TV western series was James Arness at 6' 7". Then came Chuck Connors at 6' 5½", and Fess Parker and Clint Walker tied for third at 6' 5".

Brown the bacon in a large Dutch oven. Remove bacon, crumble, and set aside. Slice the sausage into 1-inch pieces and fry in bacon fat until brown. Remove and set aside with bacon. Pour off excess fat from the pot. Brown the beef, drain, and set aside. Cook the onion, bell pepper, garlic, and jalapeño over low heat for 5 minutes. Stir in Worcestershire sauce, mustard, celery seed, and chili powder. Simmer for 10 minutes. Mash tomatoes, and add with liquid and meats to onion mixture. Stir in cayenne pepper. Heat to boiling. Reduce heat and simmer for 30 minutes, stirring occasionally. Add beans with liquid and wine and heat to boiling. Reduce heat and simmer for 1 hour, stirring occasionally.
Makes 10 servings.

Ty Murray, rodeo champion
Courtesy of Cajun Country Cookbook *by Tony Chachere*

CADILLAC RANCH CHILI

Top of the line.

2 pounds hamburger
1 garlic clove, chopped
1 green bell pepper, chopped
½ cup chopped onions
1 16-ounce can tomato sauce
1 bay leaf
2 to 3 tablespoons chili powder
1 to 2 15-ounce cans chili beans

Fry hamburger, garlic, green pepper, and onions on medium heat until meat is browned. Drain off excess drippings. Add tomato sauce, bay leaf, chili powder, and beans. Cook for 30 minutes to 1 hour and eat!
Makes 8 to 10 servings.

Chris LeDoux, rodeo cowboy and singer/songwriter

Cowboy singer Chris LeDoux was a world champion bronc rider in the 1970s. In 1993 he had a gold record when he and Garth Brooks collaborated on "Whatcha Gonna Do with a Cowboy?"

Who's "easy lopin', cattle ropin', carefree as the tumbleweeds"? Why, Sugarfoot (Will Hutchins), of course. Hutchins was the star of *Sugarfoot* from 1957 to 1961.

RIO GRANDE CHILI

Sugarfoot's favorite.

1   tablespoon vegetable oil
1   medium onion, chopped
2   garlic cloves, chopped
1   pound ground beef
1   14½-ounce can peeled tomatoes
1   8-ounce can tomato sauce
2   15-ounce cans kidney beans
1   jalapeño pepper, chopped
2½ cups water
1   tablespoon chili powder
1   teaspoon sage
1   teaspoon oregano
1   teaspoon cumin
1   teaspoon dill seed
1   teaspoon pepper
   Dash of salt
   Chopped onions for garnish

Heat oil in a large skillet or Dutch oven. Add onion and garlic, and brown. Add beef and brown. Drain off excess drippings. Stir in remaining ingredients and bring to a boil, stirring constantly. Lower heat and let simmer. Uncover for 1 hour. Top with a heap of raw chopped onions, and serve with pan-fried cornbread.

Makes 4 servings.

Will Hutchins, actor

"I reckon so."
—Clint Eastwood throughout *The Outlaw Josey Wales*

Johnny Cash made his acting debut in 1971's *A Gunfight* opposite Kirk Douglas.

JOHNNY CASH'S "OLD IRON POT" FAMILY-STYLE CHILI

This recipe is taken from Recipes & Memories from Mama Cash's Kitchen, *a collection of recipes passed down in our family through the last seventy years.*

5   pounds sirloin steak, chopped
     Shortening
3   packages McCormick's chili seasoning*
3   to 4 15-ounce cans red kidney beans
3   to 4 16-ounce cans whole tomatoes
     Cumin*
     Thyme*
     Sage leaves*
     Garlic powder*
     Onion powder*
     Salt to taste
     Chopped onions*
     Chopped chili peppers*
1   4-ounce can tomato paste
2   tablespoons sugar
     Mexene chili powder*
     Spice Island chili con carne seasoning*

Brown steak with a little shortening until medium. Add chili seasoning, and cook for 5 minutes. Add beans, tomatoes, spices, onions, chili peppers, sugar, chili powder, and/or chili con carne seasoning. Taste. (If chili is too hot, add 1 to 2 cans tomatoes.) Add tomato paste. If chili seems too thick, add water. Simmer on low for 20 minutes. Serve with soda crackers and soda. This chili will be better tomorrow than today, if properly taken care of overnight. I have also been known to substitute things, such as snake meat, for the steak.

Serves 12 people, 3 helpings each!

*You must guess at the amounts to use—I never measure them!

Johnny Cash, singer/songwriter and actor

HUGH'S FAVORITE NO BEANS CHILI

Loved Farr and wide.

    Ground meat
    Garlic cloves
    Chili powder
    Black pepper
    Hot dried red peppers
    Cumin
    Oregano
    Tallow
    Salt

Hugh would have the meat department grind a very fine piece of meat (coarse ground, the size of a large pea). He would put that in a large cast-iron skillet. He would add fresh garlic, chili powder, and fresh ground black pepper. He would crumble up these real hot dried red peppers, and add a very delicate amount of cumin. Then a little oregano, and a piece of tallow for richness. He would cover all of that with cold water and cook it on a very low boil. From time to time he would add water. He didn't cover the skillet, and he added salt at the end. He would cook it so it was very tender. After it was finished he would serve it with regular crackers, oyster crackers, or breadsticks. There are no beans in this chili.

Mrs. Hugh Farr, Sons of the Pioneers

Sons of the Pioneers have Roy Rogers and Dale Evans surrounded. (Courtesy of Fred Goodwin Collection)

The TV movie *Wild Horses* brought Ben Johnson, Kenny Rogers, and Richard Farnsworth (l-r) together in 1986.

CHILIS

THE GAMBLER'S FIRE AND ICE CHILI

Great for when the dealin's done.

Good food shared with family and friends is one of the real pleasures in life. I'm on the road so much performing, recording, or filming, that it's really a treat to sit down and enjoy a relaxing meal. I'm pleased to share this recipe with you. It's a favorite of mine and believe me, it is meant to warm a southern boy's heart and soul!

1 20-ounce can pineapple chunks in syrup
1 28-ounce can whole tomatoes, with juice
1 6-ounce can tomato paste
1 4 ounce-can diced green chilies
3 garlic cloves, pressed or minced, divided
2 medium-size yellow onions, chopped, divided
1 green bell pepper, seeded and chopped
¼ cup chili powder
4 teaspoons ground cumin
1 tablespoon diced jalapeño chilies
2 teaspoons salt
2 tablespoons olive oil
2 pounds lean boneless pork butt, cut into 1-inch cubes
Sliced green onions
Shredded light Cheddar cheese
Light sour cream

Drain pineapple, reserving syrup. Drain and chop tomatoes, reserving juice. In a large bowl, combine reserved pineapple syrup, tomatoes and juice, tomato paste, green chilies, 2 garlic cloves, half of the chopped onions, bell pepper, chili powder, cumin, jalapeño chilies, and salt. Heat olive oil in a Dutch oven until very hot. Brown pork on all sides in batches. (Don't crowd the pot. Add just enough pork to cover bottom.) With all browned pork in the pot, add remaining garlic and onions. Cook until onions are soft. Add tomato mixture to pork mixture. Cover and simmer for 3 hours, stirring occasionally. Add pineapple for the last 30 minutes of cooking. For more fire, add 2 tablespoons jalapeño chilies. Serve with onions, cheese, and sour cream.

Makes 8 to 10 servings.

Kenny Rogers, singer and actor

Kenny Rogers—The Gambler

DIAMOND D BUFFALO CHILI

1 small bag pinto beans (soaked overnight in 3 quarts water)
1 medium Bermuda onion, chopped
1 pound ground buffalo meat
1 tablespoon olive oil
1 16-ounce can stewed tomatoes
2 tablespoons chili powder
1 teaspoon garlic salt, or to taste
1 teaspoon pepper
½ cup medium salsa

Cook the pinto beans without any seasoning until done. In a frying pan, brown the onion in the olive oil. Remove onion and set aside. Add the buffalo meat to pan, and cook until browned. Combine the onion, tomatoes, spices, and salsa with the meat. Mix well, then add to the pinto beans. Let simmer for 1 hour.

Makes 4 to 6 servings.

Richard Farnsworth, actor

TILLI'S CHILI

1   pound ground meat
1   16-ounce can mild chili
1   16-ounce can tomatoes
1   16-ounce can vegetables (like beans)
    Ketchup to taste
    Toast
    Cheese

Stir-fry the ground meat. Drain off excess drippings. Add the chili and stir while heating. Add tomatoes, vegetables, and ketchup to taste. Serve on toast, topped with cheese.

    Hope you like it!

    Makes 4 servings.

Floyd Tillman, singer

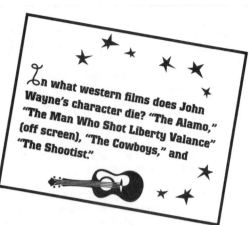

In what western films does John Wayne's character die? "The Alamo," "The Man Who Shot Liberty Valance" (off screen), "The Cowboys," and "The Shootist."

Oklahoma-born Floyd Tillman is one of the top western honky-tonk singer-songwriters of all time. He wrote "Slipping Around," among other hits.

Steven R. Stevens of the Cowboy Agency knows how to ride the L.A. range. Besides representing many of television's top cowboy actors, Stevens competes in team roping at rodeo events. His son is an athlete in the Pro Rodeo Cowboy Association.

FASTEST CHILI IN THE WEST

2   tablespoons olive oil
1   garlic clove (can use precut in juice), minced
2   16-ounce cans chili, with or without beans (I prefer Stagg)
1   15-ounce can sweet corn
2   pounds spaghetti
    Grated cheese (optional)

Put oil in a big frying pan. Add the garlic and corn; simmer until brown. Add the chili. Boil 2 quarts water and add the spaghetti. Spaghetti and chili should be ready around the same time. Mix together and top with grated cheese if you wish.

Makes 4 to 6 servings.

Steven R. Stevens, cowboy talent agent

The chuck wagon was invented in 1866 by Col. Charles Goodnight so that he could feed his cowboys on the long trail drives to the railheads.

The initials in the "O.K." Corral don't stand for okay, they stand for "Old Kinderhook."

SCORPION CHORIZO CORN CHILI

Stings your taste buds with flavor.

2   medium jalapeño peppers, chopped
1   3-ounce can green chilies
1   16-ounce can tomatoes
4   tablespoons fresh cilantro, chopped
2   to 3 cups beef broth, divided
1½ pounds Chorizo (spicy Mexican sausage)
1   large onion, chopped
1   green bell pepper, diced
4   garlic cloves, minced
1   tablespoon oregano
2   tablespoons fresh thyme, chopped (or 1 tablespoon dried)
1   tablespoon cumin
2   tablespoons chili powder
1   tablespoon cayenne pepper
1   tablespoon black pepper
1   tablespoon fresh rosemary, chopped
1   16-ounce can kidney beans
1   16-ounce can corn
    Salt to taste
    Crushed tortilla chips
    Shredded Cheddar cheese
    Sliced green onions

In a medium saucepan, combine jalapeños, green chilies, tomatoes, fresh cilantro, and 1 cup beef broth over high heat. Bring to a boil, then lower to a simmer for 10 minutes. Pour this mixture into a blender or food processor and purée. Set aside.

In a large pot, over medium heat, brown Chorizo for 10 minutes, breaking up large pieces with a spoon. Add onions and cook until well browned. Then add green peppers, garlic, and remaining spices. Continue to cook for 5 more minutes, stirring occasionally. Add kidney beans, puréed mixture, and remaining beef broth. Simmer on low heat for 45 minutes to 1 hour. Add salt and corn. To serve, garnish with tortilla chips, cheese, and onions.

Makes 10 to 12 servings.

Joe Cobb, Skyline Guest Ranch
Telluride, Colorado

BRETECHE CREEK MEATLESS BLACK BEAN CHILI

2   tablespoons vegetable oil
2   yellow onions, diced
4   garlic cloves, minced
2   green bell peppers, seeded and diced
1   yellow bell pepper, seeded and diced
1   red bell pepper, seeded and diced
1   jalapeño pepper, seeded and finely diced
2   15-ounce cans black beans
1   16-ounce can whole tomatoes
1   4-ounce small can tomato purée
2   tablespoons chili powder
¼   teaspoon cayenne pepper
1   tablespoon cumin
    Salt to taste
    Chopped onions
    Shredded Monterey Jack cheese
    Sour cream

Heat oil in a heavy skillet or Dutch oven. Add onions and garlic, and sauté for several minutes. Add bell peppers and jalapeño pepper, and sauté for several more minutes. Add beans, tomatoes, tomato purée, and spices and simmer gently for 1 hour or so. Ladle into bowls and garnish with onions, cheese, and sour cream. Serve with tortilla chips or warm whole-wheat rolls.

Makes 8 to 10 servings.

Breteche Creek Ranch
Cody, Wyoming

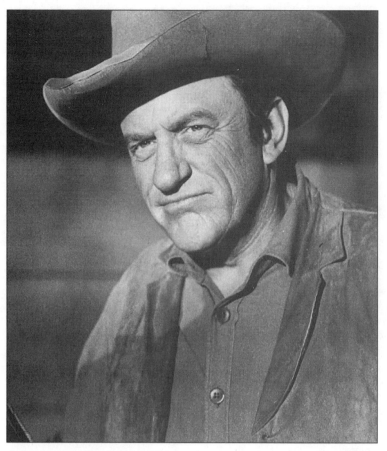

James Arness—Marshal Matt Dillon

GUN-SMOKIN' CHILI

Draws, fires.

4   to 5 pounds ground lean beef or venison
4   to 5 onions, chopped
4   to 5 tablespoons chili powder (1 per pound of meat)
1   4-ounce can green chili peppers, chopped
1   15-ounce can tomatoes, chopped
1   to 2 tablespoons cumin
1   to 2 tablespoons ground coriander
1   to 2 tablespoons red pepper
2   fresh jalapeño peppers, chopped

2   15-ounce cans chili beans
¼   cup Pace hot picante sauce
3   cups water
2   tablespoons lime juice
½   can beer (optional)

Brown the meat in a large Dutch oven. Add remaining ingredients. Cook, covered, for 4 hours. (If less hot chili is desired, omit the jalapeños.) Add more water, if needed, while cooking.

Makes 8 servings.

James Arness, actor

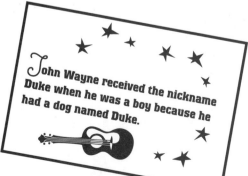

John Wayne received the nickname Duke when he was a boy because he had a dog named Duke.

Don Collier starred in three TV westerns: As Deputy Marshal Will Forman in *The Outlaws* from 1960 to 1962, as ranch foreman Sam Butler in *The High Chaparral* from 1967 to 1971, and as Noah Dixon in *The Young Riders* from 1990 to 1991. More recently, TV watchers have spotted him as the good guy in the Hubba-Bubba bubblegum commercials.

HIGH CHAPARRAL GREEN CHILI STEW

The Butler did it. (Hubba-Bubba!)

2   pounds extra lean chuck, cut into ½-inch cubes
      Vegetable oil
½   onion, chopped
3   large potatoes, peeled and cubed
3   large zucchini, peeled and cubed
12   large green chili peppers, roasted, peeled, and chopped (or 2 4-ounce cans chopped green chilies)
1   teaspoon garlic salt
1¼   teaspoons salt
6   cups water

Brown the meat in a bit of oil in a large cast-iron skillet. Add the onion and potatoes. When browned, drain off excess drippings. Add zucchini, chili peppers, garlic salt, salt, and water. Bring to a boil and let simmer for 45 minutes. Serve with your favorite bread.

    Makes 6 servings.

Don Collier, actor

CHUCK WAGON

BILL'S DARING BEER STEW

Taking this dare'll be rewarding.

¾	cup flour
	Salt and pepper to taste
3	pounds lean beef chuck, cut into cubes
½	cup vegetable oil
¼	cup tomato paste
⅛	teaspoon thyme
⅛	teaspoon minced dry garlic
6	parsley sprigs, chopped
1	bay leaf
3	cups beer
6	to 8 medium carrots, cut into rounds
3	large onions, diced
	Hot, cooked egg noodles

Put the flour and salt and pepper in a brown paper bag. Add meat and shake to coat meat evenly. Put oil in a large skillet and heat. Add meat to skillet and brown on all sides. Add seasonings and beer to browned meat. Bring to a boil. Reduce heat, partially cover, and simmer for 1½ hours. Remove bay leaf. Add carrots and onions and continue to simmer for 1 more hour. Serve on egg noodles.

William Sanderson, actor

William Sanderson played Lippy in the TV mini-series *Lonesome Dove* and the sequel *Return to Lonesome Dove.* Other western films in which he has appeared are *Ballad of Gregorio Cortez, Wagons East,* and *Saringo.* He also starred in the lead role on stage in *The Authentic Life of Billy the Kid,* directed by Tommy Lee Jones.

One of cowboydom's greatest sidekicks was Smiley Burnette. He rode alongside Charles Starrett, Gene Autry, and Roy Rogers. (Courtesy of Fred Goodwin Collection)

SMILEY'S CORN AND SALMON LOAF

1 #2 can cream-style corn
1 #1 can salmon
1 cup fine bread or cracker crumbs
2 eggs, beaten
1 cup milk
1 tablespoon melted butter
1 teaspoon lemon juice
    Salt and pepper to taste

Remove bones and skin from salmon and combine with other ingredients. Bake in a greased loaf pan for 50 to 60 minutes in a 325° oven. Serve hot with buttered peas and crisp tart salad. This may be used a sandwich filling when cold.
    Makes 6 to 8 servings.

Smiley Burnette, actor

WICHITA MEATLOAF

1 pound ground meat
¾ cup oatmeal
    About 2 tablespoons wheat germ
1 onion
1 green bell pepper
    Mushrooms
3 garlic buds
2 eggs
3 tablespoons Worcestershire sauce
1½ tablespoons soy sauce
1 tablespoon Italian seasoning
1 small can tomato sauce

Combine all ingredients except tomato sauce. Spread tomato sauce over top and bake at 350° for a little more than 1 hour. Before serving, add ketchup for flavor. Serve with mashed potatoes and green beans.

Dusty and Jody McCrea, actors

Don't Look Back, They Might Be Gainin'—Joel McCrea has ridden tall in the saddle in many a fine western. He starred in such films as *Buffalo Bill, Four Faces West, The Oklahoman,* and *Wichita.* And he was the voice of Ranger Pearson in radio's *Tales of the Texas Rangers.*

Hoot Gibson won the title of Cowboy Champion of the World in 1912 and then moved to Hollywood, where he worked as a stuntman before becoming one of the western greats of silent films. During the 1920s, he was Universal's top western star. (Courtesy of Fred Goodwin Collection)

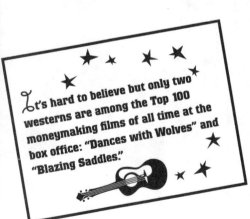

It's hard to believe but only two westerns are among the Top 100 moneymaking films of all time at the box office: "Dances with Wolves" and "Blazing Saddles."

HOOT'S ENCHILADAS

We like to make these enchiladas in pans and freeze them for future use.

2   medium onions, chopped
    Peanut oil for frying
1   pound ground round
3   small cans chopped ripe olives
½   pound Cheddar cheese
4   small cans tomato sauce diluted with same amount of water
½   teaspoon chili powder
1   level tablespoon flour mixed with ½ cup water
2   dozen tortillas
    Grated cheese for topping

Fry the onions in peanut oil, sauté the ground round in with onions, and turn off the flame. Add the olives and cheese. Cover, and allow cheese to melt through the meat, olives, and onions. To make the hot sauce, place the diluted tomato sauce and the chili powder in another pan. When the mixture comes to a boil, thicken it with the flour and water. One at a time, dip each tortilla into the hot sauce, place in another pan, and fill in the center with diluted tomato sauce and meat. Roll and fasten with a toothpick and place on a greased pan. Cover the pan of enchiladas with remaining hot sauce and grated Cheddar cheese. Bake for 45 minutes at 350°. Be sure to place a pan of water in the bottom of the oven to keep the enchiladas moist.

Dorothy and Hoot Gibson, actor

BOOT KICKING RANGE TOP CASSEROLE

This is a fast top-of-the-stove meal after helping your rancher husband work cattle. You can get right off your horse and kick around the kitchen in your boots.

1   pound ground meat
1   onion
4   carrots
1   cup shredded cabbage
2   cans kidney beans
2   garlic buds
    Optional: Italian seasoning, salt, pepper, mushrooms, crushed chili peppers

Brown the meat. Add the onion and garlic. Cut up the carrots, and add carrots and kidney beans to the mixture. Fry for about 45 minutes.

Frances Dee and Joel McCrea, actor

As Hopalong Cassidy, actor William Boyd was beloved as one of the Silver Screen's and TV's greatest cowboy heroes of all time. He and his horse, Topper, made sixty-six Hoppy films before the popular television series (with a total of ninety-nine episodes) started in 1948. (Courtesy of Fred Goodwin Collection)

HOPPY'S FRIED CHICKEN

This is a fine recipe that will be utterly ruined if you cook the chickens over too hot a flame.

2 young chickens, 2¼ pounds each
    Salt and pepper
3 strips bacon
3 cups flour
1 pound butter
1½ cups whole milk
    Parsley

Cut up the chickens. Wash and drain, but do not wipe dry. Season with salt and pepper. Roll in flour. Fry out the bacon until there is deep fat in the pan. Add butter and chicken. Cook slowly in hot fat, turning frequently until chicken is well browned. Remove chicken to a hot platter. Add bacon and milk to the cooking fat. Stir thoroughly. Let simmer for 15 minutes. Pour over chicken. Garnish with parsley.

*Hopalong Cassidy (William Boyd), actor
Used with permission from* Hoppy Talk, *the Hopalong Cassidy fan club newsletter.*

"CRASH" CORRIGAN'S CHICKEN SHERRY

3 half breasts skinless, boneless chicken
    Soy sauce
    Sliced mushrooms
    Butter
    Sherry
    Pinch of cornstarch

Dip the chicken in a mixture of melted butter and soy sauce. Lightly sauté to just brown. Remove and put in a separate pan. In the same pan used to brown the chicken, add mushrooms and a little more butter. Brown the mushrooms. Put butter and sherry in with the chicken and heat to medium. When the chicken is done, remove and put on a platter. Add cornstarch to juices in that pan until it thickens or reduces. Sauté mushrooms. Put mushrooms on top of chicken and cover with sauce.

Ray "Crash" Corrigan, actor

Ray "Crash" Corrigan was one of the top stars of B westerns. He was one of the original Three Mesquiteers, for which he partnered with Bob Livingston and John Wayne. After nineteen Mesquiteer films, he made nearly three dozen Range Buster films. Following that series, he retired from the screen and devoted most of his time to his ranch and western town, Corriganville, where many A and B westerns were filmed, including *Fort Apache.* His son Tom operates Corrigan's Restaurant in Thousand Oaks, California.

As Wishbone, Paul Brinegar cooked up many a pot of stew for the drovers on *Rawhide*. In real life, he admitted he couldn't cook worth a darn.

WISHBONE'S BRISKET OF BEEF

3   to 4 pounds beef brisket
1   medium or large onion, sliced
1   cup chili sauce
1   garlic clove, minced
1   12-ounce can beer
½   cup water

Place all ingredients in a baking pan. Cover tightly with foil. Bake at 350° for 3½ hours. Remove foil. Brown, uncovered, at the same temperature, for 20 to 30 minutes or until tender. Serve sliced, with juices spooned over top. Great with French rolls and steamed broccoli.

Paul Brinegar, actor

DOC'S MEATLOAF

2 pounds ground chuck
1 cup chopped onions
½ cup chopped green bell peppers
1 cup seasoned bread crumbs
1 cup undiluted evaporated milk
2 eggs, slightly beaten
1 teaspoon salt
¼ teaspoon pepper
1 teaspoon dry mustard

Combine all ingredients and bake at 350° for 1 hour and 10 minutes.

Milburn Stone, actor

DOC'S LEG OF LAMB

Leg of lamb
⅓ cup lemon juice
⅓ cup Worcestershire sauce
⅓ cup ketchup
Bay leaves to taste
Rosemary to taste

Combine all ingredients except the lamb. Pour over lamb and bake, uncovered, in a slow oven. Taste as you go along.

Milburn Stone, actor

A friendly game of checkers in the Longbranch between Marshal Dillon (James Arness) and Doc (Milburn Stone) as Kitty (Amanda Blake) kibitzes.

Sons of the Pioneers in 1941—(clockwise from top) Bob Nolan, Karl Farr, Lloyd Perryman, Tim Spencer, Hugh Farr, and Pat Brady

YANKEE POT ROAST

1 3-pound chuck roast
Salt and pepper
1 cup chopped celery
1 cup chopped onions
2 cups sliced carrots
2 tablespoons vinegar
1 12-ounce can tomatoes (I use S & W bits & pieces)

Sprinkle meat on both sides with salt and pepper. Place in a Dutch oven. Roast at 375° until brown, about 30 minutes. Add onions, celery, and carrots. Stir vinegar into tomatoes. Add all to roast. Cover and bake for 2½ hours or until tender. Great with mashed potatoes.

Jerry Scoggins, singer

PIONEER FLANK STEAK

¼ cup lemon juice
½ cup soy or barbecue sauce
1 teaspoon garlic powder
1 teaspoon ground pepper
Finely chopped green onions
Approximately 2 pounds flank steak

Combine all ingredients except steak in a bowl. Score steak diagonally on both sides. Place the meat in a dish and pour marinade over the meat. Leave at room temperature for 4 to 5 hours. Turn steaks at least once. Remove meat from marinade. Grill 4 to 5 minutes on each side. Don't overcook, because the meat toughens easily.

Bob Nolan, Sons of the Pioneers

Brian Keith made a number of great westerns, such as *Arrowhead, Nevada Smith, The Rare Breed,* and *Scandalous John,* but he also starred in the 1960 Sam Peckinpah TV series *The Westerner* along with Brown, the same dog featured in Walt Disney's *Old Yeller.*

"And you want to plan your moves, pick your place to fight, don't make any threats, and don't you ever walk away from one either."—Brian Keith to Steve McQueen in *Nevada Smith*

"We deal in lead, friend."—Steve McQueen to Eli Wallach in *The Magnificent Seven*

WESTERNER STUFFED STEAK FOR TWO

It's great! (I wouldn't steer you wrong.)

2   same-sized flank steaks
½   pound bacon, cooked and crumbled
    Bacon drippings
    Sliced mushrooms
    Sliced onions
    Garlic salt to taste
    Pepper to taste
    Oysters

Fry the bacon until crisp, and crumble it in a bowl. Fry up a lot of sliced mushrooms and onions in the bacon fat with garlic salt and pepper—red pepper if you like it hot. When the mushrooms and onions are almost done, put in some small oysters—as many as you want—just heat them until the edges curl and there's your stuffing. Mix the whole mess with the bacon and spread it thick all over on steak. Put the other steak on top and sew them together. Grill the steak and don't forget to pull out the string! Steak should be rare or else it's tough. Louisiana cowboys will eat two of these. Women aren't crazy about it, and I don't know why.

Brian Keith, actor

LONGHORN LEMON BAKED BEEFSTEAK

3   pounds steak
2   tablespoons butter
2   teaspoons salt
¼   teaspoon pepper
1   large lemon, thinly sliced
2   medium onions, sliced
1   cup ketchup
1   tablespoon Worcestershire sauce
¼   cup water

Preheat the oven to 350°. Combine all ingredients in a large ovenproof dish. Cover tightly. Bake for up to 2 hours or until tender.
    Makes 8 to 12 servings.

Carolyn and Bill Hearne, music publishers

BUFFALO BILL JR.'S TEX-MEX STEAK

Besides good old "charred" broiled steaks and rare roast beef, this is my next favorite meat dish.

- 1 **tablespoon chili powder**
- ½ **teaspoon ground cumin**
- ½ **teaspoon salt**
- ¼ **teaspoon ground red pepper**
- 1 **big top sirloin steak, cut 1½ inches thick (minimum)**
- 1 **15-ounce can black beans, rinsed and drained**
- 1 **cup thick salsa (to your taste—I like it hot)**
   Fresh cilantro sprigs for garnish (optional)

In a small bowl or cup, combine chili powder, cumin, salt, and red pepper. Trim the fat from the steak and press the seasoning mixture evenly into both sides of the steak. Let it stand while you preheat the barbecue grill until the coals have flamed down and have formed a gray covering ash. Place the steak on the grill, 4 inches from the coals, and grill for 20 to 25 minutes for rare to medium meat (turning occasionally). Remove the steak from the grill and let it stand for 10 minutes before carving. Meanwhile, in a medium bowl, combine the beans and salsa. Mix until well blended. Slice the steak on the bias, across the grain, and arrange on a preheated serving platter. Top with the salsa mixture and garnish with cilantro sprigs if desired. Goes good with garlic-cheese toast and a tossed salad.

Makes 4 servings (3 for the hungry ones).

Dick Jones, actor

Dick Jones starred opposite Jock Mahoney as Dick West in *Range Rider* from 1951 to 1952. During the mid-1950s, Dick Jones starred on TV as Buffalo Bill Jr. At age four, Jones began his career appearing in rodeos as the "World's Youngest Trick Rider and Roper." He was discovered by cowboy movie star Hoot Gibson, and at age eleven was selected by Walt Disney to be the voice of Pinocchio in the animated film classic. He made a number of western films, including eight with Gene Autry.

Most folks remember Claude Jarman Jr. as young Jody in *The Yearling*, but he played the son of John Wayne and Maureen O'Hara (pictured) in the John Ford classic *Rio Grande*, where he performed some outstanding Roman riding as he jumped fences astride two horses.

THE BEST OF THE WEST

Scene Five

Match the actor to the lawman, western hero, or cowboy he portrayed.

1. James Drury	A. Johnny Yuma
2. Doug McClure	B. The Virginian
3. Lee Majors	C. Heath Barkley
4. Ward Bond	D. Chester Goode
5. Nick Adams	E. Trampas
6. Steve McQueen	F. Nichols
7. Guy Madison	G. Josh Randall
8. Guy Williams	H. Wild Bill Hickok
9. Dennis Weaver	I. Seth Adams
10. James Garner	J. Zorro

Solution: 1. B; 2. E; 3. C; 4. I; 5. A; 6. G; 7. H; 8. J; 9. D; 10. F

CODE OF THE WEST PEPPER STEAK WITH COGNAC CREAM

	Cracked pepper (black, red, or green)
1	2½-pound filet mignon
4	to 5 tablespoons cognac
⅓	cup heavy cream

Press cracked pepper (as much as desired) on both sides of steak. Let it sit for 1 hour. Pan fry almost to desired doneness. Pour cognac over steaks and stir in cream. Heat until warmed through. Place steaks on a plate and cover with sauce. Serve with pan-fried potatoes, steamed cauliflower, and salad.

Makes 6 to 8 servings.

Katie and Claude Jarman Jr., actor

Gunsmoke Portrait—Taking a break in the streets of Dodge City are Marshal Matt Dillon (James Arness), Galen "Doc" Adams (Milburn Stone), Miss Kitty Russell (Amanda Blake), Quint Asper (Burt Reynolds), and Festus Haggen (Ken Curtis).

MARINATED STEAK À LA BURT

Quint's essential meal.

- 1 tablespoon lemon juice
- ½ cup soy sauce
- ½ teaspoon Worcestershire sauce
- 1 teaspoon sugar
- ½ garlic clove, crushed
- 2 tablespoons of your best brandy or bourbon
  Dash of liquid red pepper seasoning
  Dash of ground ginger
  Thick-cut steaks (your choice)

Combine the first eight ingredients. Let steaks marinate in this mixture for at least 30 minutes—1 hour is even better. To broil or barbecue steaks, trim excess fat. Slash remaining fat just to the meat (not into it). Place on grill about 4 inches from hot coals to sear. For a 1½-inch steak sear on high, direct heat 3 to 5 minutes on the first side. Turn with tongs and cook the second side on medium to low heat. Cook 5 to 8 minutes for medium and 12 to 15 minutes for well done. Because grills and broilers vary, it is best to check doneness by slitting close to the bone or in the thickest part of the meat to peek. Enjoy!

Burt Reynolds, actor

Whatever happened to Randolph Scott? Some cowboy heroes live forever in our hearts.

HIGH COUNTRY NEW YORK STRIPPER

10   ounces ketchup
     White pepper
     Pinch of garlic powder
3   tablespoons molasses
3   ounces white wine vinegar
     Cayenne pepper
1   tablespoon sugar
     New York strip steaks (1 per person)

Two hours before cooking, combine the first seven ingredients and spread an even coating of the mixture on the meat. On a charcoal grill, set coals and light, allowing at least 30 minutes for coals to heat evenly. Set the grate fairly close to the fire. Cooking time will vary with the size of the steaks. When you turn the steaks, spread more sauce lightly over top. The steaks will be complimented by the flavor of the sauce, so don't use too much.

Note: All spices are to taste. Start out with a little and experiment. It's the only way to achieve the right flavor.

Randolph Scott, actor

CURLY JOE'S ROAST BEEF

Easy to throw together.

1   2-pound tri-tip beef roast
1   package dry onion soup mix
1   teaspoon garlic powder or to taste
2   10¾-ounce cans mushroom soup
     Diced carrots or potatoes (optional)

Preheat the oven to 350°. Line a baking dish with foil. Place roast on top of foil. Sprinkle with onion soup mix and garlic powder. Pour mushroom soup on roast with ½ cup water added for each can of soup. If desired, add carrots and/or potatoes around the roast. Fold foil over roast and seal over the baking dish. Bake for about 2 hours or until beef is tender. This makes a delicious gravy.

Makes 8 to 10 servings.

Joe De Rita, actor

The Three Stooges (Curly Joe, Larry, and Moe) turn cowboys in *The Outlaws Is Coming* (1965), their last film. (Courtesy of Steve Cox Collection)

CHEYENNE CHICKEN FRIED STEAK

- 2 pounds lean, tenderized round steak
- 1 cup all-purpose flour
- 2 teaspoons salt
- 1 teaspoon pepper
- 1 egg, beaten
- 1 cup milk
- 1½ cups canola or vegetable oil

Cut the steak into serving pieces. Mix flour, salt, and pepper, and place on a plate or wax paper. Mix egg and milk in a small, flat bowl. Dredge meat in flour mixture, and dip in egg mixture and into flour mixture again. Heat oil in a large skillet until very hot, but not smoking. Add steaks to hot oil and cook for about 5 minutes on each side or until golden brown. Drain on paper towels; serve warm with Cream Gravy.

Note: Buttermilk may be substituted for egg-milk mixture.

Makes 6 to 8 servings.

Cream Gravy:
- 4 tablespoons pan drippings
- 3 tablespoons all-purpose flour
- 2 cups milk
- 1 teaspoon salt
- ¼ teaspoon pepper

Pour off drippings, leaving 4 tablespoons. Blend flour, stirring constantly, until bubbly. Stir in milk. Add salt and pepper. Continue stirring until thickened. If too thick, add a little more milk.

Makes 8 servings.

Bill Cody, disc jockey

Lee Aaker starred as Rusty, a dog's best friend, in *The Adventures of Rin Tin Tin* from 1954 through 1959.

RUSTY'S PORK CHOPS

- 4 medium pork chops
- 1 16-ounce package elbow macaroni, cooked
- 1 8-ounce package Velveeta cheese
- 1 cup milk
- 1 10¾-ounce can mushroom soup
- 2 soup cans water
  Grated cheese

Preheat the oven to 350°. Brown pork chops and pour off grease; set aside. Chop Velveeta cheese loaf into small pieces; set aside.

Combine milk, soup, and water. Mix together; add cheese. Layer 2 chops and half of the macaroni into a greased casserole dish. Top with half of the white sauce. Repeat with another casserole dish. Bake for 1 hour. Season to taste. Sprinkle with grated cheese.

Makes 2 casseroles.

Lee Aaker, actor

"My profession—you trust too much, you don't celebrate many birthdays. I kinda like it around here."—John Wayne to Jimmy Stewart in *The Shootist*

FALL GUY BEEF STROGANOFF

½   pound fresh mushrooms, sliced
1   large onion, chopped
½   stick butter or margarine, divided
2   pounds top sirloin
    All-purpose flour
1   teaspoon salt
1   10½-ounce can beef broth, diluted with water to make 2 cups
1   cup sour cream, at room temperature
    Hot, cooked rice or noodles

Sauté the mushrooms and onion in 2 tablespoons butter and remove from pan. Cut the meat into strips. Melt butter in a heavy skillet. Coat meat with flour and brown in butter. Add salt and broth mixture. Simmer, stirring occasionally, for about 45 minutes, or until meat is tender. Add mushrooms-onion mixture. Add sour cream a little at a time so it won't curdle. Simmer until blended. If thicker gravy is desired, add flour mixed with cold water to the sauce and simmer until desired thickness. Serve over hot rice or noodles.
    Makes 8 servings.

Rick Arnold, stuntman

Ronnie Dunn, half of award-winning country duo Brooks & Dunn with Kix Brooks, was born in Tulsa. Among the many Brooks & Dunn hits are "Next Broken Heart," "Brand New Man," and the monster that ate the country charts, "Boot Scootin' Boogie."

BOOT-SCOOTIN' PORK CHOPS AND SAUERKRAUT

Best served on a platinum platter!

4   butterfly pork chops
¼   cup butter
½   small onion, chopped
    Cavender's seasoning mix
    Black pepper
1   jar Vlasic sauerkraut

Season pork chops generously with Cavender's and pepper. Sauté pork chops and onion together until brown. Add sauerkraut (partially drain liquid), and simmer for 1 to 2 hours. Serve with mashed potatoes and vegetables of your choice.
    Makes 4 servings.

*Ronnie Dunn of Brooks & Dunn,
singer/songwriter*

Rick Arnold was a Hollywood stuntman for about twenty-five years and worked regularly in such TV series as *Laramie, Wagon Train, Laredo,* and *Rawhide,* plus he did stunt work in such films as *How the West Was Won* and *The Shakiest Gun in the West.*

WESLEY REXRODE'S BARBECUE FLATJACKS

You'll love 'em even better than you did then.

1   pound ground beef
¼   cup chopped onions
½   cup barbecue sauce
½   teaspoon Tabasco sauce
1   9½-ounce can canned biscuits
1   cup shredded sharp cheese

Preheat the oven to 375°. In a large frying pan, brown ground beef and onions; drain. Stir in sauces. Simmer while preparing crust. Make crust in a 13x9-inch pan; press biscuits together over bottom and sides. Spread with hot meat mixture. Sprinkle with cheese. Bake for 15 to 20 minutes.
    Makes 6 servings.

Deborah and Don Reid, the Statler Brothers

FORTUNE HUNTER'S BARBECUED BEEF

Very rewarding.

¾   cup water
2   pounds round steak, cut into 1-inch chunks
½   cup ketchup
½   cup chili sauce
4   teaspoons brown sugar
1   tablespoon cider vinegar
½   teaspoon salt
1   medium onion, minced

About 1½ hours before serving, mix all ingredients in a large skillet. Cover and chill for 30 minutes in the refrigerator. Over medium-low heat, cook, covered, for about 50 minutes or until steak is fork tender.
    Makes 6 main-dish servings.

Jimmy Fortune, the Statler Brothers

RED'S EASY OVEN-BARBECUED BRISKET

4   to 5 pounds brisket
1   teaspoon onion salt
1   teaspoon celery salt
1   teaspoon garlic salt
½   a 3½-ounce bottle liquid smoke
    Salt and pepper to taste
3   tablespoons Worcestershire sauce

Trim brisket well and place in a pan deep enough so foil placed across top of pan will not touch meat. Sprinkle with seasoning salts and pour liquid smoke over meat. Cover with foil and marinate in the refrigerator overnight. Preheat the oven to 275°. Sprinkle with salt, pepper, and Worcestershire sauce. Cover tightly with heavy-duty foil. Bake for 4½ hours or until tender.

Sauce:
½   cup ketchup
¼   cup water
¼   cup packed brown sugar
1   tablespoon vinegar
1   tablespoon liquid smoke
1   tablespoon Worcestershire sauce
1   tablespoon chili powder
½   teaspoon pepper
½   teaspoon Tabasco sauce
1   small onion, chopped

Mix sauce ingredients and simmer for 10 minutes. Cool brisket; slice thin. Pour sauce over meat. Bake, uncovered, at 325° for 30 minutes.
    Makes 15 to 20 servings.

Red Steagall, singer

THE BEST OF THE WEST

Scene Six

Match the actor to the lawman, western hero, or cowboy he portrayed.

1. Ken Berry   A. Rango
2. Michael Landon   B. Hoss Cartwright
3. David Carradine   C. Festus Haggen
4. Ken Curtis   D. Buck Cannon
5. Tim Conway   E. Kwai Chang Caine
6. Dan Blocker   F. Little Joe Cartwright
7. Ben Murphy   G. Capt. Wilton Parmeter
8. Lorne Greene   H. Jed "Kid" Curry
9. Cameron Mitchell   (Thaddeus Jones)
10. Leif Erickson   I. Big John Cannon
           J. Ben Cartwright

Solution: 1. G; 2. F; 3. E; 4. C; 5. A; 6. B; 7. H; 8. J; 9. D; 10. I

Baxter Black—World champion cowboy poet

COWBOY POET'S BARBECUE RIBS 'N' GRITS

Selection of a fire pit location is essential for this recipe. Our pit is 3' x 1½' x 1' deep. The grill is expanded metal and level with the ground. Outdoor tables and chairs made of cottonwood stumps are gathered around the west end of the grill. It is an area of intense visiting and activity when company comes. The Colorado dirt is kept dry and pulverized.

Those familiar with weather in the west know that certain atmospheric changes occur at sundown. The earth's crust cools, and the wind, usually imported from Wyoming, can appear with surprising force and suddenness! The proper combination of ground level ribs dripping in sticky barbecue sauce, enough company to loosen the dirt, and a twilight zephyr of 30 knots will result in a thick coating of sand and dirt on each succulent rib. If you are lucky, at the same time, the wind will turn the underlying coals into a blast furnace and blacken the bottom side of the ribs. After

hosing off at the nearest hydrant, the ribs are ready to eat. Serve with a pine needle and corral dust garnish.

1	cup ketchup
¼	cup vinegar
3	tablespoons Worcestershire sauce
½	teaspoon paprika
¾	cup packed brown sugar
1	teaspoon salt
¼	cup lemon juice
1	6-ounce can tomato paste
1	tablespoon brown mustard
16	good-sized country style pork ribs

Combine all ingredients well. Soak ribs in the sauce for a few hours before cooking, overnight if possible.

Note: It's handy to keep a covered pot of fresh corn on the cob for those guests who don't like their ribs served with such earthy grits.

Makes 8 servings (2 ribs each).

Cindy Lou and Baxter Black, poet

MAMA MEAT'S GOULASH (EXCEPT IT AIN'T REALLY GOULASH)

1 cup macaroni, uncooked
Margarine
1 onion, diced
1 pound ground chuck
2 cups stewed tomatoes
Grated cheese

Add macaroni to boiling salted water 'fer about 10 minutes. Preheat the oven to 350°. Melt some margarine in a frying pan and add onion. When it's kinda transparent add ground chuck and brown. Mix drained macaroni and stewed tomatoes with hamburger mixture. Put in a baking dish and top with grated cheese. Bake 'fer 1 hour. Stand back cause the young'uns will trample you trying to get to the dinner table.
Makes 4 to 6 servings.

Sidemeat, trail cook for Riders in the Sky

LAUGHING WATER BARBECUED BEEF

Even better the second day.

3 pounds chuck roast
1 14-ounce bottle ketchup
3 large onions, chopped
1 rib celery, chopped
1 tablespoon vinegar
1 tablespoon Worcestershire sauce
1 tablespoon chili powder
2 ketchup bottles water
1 tablespoon brown sugar
1 tablespoon cinnamon
Salt and pepper
Hamburger buns

Preheat the oven to 350°. Place the roast in a roasting pan. Top with remaining ingredients; cover. Roast for 3 to 3½ hours. Cool slightly. Pull meat apart with forks. Return to the roaster. Use a potato masher to break up chunks. Heat and serve on buns.
Makes 12 to 16 servings.

Shirley Mikita, Laughing Water Ranch
Fortine, Montana

BEST-EVER POT ROAST

1 3- to 5-pound rump, round, or ball tip roast
1 tablespoon vegetable oil
1 package dry onion soup mix
2 10¾-ounce cans beefy mushroom soup
½ soup can water
Dash of oregano
Salt and pepper to taste

Brown the roast in oil. Place in a Crock Pot. Add remaining ingredients, and cook on HIGH for 6 hours. Turn on LOW until gravy thickens. Serve with creamed potatoes and hot biscuits.
Makes 12 to 20 servings.

Kay Galyon, Sky Corral Ranch
Bellvue, Colorado

Sidemeat can't figure out whether to sample his wares before serving it up to the Riders in the Sky.

PIONEER CHICKEN FRIED STEAK

3 to 4 tablespoons shortening
1 top round steak, tenderized
2 to 3 tablespoons all-purpose flour, plus
extra for dusting
Salt
Pepper
Lawry's seasoned salt
Garlic salt
Milk

Place the shortening in a cast-iron frying pan. Cut steak into 2 or 3 pieces and dust with flour and seasonings. When grease is hot, add steak and cook until brown on both sides. Remove steak and make gravy by adding 2 or 3 tablespoons of flour to the grease and steak residue in pan. Stir until well mixed. Add milk (amount depends on whether you like your gravy thick or thin). Continue stirring so the gravy won't be lumpy. When desired consistency is reached, boil for 1 or 2 minutes. Now it's ready to serve.

I like biscuits and gravy with my steak. Also, I like sorghum syrup mixed with butter.
Makes 2 servings.

Karl Farr, Sons of the Pioneers

CREOLE POT ROAST

1 4-pound roast
2 tablespoons vegetable oil
1 15-ounce can tomato sauce
4 dashes of Tabasco sauce
¼ teaspoon Worcestershire sauce
2 cups sliced onions
¾ cup sliced green olives, drained, reserving
¼ cup liquid

In a heavy pan, brown the meat in oil. Add tomato sauce, Tabasco sauce, Worcestershire sauce, onions, and olives and liquid. Bring to a boil. Lower heat and simmer for 3 hours. Add water, if needed.

*Mabel Boehm, Peaceful Valley Lodge
Lyons, Colorado*

DIANA'S SPICED ROAST BEEF

5 to 8 pounds cross rib roast
2 tablespoons vegetable oil
1 large can tomato juice
1 bay leaf
1 teaspoon cinnamon
1 teaspoon allspice
1 teaspoon ground cloves
1½ teaspoons salt
1 teaspoon pepper
2 large onions, sliced

Brown the roast in oil. Combine with remaining ingredients in a large pot. Bring to a boil, then simmer for about 6 hours or until meat falls apart. Serve with pan gravy.
Makes 20 to 30 servings.

*Diana Haynes, Wapiti Meadow Ranch
Cascade, Idaho*

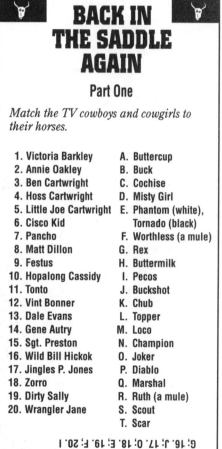

BACK IN THE SADDLE AGAIN

Part One

Match the TV cowboys and cowgirls to their horses.

1. Victoria Barkley
2. Annie Oakley
3. Ben Cartwright
4. Hoss Cartwright
5. Little Joe Cartwright
6. Cisco Kid
7. Pancho
8. Matt Dillon
9. Festus
10. Hopalong Cassidy
11. Tonto
12. Vint Bonner
13. Dale Evans
14. Gene Autry
15. Sgt. Preston
16. Wild Bill Hickok
17. Jingles P. Jones
18. Zorro
19. Dirty Sally
20. Wrangler Jane

A. Buttercup
B. Buck
C. Cochise
D. Misty Girl
E. Phantom (white), Tornado (black)
F. Worthless (a mule)
G. Rex
H. Buttermilk
I. Pecos
J. Buckshot
K. Chub
L. Topper
M. Loco
N. Champion
O. Joker
P. Diablo
Q. Marshal
R. Ruth (a mule)
S. Scout
T. Scar

Solution: 1. D; 2. A; 3. B; 4. K; 5. C; 6. P; 7. M; 8. Q; 9. R; 10. L; 11. S; 12. T; 13. H; 14. N; 15. G; 16. J; 17. O; 18. E; 19. F; 20. I

TUCK'S IRISH STEW

4   pounds lean stew beef
½   cup flour
    Salt
    Pepper
½   cup vegetable oil
2   8-ounce cans tomato sauce
2   8-ounce cans black bean soup
8   medium onions, peeled
8   medium potatoes
1   pound carrots, peeled and sliced
1   bunch celery, sliced
1   cup water

Shake the stew beef in a paper bag with flour, salt, and pepper. Brown meat in oil. Mix tomato sauce and black bean soup together in a blender and pour over meat. Simmer for 1 hour. Add onions, and simmer for 1 hour. Add remaining vegetables and enough water (1 cup) to cover. It should be done in 3 hours, but it won't hurt to stay on a low simmer for 1 more hour.

Makes 12 to 16 servings.

Forrest Tucker, actor

RANCHER DAVID'S ONE-POT DINNER

This is one of our favorite dinners on cattle-working days. It always goes well with Bread.

½   to 1 pound ground beef
¾   pound bacon, cut into small pieces
1   cup chopped onions
2   1 pound, 15-ounce cans pork and beans
1   16-ounce can kidney beans, drained
1   16-ounce can butter limas, drained
1   cup ketchup
¼   cup packed brown sugar
1   tablespoon liquid smoke
3   tablespoons white vinegar
1   teaspoon salt
    Dash of pepper

Brown the ground beef in a skillet; drain off excess drippings. Place beef in a Crock Pot. Brown bacon and onions; drain. Add bacon, onions, and remaining ingredients to the pot. Stir together well. Cover and cook on Low for 4 to 6 hours. Add a salad and French bread to complete the meal.

Makes 6 servings.

Mr. and Mrs. David Gates, singer and rancher

BURT'S BEEF STEW

3   slices bacon, cut into small pieces
4   tablespoons all-purpose flour
¼   teaspoon pepper
    Bacon drippings
2   pounds lean beef (I like chuck), cut into chunks
    Vegetable oil (optional)
1   large onion, chopped
2   garlic cloves, minced
1   28-ounce can tomato sauce
1   cup beef broth
1   cup dry red wine
1   bay leaf (optional)
    Pinch of thyme
4   carrots, cut up coarsely
2   ribs celery, cut up coarsely
4   large potatoes, peeled and cut into 4 pieces each
10 to 12 mushrooms, sliced

In a large pot or Dutch oven, cook bacon until light brown. Combine the flour and pepper in a bowl, and dip the meat in the flour mixture to coat completely. Brown in bacon drippings, turning often. Add a little vegetable oil if needed. Add onion and garlic and brown them a little. Add tomato sauce, broth, wine, bay leaf, and thyme. Cover and cook slowly for about 1½ hours. Add carrots, celery, potatoes, and mushrooms. Cook, covered, for 30 more minutes or until vegetables are tender. Serve with hot Italian bread, a large salad, fine wine, and good friends.

Makes 6 to 8 servings.

Burt Reynolds, actor

LONG X RANCH PRIME RIB

    Boneless prime rib
    Olive oil
    Salt to taste
    Cracked black pepper to taste
    Cavender's seasoning to taste

Rub the prime rib generously with olive oil. Season with salt, pepper, and Cavender's. Place approximately 2 feet above live coals for approximately 2 hours prior to serving. Start with the fat side up. Turn as needed.

Note: During windy conditions meat can be protected with an upside-down Dutch oven and covered with coals.

*Cliff Teinert, Long X Ranch
Kent, Texas*

Forrest Tucker starred as Sgt. Morgan O'Rourke on *F Troop* from 1965 to 1967. He made his film debut in 1940 in *The Westerner*.

STRAIT FROM THE HEART CARNE GUISADA

2 tablespoons butter
1 pound round steak, cut into cubes
¼ medium onion, sliced
¼ green bell pepper, sliced
1 tablespoon all-purpose flour
2 garlic cloves, peeled
   Pinch of ground cumin
   Pinch of coarse ground black pepper
½ a 10-ounce can tomatoes
   Strait-Shootin' Spanish Rice (p. 53)

Melt the butter in a skillet and cook the meat, turning occasionally, until brown. Add onion and bell pepper. Add flour and let flour brown while stirring. Mash garlic, cumin, black pepper, and tomatoes. Pour over meat and let simmer for 20 minutes, adding water, if necessary, for desired thickness. Serve with Strait-Shootin' Spanish Rice (p. 53).

Makes 2 to 4 servings.

George Strait, singer, actor, and rancher

SONS OF THE PIONEERS STEAK AND PINTO BEANS

½ cup all-purpose flour
1 teaspoon salt
½ teaspoon fresh ground pepper
1 pound boneless round steak, cut into 1-inch pieces
⅛ cup vegetable oil
1 16-ounce can tomatoes
1½ cups chopped celery
1½ cups sliced carrots
1½ cups chopped onions
⅔ cup water
⅔ cup chili sauce
1 16-ounce can pinto beans (with jalapeño peppers)

Mix the flour, salt, and pepper. Coat the beef with the flour mixture. Brown beef in oil. Stir in tomatoes, celery, carrots, onions, water, and chili sauce. Simmer, covered, for about 1 to 1½ hours or until beef is tender. Add beans and simmer for 20 more minutes. Enjoy!

Makes 6 servings.

Carolyn and Luther Nallie, Sons of the Pioneers

CLINT EASTWOOD'S SPAGHETTI WESTERN

Many of Clint Eastwood's cowboy movies were filmed in Italy, hence they became known as spaghetti westerns. A few years ago he participated in a gourmet gala, the Flavors of Monterey, to benefit the March of Dimes. His edible Spaghetti Western brought him top honors. You know it's got to be Good!

    Juice of 1 lemon, divided
12 tablespoons olive oil, divided
12 baby artichokes
1   8-ounce package spaghetti
2   large garlic cloves, diced
¼   cup finely chopped celery
¼   cup chopped shallots
½   cup tomato purée
½   cup fish stock
    Salt and fresh ground black pepper to taste
¼   teaspoon thyme
1   bay leaf
2   tablespoons chopped parsley
    Saffron
2   tablespoons tomato paste
½   teaspoon anchovy paste
4   clams, chopped
4   Monterey Bay prawns or jumbo shrimp
12 large mussels
½   cup brandy
1   red bell pepper, thinly sliced
1   yellow bell pepper, thinly sliced
2½ tablespoons Pernod
½   cup heavy cream
8   large sea scallops, quartered

Stir juice from ½ lemon and 2 tablespoons olive oil into a large pot of salted, boiling water. Add artichokes and boil for 5 minutes or until almost tender. Remove artichokes and cool under cold running water. Reserve artichoke cooking water. Peel outer leaves from 8 artichokes down to tenderest part (leave 4 artichokes with leaves intact). Cut off stems. Cut peeled artichokes into bite-size pieces (about 1½ inches long). Set aside.

Add additional salted water to leftover artichoke water. Bring to a boil and cook pasta. Drain and return to pot.

In a large sauté pan heat 7 tablespoons olive oil. Sauté garlic, celery, and 2 tablespoons shallots until golden. Add tomato purée, fish stock, salt, pepper, thyme, bay leaf, parsley, 2 generous pinches of saffron, tomato paste, anchovy paste, and clams. Bring to a low simmer and cover.

In a large sauté pan, heat 3 tablespoons olive oil and sauté 2 tablespoons chopped shallots. Season with black pepper. Add

Rawhide Regulars—Driving the dogies to Abilene were (l-r) ramrod Rowdy Yates (Clint Eastwood), cook Wishbone (Paul Brinegar), and trail boss Gil Favor (Eric Fleming) in this 1960 *Rawhide* publicity still.

prawns and mussels, cover with brandy, and ignite. Remove from heat and when flame subsides, set aside.

Add red and yellow peppers, artichokes, mussels, and brandy to sauce and simmer for 5 minutes. Add Pernod and cream to sauce and cook for 1 minute, stirring constantly. Remove from heat. Use a slotted spoon to remove peppers from sauce; add peppers to spaghetti. Rinse the spaghetti mixture in hot water and drain (to remove traces of the sauce).

Cover the bottom of 4 flat bowls with a few tablespoons of sauce. Arrange ¼ of the spaghetti in each bowl, leaving a hollow in the center. Place 2 quartered raw scallops in the center. Arrange 3 mussels on edge of plate and, on the opposite side, place 3 artichokes. On each plate, place a reserved, uncut artichoke over the scallops. Spoon remaining sauce over scallops and mussels. Place 1 prawn in the center. If preparing in advance, cover with foil and set aside. To serve, re-heat in a 325° oven for 20 minutes.

Makes 4 servings.

Clint Eastwood, actor and director

Lash LaRue—The "King of the Bullwhip" astride his steed Black Diamond

LASH'S LINGUINE

Whip-smacking!

1 pound extra lean ground beef or ground chuck
½ cup chopped onions
2 garlic cloves, finely minced
2 15-ounce cans plain tomato sauce
1 12-ounce can plain tomato paste
2 14½-ounce cans chopped tomatoes with juice
1 to 1½ tablespoons dry Italian seasoning
¼ cup to ½ cup burgundy
1 3-ounce can sliced black olives, drained
1 jar marinated artichoke hearts, drained and chopped
1 can hearts of palm, drained and chopped
1 pound linguine
   Vegetable oil
   Parmesan cheese, grated

Brown the beef in a large pot. Remove from the pan, and cook the onions and garlic in the remaining beef juices until tender. Remove onions and garlic from the pan. Heat the tomato sauce slightly, whisk in the paste, and add the chopped tomatoes. Stir in the Italian seasoning and burgundy. Start with smaller amounts, then add more after the sauce has immersed a bit (amounts will differ according to flavor desired). Simmer over very low heat for 15 minutes. Add the following as desired: black olives, artichoke hearts, and hearts of palm. Simmer, semi-covered, for 30 more minutes. Adjust seasonings as desired. Add salt or pepper if needed. This is best made a day ahead and slowly re-heated.

Use 4 quarts of boiling, salted water with 1 tablespoon oil added for 1 pound of linguine. Add linguine, wait for re-boil. Stir frequently and cook until al dente (firm to the bite), about 10 to 11 minutes. Drain. Serve with sauce and grated Parmesan cheese.

Makes 6 to 8 servings.

Lash LaRue, actor

PEE WEE'S MEATLOAF AND POTATOES

1½ to 2 pounds ground chuck
    Salt and pepper to taste
1   egg
1   small onion, chopped
2   slices bread, moistened and cubed
3   to 4 potatoes, quartered
¼   cup chopped celery
1   10¾-ounce can celery soup
½   cup water

Preheat the oven to 325°. Combine beef, salt and pepper, egg, onion, bread, and celery. Form into a loaf and place in a roaster. Bake for 45 minutes. Place the potatoes around the meat. Mix soup with water and pour over all. Cover and bake for 30 more minutes or until done.

Makes 6 to 8 servings.

Pee Wee King, singer/songwriter

LOW-FAT MEATLOAF JOHNNY WESTERN

1   pound ground venison
1   pound ground buffalo
1½ cups Italian-style bread crumbs
2   egg whites
1   large onion, chopped
2   8-ounce cans tomato sauce
    Dash of salt and pepper
    Dash of garlic powder (optional)
    Dash of oregano

Preheat the oven to 375°. Combine all ingredients well. Place in a loaf pan and bake for 45 minutes to 1 hour.

Makes 8 to 10 servings.

Johnny Western, singer/songwriter

Marty Robbins wrote and performed one of the most popular cowboy ballads ever, "El Paso," which was on his classic cowboy album, *Gunfighter Ballads and Trail Songs.* He also starred in the western film *Guns of a Stranger* in 1973. (Courtesy of Marty Robbins Enterprises)

MARTY'S CAMPFIRE CASSEROLE

1   pound ground beef
1   medium onion, chopped
2   teaspoons cumin
1   to 3 teaspoons ground red pepper (optional, to taste)
2   teaspoons oregano
1   large potato, shredded with grater
    Vegetable oil (optional)
6   eggs, beaten
    Salt and pepper

Brown the meat, onion, and spices in a large skillet; drain. Add the potato to the meat mixture, stirring briskly to keep from sticking. Add a small amount of vegetable oil if necessary. Add the eggs to the mixture when potatoes are browned. Continue to stir until eggs are done. Salt and pepper to taste.

Marty Robbins, singer/songwriter and actor

DEBBIE'S COWBOY MEATLOAF

This is an easy, filling main dish that the cowboys at the ranch enjoy.

1½ pounds ground beef
1   package Lipton Onion soup mix
½   cup ketchup
2   eggs
1   cup cooked rice, crackers, or dried bread crumbs
1   teaspoon mustard
1   pound sliced or grated mozzarella cheese

Preheat the oven to 325°. Mix all ingredients except cheese in a large bowl. Roll out on a sheet of wax paper, and spread cheese evenly. Roll up jelly-roll style and place in a loaf pan. Crimp down edges to keep cheese inside. Bake for 1 hour and 35 minutes.
    Makes 6 to 8 servings.

Allen Ranch
Bixby, Oklahoma

JESSE'S 1950s WESTERN MEATLOAF

1 tablespoon minced garlic
1 cup chopped onions
1 cup chopped green peppers
1 tablespoon butter
3 pounds ground beef
3 eggs, beaten
2 packages Lipton onion dip mix
1 teaspoon basil
1 tablespoon cayenne pepper
½ cup sour cream
1 cup chopped parsley
1 teaspoon dry oregano
1 teaspoon steak sauce
1 tablespoon ketchup
½ cup raisins
⅔ cup cracker crumbs
½ cup tomato paste

Preheat the oven to 350°. Sauté garlic, onions, green peppers, and butter. Mix all ingredients together in a large bowl. Place in a loaf pan. Bake for 1 hour and 45 minutes.
    Makes 12 to 16 servings.

Jesse Wayne, stuntman

HOYT'S HAMBURGER À LA BRANDY

Hoyt cuisine.

1 stick butter
8 ounces cherry brandy
1 pound ground round
1 8-ounce package grated Cheddar cheese

Melt butter over low heat. Add cherry brandy, and bring to a simmer. Make 1 large patty from the ground round and add to pan. Simmer for10 minutes per side over medium heat. Wrap and seal in foil. Refrigerate for 12 hours. Preheat oven to 300°. Cover with grated cheese and warm in the oven for about 5 minutes.
    Makes 4 servings.

Hoyt Axton, singer/songwriter and actor

Hoyt Axton is a mighty fine singer and songwriter, and occasionally plays cowboys, as he did in the 1966 film *Smoky*.

Sons of the Pioneers in 1956—(clockwise from top) Lloyd Perryman, Tommy Doss, Karl Farr, George "Shug" Fisher, Hugh Farr, and Dale Warren

TUMBLING TUMBLEWEEDS TACO BURGERS

½   pound lean ground beef
1   medium onion, chopped
1   14½-ounce can tomatoes
2   tablespoons ketchup
1   to 2 teaspoons chili powder
1   teaspoon salt
4   large hamburger buns, split
1   cup shredded Cheddar cheese
2   cups shredded iceberg lettuce
    Diced tomatoes for garnish
    Taco sauce

In a skillet, sauté the beef and onion until meat is no longer pink and onion is tender. Stir in tomatoes, ketchup, chili powder to taste, and salt. Simmer, uncovered, for 10 minutes or until most of the liquid has evaporated. Spoon meat mixture onto hamburger buns. Top with shredded cheese and lettuce. Sprinkle with diced tomatoes. Serve with taco sauce.

Makes 4 servings.

Valarie and Gary LeMaster, Sons of the Pioneers

RANCH BURGERS

These are a family favorite.

1¼   pounds ground beef
 1   tablespoon vegetable oil
 1   large onion, chopped
 1   green bell pepper, chopped
 1   teaspoon salt
 ¾   cup ketchup
 2   tablespoons sugar
 2   tablespoons mustard
 1   tablespoon vinegar
     Hamburger buns, toasted

Brown the meat in oil. Drain excess drippings. Add all other ingredients and simmer for 30 minutes. Serve on toasted buns.
   Makes 6 to 8 servings.

Elsie and Clyde Frost, rodeo cowboy

POOHAWK PEMMICANBURGERS

If buffalo meat is not available, beef purchased in Buffalo will do. Or, in a pinch, chopped sirloin over which you've chanted "Go, you Buffalo Bills!"

 2   pounds finely chopped buffalo meat
 ½   cup diced onions
 ¼   cup shredded jerky (bacon bits okay)
 2   tablespoons Gray Pooh-Pooh mustard (if not in Poohawk Territory, Grey Poupon will do)
     Hamburger buns

Knead onions, jerky, and mustard thoroughly into meat. Grill to taste over an open fire or grill. Serve on buns with eagle, turkey, or bogus feather protruding from top.
   Makes 8 servings.

Tom K. Ryan, artist

©1995 Tom K. Ryan;

GILLEY'S FAJITAS

16   ounces choice skirt meat
1   package Gilley's mesquite marinade
2   large green bell peppers, cut into match-
      stick-size pieces
1   medium red bell pepper, cut into match-
      stick-size pieces
1   medium yellow onion, cut into matchstick-
      size pieces
½   lime
2   cups shredded lettuce
2   cups grated Cheddar and Jack cheeses
2   cups pico de gallo sauce
12   6-inch flour tortillas, heated and browned
      slightly

Have skirt meat cleaned and tenderized.
Marinate beef according to instructions on
the Gilley's mesquite marinade package.
Charbroil or sauté beef and cut into strips.
Sauté onion and bell peppers. Serve on a siz-
zling hot platter. Squeeze fresh lime over
beef, bell peppers, and onions to finish.
Serve shredded lettuce, cheese, pico de
gallo, and tortillas on the side. Enjoy!
    Makes 12 servings.

Mickey Gilley, singer

GREAT SOUTHWEST BEEF ENCHILADAS

Enchiladas:
      Inexpensive cut of beef
      Water to cover
1   garlic clove, crushed
      Garlic salt
      Chili powder
      Cumin

Sauce:
      Flour
      Chicken bouillon
2   garlic cloves, crushed
      Chili powder
      Cumin
      Garlic salt
1   10-ounce can chopped green chilies
      Shredded Jack and Cheddar cheeses

Combine all enchilada ingredients and boil
for several hours, until the meat shreds. Add
more water if necessary. In a large skillet,
lightly brown enough flour to cover bottom
of pan. Remove from heat and slowly add
chicken bouillon (lots), stirring with whisk
until smooth. Add remaining ingredients,
mixing well. Return to heat. Bring to a boil.

Reduce heat and simmer for several hours,
stirring occasionally. Before cooking time is
over, add some liquid from cooking meat.
Sauce should be slightly thick.
    Put each corn tortilla into hot oil on both
sides for a second or two. Drain on paper
towels. Dip each tortilla into sauce and fill
with meat, black olives, onion, and cheese.
Preheat the oven to 350°.
    Roll and place enchiladas, seam sides
down in a 9x13-inch pan, the bottom of
which has been covered with some sauce.
Pour remaining sauce over enchiladas. Top
with cheeses. Bake until bubbly.
    Makes 6 generous servings.

Lloyd Perryman, Sons of the Pioneers

Urban Cowboy Hitmaker—Mickey Gilley invites
you to ride a bull any night at Gilley's, his world-
famous Houston honky-tonk.

Rex Allen—The "Arizona Cowboy" and his horse Koko

THE ARIZONA COWBOY ENCHILADA

Sauce:
- 2 pounds hamburger meat
- 1 garlic clove, minced
- 1 tablespoon chili powder
- 1 16-ounce can tomato sauce

Enchiladas:
- 3 cups Bisquick
- 1 cup all-purpose flour
- 1 cup cornmeal
  - Milk
  - Eggs
- 2 cups finely chopped onions
- 2 cups shredded Cheddar cheese

Brown the hamburger and drain. Add the next three ingredients to meat and cook for 1 hour. For enchiladas, mix Bisquick, flour, and cornmeal with enough milk to make the batter. Make pancakes 8 inches in diameter. Fry 2 eggs sunny side up for each pancake. Top with onions and cheese. Cover enchiladas with sauce.

Makes 8 to 10 servings.

Rex Allen, singer and actor

MOM'S MEATBALLS

3   pounds ground chuck or stewing beef (put through meat grinder twice)
1   loaf French or Italian bread (¼ loaf per 3 pounds ground meat)
    Milk
6   eggs (2 eggs per pound of beef)
    Sweet basil
    Fresh parsley
    Salt and pepper (use cayenne pepper for that extra touch)
    Grated Parmesan cheese
¼   cup vegetable oil
    Tomato sauce

Place the meat in a large bowl. In another bowl, break up the bread into small pieces and dampen with milk. Beat the eggs and add to meat. Add seasonings to taste. Mix well. Form the meatballs and place on waxed paper. Heat a cast-iron skillet with oil on low heat. Brown the meatballs. Drain on paper towels.

Now, what are meatballs without a great tomato sauce? Find an old Italian recipe or use one of those store-bought bottled types and season it with a bay leaf. (Don't forget to remove the bay leaf before serving. People have choked on them.)

In a large kettle of hot tomato sauce, sink the drained meatballs and cook on Low for 2 hours. The flavor of the sauce will permeate the meatballs. They'll melt in your mouth.

Makes 12 to 16 servings.

Jesse Wayne, stuntman

Stuntman Jesse Wayne worked in just about every TV western of the 1960s and doubled such young stars as Johnny Crawford of *The Rifleman* and Kurt Russell in *The Travels of Jaimie McPheeters*. This shot is from the TV pilot of *The Wrangler* in 1959.

BIG TIMBER SLOPPY JOES

1   pound hamburger
4   tablespoons vinegar
1   cup ketchup
1   tablespoon brown sugar
1   tablespoon dry mustard
2   cups chopped celery
1   cup chopped onions
1   teaspoon salt
2   tablespoons lemon juice
   Hamburger buns

Brown the hamburger in a large pot and drain excess drippings. Add remaining ingredients, stirring well to mix thoroughly. Heat through and serve on hamburger buns.
   Makes 4 to 6 servings.

Sweet Grass Ranch
Big Timber, Montana

STUFFED GREEN PEPPERS PETTY

6   bell peppers, cut in half and cleaned
1½ pounds ground beef
1   medium onion, finely chopped
1   tablespoon chili powder
2   eggs
1   cup ketchup
1   cup cornflakes
   Salt and pepper to taste

Sauce:
2½ cups combined ketchup and tomato paste (more ketchup than paste)
2   tablespoons brown sugar
2   tablespoons ground mustard
1   tablespoon vinegar

Boil the peppers for 5 minutes. Mix the next seven ingredients together. Stuff peppers with the mixture and arrange in a large glass dish. Preheat the oven to 375°. Mix all sauce ingredients together. Pour over peppers. Bake for 30 to 40 minutes.
   Makes 6 servings.

Lynda and Richard Petty, stock car champion

ITALIAN DELIGHT

You'll enjoy every Nichols' worth.

   Vegetable oil
1   garlic clove, chopped
1   green bell pepper, chopped
1   small onion, chopped
1   pound ground sirloin steak
1   16-ounce can whole tomatoes, drained
1   15-ounce can cream-style corn
1   10¾-ounce can tomato soup
1   cup grated sharp Cheddar cheese
   Chili powder to taste
   Cayenne pepper to taste
   Salt and pepper to taste
¾   pound spaghettini or penne pasta

In hot oil, fry the garlic, green pepper, and onion until thoroughly cooked. Add ground sirloin, cook until browned. Add the tomatoes, corn, and tomato soup; mix well. Add the grated cheese, and stir until melted. Stir in the chili powder, cayenne pepper, and salt and pepper to taste. Remove from heat and set aside.
   Cook spaghettini according to package directions. Drain. Add sauce. Mix thoroughly, and divide into 2 casseroles. Preheat the oven to 325°. Bake, uncovered, just until hot. (For a lighter version, try the light recipe found below.)
   Makes 6 to 8 servings.

ITALIAN DELIGHT LIGHT

   Vegetable oil
1   garlic clove, chopped
1   green pepper, chopped
1   small onion, chopped
½   pound ground steak
½   can whole tomatoes, drained
½   a 10¾-ounce can tomato soup
   Chili powder
   Cayenne pepper
   Salt and pepper
½   cup grated Cheddar cheese
¾   pound pasta

Cook according to preceding directions. This lighter version is just as tasty.
   Makes 6 to 8 servings.

James Garner, actor

WILD, WILD WEST VENISON ROAST

¾   cup raspberry vinegar
1   bottle red wine, divided
3   bay leaves, divided
3   cloves, divided
3   pounds venison roast
1½ jars McCormick soup greens
1   onion, diced
1   garlic clove, minced
1   to 1½ 12-ounce cans tomato paste
1   to 2 teaspoons curry paste mild, medium, or hot (according to taste)
1   to 2 teaspoons Worcestershire sauce
1   bottle Kikkoman soy sauce
1   10-ounce jar lingonberries (can substitute red currant jam or cranberries)
3   tablespoons juniper berries
1   tablespoon green dried pepper
¼   teaspoon margarine
   Butter
   Whipping cream
   Cornstarch

For the first marinade, mix the raspberry vinegar with ¼ cup wine (or 50–50 mixture). Soak a cheesecloth in the marinade, and wring out; pin 2 bay leaves, by sticking 2 cloves through them, onto each side of the meat; wrap meat in soaked cheesecloth for about 24 hours (if the meat is from an older deer, soak longer, but no longer than 48 hours; for a young deer soak only about 12 hours).

To prepare the second marinade, mix the soup greens (grind to powder in food processor), diced onion, diced garlic, tomato paste, curry paste, Worcestershire sauce, soy sauce, 1 to 3 cups red wine (to thin the marinade), or half wine, half water if you like it less strong, and lingonberries (pureed in food processor). In a tea ball or cheesecloth combine juniper berries, green dried pepper, 1 bay leaf, 1 whole clove, margarine, and thyme. Add the tea ball to the marinade.

Take the meat out of the cheesecloth, remove the bay leaves and cloves, and soak the meat in the second marinade for at least 8 hours, but not longer than 2 days (if the meat is from an older deer, soak longer, but no longer than 48 hours; for a young deer soak only about 8 to 12 hours).

Take the roast out of the marinade, and scrape the marinade off the meat. Brown meat slightly in butter, never in oil. Add the thick marinade mixture, and dilute with water or wine to your liking. Slowly simmer meat until tender.

To complete the gravy, add 1 to 2 cups whipping cream according to taste; for thickening add cornstarch or a package of brown gravy mix (if you prefer stronger seasoning taste). Season to taste by increasing the appropriate amount of the marinade ingredients.

Makes 4 to 5 servings.

Iris Behr, Hidden Creek Ranch
Harrison, Idaho

DAVY CROCKETT'S PORK SCALLOPS WITH DIJON SAUCE

1 tablespoon vegetable oil
1 tablespoon butter
1¼ pounds lean pork scallops
½ cup dry white wine, divided
½ cup chicken broth
1 cup heavy cream
1 teaspoon Dijon mustard
    Salt and pepper to taste

Divide the butter and oil into two large, heavy skillets over medium heat. Arrange the scallops so they do not overlap in the pans. If crowded, they will steam rather than brown. Cook 1 minute or until brown. Transfer to a plate and keep warm. Discard the fat from the skillets. Add half of the wine and broth to each pan. Cook over high heat, scraping bits from the bottom. Add the rest of the wine and broth and boil until reduced. Remove from heat and whisk in cream and mustard. Pour over pork scallops.

Note: The production of pork has been redesigned so that it is leaner and more tender than what was available in the past, providing a delicate yet flavored meat. I serve this with thinly sliced potatoes roasted in olive oil or wild rice. A selection of vegetables in season completes the plate. For dessert I prefer something simple, such as an apple tart or a chilled poached pear with a light caramel or raspberry sauce on a cloud of hand-whipped cream.

Makes 6 servings.

Marcy and Fess Parker, actor

PARKER KABOBS

1 to 1½ pounds pork or beef, cubed
½ cup extra virgin olive oil
2 heaping tablespoons ground cumin
    Soy sauce
1 yellow bell pepper
1 red bell pepper
2 red onions

Cut the meat into 1½- to 2 inch-cubes (or have the butcher do it for you). There should be 16 pieces. Mix the olive oil, cumin, and a dash of soy sauce in a large bowl. Add meat and toss. Create more marinade if this is an insufficient amount. Marinate for 4 to 5 hours, stirring every hour or so. Cut red and yellow peppers in half. Take each half and cut in half again and then into 3 pieces. Peel and halve the onions.

Cut each half into half again and then into 3 pieces. On four 12- or 18-inch wooden skewers alternate with 4 meat pieces, 3 onion pieces, 3 to 4 red pepper pieces, and 3 to 4 yellow pepper pieces. Baste kabobs with marinade, then grill or broil for about 10 to 15 minutes on each side until brown and crusty. Serve with brown rice or couscous in which a bit of chicken broth has replaced the water in cooking. A simple green salad and fresh French bread complete the meal.

Makes 4 servings (1 skewer each).

Marcy and Fess Parker, actor

PIONEERS POSOLE

This may sound like a Mexican dish, but really it is an international entrée. I was introduced to it by a beautiful French lady, who on numerous occasions invited Tim and me to dinner at her house. Tim loved it!

2 15½-ounce cans white hominy
2 4-ounce cans green chilies
¼ cup chopped onions
4 lean loin pork chops, cut into small cubes
1 garlic clove, minced
    Olive oil

Combine the hominy, chilies, and onions in a medium pot. Brown the cubes of pork and garlic in olive oil and add to other ingredients. Simmer slowly, adding water as necessary to maintain a rather thick consistency. Serve with a hearty tossed green salad with creamy Italian dressing, garlic bread, and white wine.

Makes about 4 servings.

Velma and Tim Spencer, Sons of the Pioneers

Stuntwoman Donna Hall worked in Hollywood for forty-two years, specializing in horseback tricks. She was the stunt double for Gail Davis on the *Annie Oakley* TV series, for Doris Day in *Calamity Jane,* for Debbie Reynolds in *How the West Was Won,* and for Jane Fonda in *Cat Ballou.* She also doubled for Barbara Stanwyck and Bette Davis, among other stars.

FALL GAL PEANUT BUTTER PORK LOIN

1   3- to 5-pound boneless pork, top loin roast
⅓   cup orange juice
¼   cup peanut butter

Insert a meat thermometer in a covered grill, and arrange coals around the drip pan. Place meat on a grill rack over the drip pan, but not over the coals. Lower the grill hood. Grill for 1¼ to 1½ hours or until thermometer reaches 140°. In a small bowl, blend orange juice into peanut butter, beating with whisk or fork until smooth. Brush roast with peanut butter mixture. Grill for 30 more minutes, brushing occasionally with mixture.

Makes 12 to 16 servings.

Donna Hall, stuntwoman

CHEROKEE PARK GRILLED PORK TENDER

2   cups vegetable oil
1   cup lemon juice
1   cup soy sauce (I use lightly salted)
1   cup chopped green onions
1½ tablespoons garlic powder
¼   cup pepper
1   cup celery seed
1   pork tenderloin

Combine all ingredients well. Cover meat with the marinade and refrigerate for 3 hours. Grill meat over medium fire for about 30 minutes. (I use aspen wood for cookouts, because it burns clean and hot.)

Makes 3 servings (1 tenderloin serves 3 people).

Eli Elfland, Cherokee Park Ranch
Livermore, Colorado

JOHNNY'S TERIYAKI PORK CHOPS

20 ounces soy sauce
1½ cups water
2½ cups packed brown sugar
¾ cup honey
½ cup red wine
1 teaspoon ginger
12 1½ inch-thick pork chops

Combine all ingredients except pork chops early in the day. Mix together over low heat and bring almost to a boil. Cool, then pour over chops in a greased roasting pan. Marinate for 4 to 6 hours. Preheat the oven to 350°. Bake, in sauce, until meat starts to shrink away from bone, approximately 2 hours. Pour off juice so chops are only half covered. Continue to cook until chops are tender and caramelized, approximately 30 minutes or more.
    Makes 12 servings.

Shepp Ranch
Boise, Idaho

TERRITORY GRILLED TERIYAKI PORK LOIN

3 cups soy sauce
1 tablespoon ginger
1 tablespoon minced garlic
    Approximately 10 pounds pork loin roast

Combine the soy sauce, ginger, and garlic. Marinate the pork loin in the sauce for 3½ hours. Preheat the oven to 350°. Bake for 2 hours or until meat thermometer registers 160°, or grill outdoors for 2 hours over a slow charcoal fire for the best flavor. Baste with sauce 4 to 5 times while cooking.
    Makes 40 servings.

Karen S. May, North Fork Ranch
Shawnee, Colorado

COWBOY'S BASIC PORK CHOPS

Pork chops, cut ¾ inch thick
Dry white wine
Garlic powder
Fresh cracked black pepper

Preheat the oven to 400°. In an ovenproof glass dish place several large pork chops. Lightly sprinkle with dry white wine. Gently shake on garlic powder and fresh cracked black pepper. Cover with lid or foil and place in oven. Bake for a little more than 1 hour. Do not overcook! The result should be tender, tasty chops.

Randolph Scott, actor

PORK CHOPS FESTUS

Pork chops
Salt
Pepper
Thyme
Vegetable oil
Red potatoes, sliced in half lengthwise
Onions
Applesauce
Hot horseradish

Preheat the oven to 350°. Season the chops with salt, pepper, and thyme. Brown in oil. Place the potatoes cut side down in a small amount of chop drippings in a heavy casserole dish. Place browned chops on top of potatoes. Top with onions. Cover and bake for 45 minutes to 1 hour.
    Serve with applesauce that has been mixed with hot horseradish (2 parts applesauce to 1 part horseradish, or to taste). Heat applesauce before serving. Serve with cooked spinach or other greens, corn bread, and cream gravy made from pan drippings.

Torrie and Ken Curtis, actor and singer

A member of the Cowgirl Hall of Fame, Patsy Montana, "America's No. 1 Cowboy Sweetheart," was the first woman in country music to sell a million copies of a record when she released "I Want to Be a Cowboy's Sweetheart" in 1935.

SHALOM'S PORK CHOPS

It's real Good food.

8 to 10 medium pork chops (fat trimmed)
   Butter
   Salt
   Pepper
   Garlic powder
   Onion powder
1 medium onion, chopped
1 ounce grape jelly
1 12-ounce bottle chili sauce

Brown the chops in butter, seasoning each side with salt, pepper, garlic powder, and onion powder to taste. Stir in onion. Do not overcook. Preheat the oven to 350°. In a pan over medium to low heat, melt grape jelly and chili sauce, stirring to blend to smooth, even consistency. Place chops with onions in long baking pan, and pour sauce over chops. Cover with foil. Bake for 1 hour. Serve with mashed potatoes, green beans, and home-made biscuits.
   Makes 8 to 10 servings.

Patsy Montana, singer

UPSTAIRS, DOWNTOWN FRIED PORK SPARE RIBS

The level best.

   Approximately 3 cups all-purpose flour
   Lemon pepper to taste
   Salt and pepper to taste
   Seasoning salt to taste
1 slab ribs

Combine all ingredients except ribs. Cut each rib apart and roll in flour mixture. Deep fry ribs until they are golden brown.

Toby Keith, singer/songwriter

Country music singer Toby Keith was a rodeo athlete in high school and later test-rode bulls and broncs for rodeos. The Oklahoman also played pro football for the Oklahoma City Drillers. His first single, "Should've Been a Cowboy," was a No. 1 hit.

145

DANIEL BOONE'S ROAST TURKEY AND OYSTER STUFFING

A big meal.

Stuffing:
- 8 cups seasoned bread crumbs (I prefer Mrs. Cubison's)
- 1 8-inch square corn bread
- 1 cup cooked rice
- 1 cup chopped onions
- 1 cup chopped celery
- 1 stick butter
  Chopped parsley to taste
  Poultry seasoning to taste
  Dried sage to taste
  Dash of Tabasco sauce
- 1 small can smoked oysters, chopped
- 1 8-ounce can mushrooms
- 1 15-ounce can Swanson chicken broth
- ½ to ¾ cup dry white wine
  Salt

Mix bread crumbs, cornbread, and rice in a large bowl. In a large skillet, sauté onion and celery in melted butter and add dry ingredients. Blend in rest of ingredients. Add white wine or more chicken broth a little at a time. You want it quite moist but not too wet.

Turkey:
- 1 12-pound turkey
- 1 onion, chopped
- 1 stick butter
  Brandy

Thoroughly clean the hen and pat dry. Salt the cavity and set aside. Put giblets (neck, gizzard) in chicken broth and water with onion and cover with lid. Liquid should cover giblets for the duration of cooking process. Simmer slowly until the turkey is finished cooking. The giblets will be used later for the gravy. Preheat the oven to 400°. Place rack in roasting pan. Take two large pieces of foil, about 24 inches long each, to form a cross and place on top of the rack. Stuff the bird in cavity and neck. Place the turkey in center of the foil. Melt the butter and baste the turkey, then pour a touch of brandy over it. Seal turkey with foil with each piece of foil going the other direction. Bake for approximately 3½ hours. Do not open oven until ready to brown. Then roll the foil back completely and continue baking for 30 to 45 more minutes.

Gravy:
- 1 onion, chopped
  Turkey giblets
- 2 tablespoons all-purpose flour
  Salt
  Pepper
  Tabasco sauce

Remove scrapings and juice from the cooked turkey to a skillet over low-medium heat. Chop giblets, gizzards, etc., very well and add to the skillet with the onion. Remove meat from neck and add. Make a roux from either flour, cornstarch, or arrowroot (chef's choice for a thickener) and add to mixture. Bring to a boil, stirring often. Season with salt, pepper, and a touch of Tabasco sauce .
Makes 12 to 16 servings.

Marcy and Fess Parker, actor

Fess Parker portrayed not one, but two of America's greatest frontiersmen as Davy Crockett in the 1950s and Daniel Boone in the 1960s.

Texas-born Mark Chesnutt is one of country music's top honky-tonk singers.

BEAUMONT BRAISED WILD GOOSE OR TURKEY

1   8-pound wild goose
2   to 3 sprigs parsley
1   stalk celery
1   bay leaf
    Pinch of thyme
1   quart stock or consommé
1   tablespoon cornstarch
2   tablespoons water

Preheat the oven to 400°. Clean, pluck, and singe the goose. Stuff the goose if desired. Truss legs and wings close to the body and cover bird with a slice of fat salt pork. Roast the bird until it is well browned. Remove the fat from the roasting pan and add parsley, celery, bay leaf, thyme, and stock. Cover the pan and continue cooking, basting often for 2 to 3 hours or until the bird is tender. Strain the gravy and thicken it with cornstarch mixed with water. Serve with cranberry sauce or applesauce and wild rice or corn fritters.

Makes 6 servings.

Mark Chesnutt, singer

ROADKILL TURKEY

The preparation time for this turkey is about 45 minutes to 1 hour, but it's worth the wait. This turkey gets its name from its flat appearance.

1   turkey, thawed
2   small bags seasoned or plain stuffing
    crumbs
    Butter
    Salt
    Pepper
    Chopped dates
    Orange juice
    Brown sugar
    Cashew nuts

Remove the backbone and ribcage from the turkey. Using a very sharp knife, slit the skin down to the backbone of the thawed, uncooked turkey. Then carefully slice the meat away from the ribs, disjointing the wings and thighs as you come to them (wing bones and thigh bones will remain intact). Continue to remove the ribcage and breast bone carefully. The turkey will obviously lose its shape and be a bit odd to handle. When the backbone, ribcage, and breast bone are removed, rinse the turkey and set aside to drain. Rub skin with butter, salt, and pepper.

Prepare your favorite dressing. For an unusual twist, use 2 small bags (depending on the size of your turkey) seasoned or plain stuffing crumbs. Prepare the stuffing according to package directions using the butter, but substituting orange juice for water and blending in brown sugar, dates, and cashews to taste. Check for seasonings.

Line the bottom of a broiler pan or large square baking pan (dish) with a double layer of foil (shiny side down). Press in the dressing mixture. Then cover with the turkey, breast on the bottom (skin side up) with the legs and wings crossed over the breast. Roast at the recommended temperature for about one-half to one-third of the time for a whole stuffed turkey. Check for juices to run clear and leg joint to be loose for doneness. Remove legs and wings and set on platter. The turkey can be easily sliced now and there is no carcass .

Makes 12 to 16 servings.

Lash LaRue, actor

Roy Rogers, King of the Cowboys

CAMPFIRE QUAIL

Because I don't suppose you want to dig a hole in your backyard and use a Dutch oven for cooking the quail, here's the way to do it in the kitchen.

>Cold biscuits, 1 per quail
>Onions, finely diced
>Bacon, finely cut
>Salt and pepper to taste
>Quail
>Vegetable oil
>Seasoned salt

Preheat the oven to 350°. Crumble cold biscuits into a container (1 biscuit for each quail). Add onions to the container, then the bacon. Salt and pepper to taste. Moisten with water and mix by hand until blended nicely. Rub quail with cooking oil and stuff with biscuit mix. Place in a shallow baking pan and sprinkle with seasoned salt. Cover the pan with foil and stab a hole in the foil here and there. Be sure baking pan is greased; bacon grease is best for flavor. Bake for 1½ hours or until quail are done. Haul the little devils out and chomp away at 'em.

Note: You can do the same thing with Cornish game hen.

Rory Calhoun, actor

ROY ROGERS' CHICKEN AND DUMPLINGS

Fit for the King.

>1   chicken
>1½ cups all-purpose flour
>2   teaspoons baking powder
>½ teaspoon salt
>3   tablespoons shortening
>¾ cup milk
>   Dashes of any and all spices you can find in the kitchen (I use pepper, garlic salt, paprika, onion salt, and celery salt)

Place the chicken in a large pot and cover with water. Boil until tender. Reserve the broth. Remove and discard the bones. Return the chicken to the broth. Mix the flour, baking powder, salt, and shortening. Blend in the milk. Drop dough by spoonful into the hot liquid. Cook, uncovered, for 10 minutes, then cover the pot and cook for another 10 minutes.

Makes 4 to 6 servings.

Roy Rogers, King of the Cowboys

FABULOUS CHICKEN-VEGETABLE BAKE

My 8-year-old grandson, Alex, and many personal friends have enjoyed this meal, as well as my ex-wife, the late Dinah Shore, who said she could eat such a meal every day. Bless her. Shortly after that she started writing her cookbooks.

1 3- to 4-pound chicken
3 tablespoons vegetable oil, divided
   Salt and pepper to taste
2 large onions, chopped
½ cup chicken broth or water
5 large potatoes, cubed
1 large green bell pepper, seeded and diced
5 large carrots, sliced
4 ribs celery, sliced

Preheat the oven to 425°. Brush chicken with 1 tablespoon oil and sprinkle with a little salt and pepper. Place in a roasting pan. Brown the chicken for 20 minutes. Sauté the onions in remaining oil until nicely browned. Stir in chicken broth or water. Arrange potatoes, green pepper, carrots, and celery around the chicken and pour browned onions over all. Sprinkle with a little pepper. Cover and bake for 1½ hours at 350°. The browned onions enhance the flavor of the chicken and other vegetables. This is a great buffet dish, along with sweet pickles, fresh green salad, hot rolls, and pie made from homegrown Montana rhubarbs.

Makes 4 servings.

George Montgomery, actor

George Montgomery played many a good guy in western films and once portrayed the Lone Ranger in a 1930s serial. His movies include *The Cisco Kid and the Lady, The Texas Rangers, Fort Ti,* and *Black Patch,* and he was the star of the TV series *Cimarron City.* Now famous for his sculpting and furniture making, Montgomery built the dining room table used by the Roy Rogers and Dale Evans family.

Louis L'Amour—The greatest cowboy writer of them all

pan. Melt the butter in the pan and spoon half over chicken. Bake, uncovered, for 45 minutes. Spoon the rest of the butter over the chicken. Bake for 10 to 15 more minutes or until tender and brown.

Makes 6 to 12 servings, depending on appetites!

Louis L'Amour, writer

YOSEMITE SAM'S CRANBERRY CHICKEN

You'll love it, you varmint!

1   **16-ounce can whole cranberries**
1   **1- to 1½-ounce envelope onion soup mix**
½   **cup creamy French dressing**
2   **3-pound frying chickens, cut up**

Preheat the oven to 350°. Mix cranberries, soup mix, and French dressing together. Dip the chicken into mixture and place on foil-lined cookie sheet. Bake for about 1 hour or until done. This goes well with Rootinest, Tootinest Rice Casserole in the West (p. 56).

Makes 4 to 5 servings.

Estelle and Mel Blanc, voice actor

Mel Blanc, the voice of Yosemite Sam and countless other cartoon legends. (Courtesy of Steve Cox Collection)

MAMU'S BAKED CHICKEN

6   **chicken breasts, boned and halved (may be skinned)**
2   **cups sour cream**
¼   **cup lemon juice**
4   **teaspoons Worcestershire sauce**
4   **teaspoons celery salt**
2   **teaspoons paprika**
4   **garlic cloves**
½   **teaspoon pepper**
    Salt to taste
1¾ **cups plain packaged bread crumbs**
1   **stick butter**

Wipe the breasts and put them in a large bowl. Mix the sour cream, lemon juice, Worcestershire sauce, celery salt, paprika, garlic, and pepper. Add salt to taste. Coat the chicken well with the sour cream mixture, being sure to use all of it. Put in refrigerator, covered, overnight. Preheat the oven to 350°. Remove the chicken from the sour cream and coat evenly in the crumbs. Arrange a single layer in a shallow baking

Clint Black—Cowboy fan

STATE OF MIND FAT-FREE FAJITAS

Fajita seasoning (or seasoning of your choice)
Defatted chicken broth
Green bell pepper, chopped
Red bell pepper, chopped
Onions, chopped
Skinless, boneless chicken breasts
Corn tortillas
Fat-free sour cream
Salsa

Add fajita seasoning to the chicken broth. Sauté the vegetables in the broth. Add strips of chicken to the above and cook until chicken is done. Place mixture in heated corn tortillas. Top with sour cream and salsa, and serve. Enjoy!

Note: Corn tortillas have no fat. Flour tortillas have added fat.

Lisa Hartman and Clint Black, actress and singer/songwriter

CAREY CURRY CHICKEN BREASTS

1   stick butter
     Mixture of flour, curry powder, and salt to taste
6   skinless chicken breasts, with ribs
¾   cup chutney
¼   cup onion flakes
3   elephant garlic cloves, or 6 regular size, peeled
1   10½-ounce can beef broth

Preheat the oven to 350°. Melt the butter, and dredge the chicken in the flour mixture. Dip chicken on both sides in melted butter. Place in a shallow casserole dish. Bake for 30 minutes. Meanwhile, in a saucepan mix chutney, onion flakes, garlic, and broth. Pour over the chicken and bake for 30 more minutes, basting often.

Marilyn and Harry Carey Jr., actor

SANTA FE TRAIL QUESADILLAS

1   pound boneless, skinless chicken breast
     Seasoned salt
     Butter
1   package flour tortillas
1   16-ounce package grated Cheddar cheese
1   4-ounce can mild, chopped green chilies
     Chopped onions

Cook the chicken in butter and seasoned salt. Grill the tortillas, one at a time, in a frying pan. Layer cheese, 1 teaspoon green chilies, and onion on one half of the tortilla. Grill until the cheese begins to melt, then fold over to make a semi-circle shape. Cut into quarters and serve with sour cream, salsa, guacamole, and Pico de Gallo.

Pico de Gallo:
3   medium tomatoes
1   medium onion
2   serrano peppers, deseeded
1   teaspoon vegetable oil
2   tablespoons cilantro
     Salt and pepper to taste

Chop all ingredients finely and combine, or for best results, blend together in a food processor for about 15 seconds. It should not be soupy.
    Makes 8 to 10 servings.

Daphne and John Nallie, Sons of the Pioneers

Harry Carey Jr. is the son of old-time western star Harry Carey. His father nicknamed him Dobe when he was just a few hours old because of the color of his red hair, which reminded him of the red adobe soil on their California ranch. Dobe made eleven feature films with John Wayne, including *Red River, The 3 Godfathers, She Wore a Yellow Ribbon, Rio Grande, The Searchers, Big Jake,* and *Cheyenne Autumn.* He has also written his autobiography, *Company of Heroes—My Life as an Actor in the John Ford Stock Company,* for Scarecrow Press. His wife, Marilyn, is the daughter of the late western character actor Paul Fix.

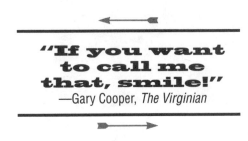

"If you want to call me that, smile!"
—Gary Cooper, *The Virginian*

CHICKEN SCACCHI

½   cup chopped onions
¼   cup chopped green bell peppers
    Butter or margarine
6   to 8 chicken breasts
    Salt and pepper to taste
1   cup white wine
1   8-ounce can tomato sauce
4   tablespoons soy sauce (more or less as
    desired)
    Hot, cooked rice

In a large heavy skillet, sauté onions and bell peppers in a small amount of butter. Place on a warm plate while preparing chicken. Remove skin from chicken breasts and season with salt and pepper. In the same skillet, fry the chicken, browning on both sides, using more or less butter as needed. Add the wine, tomato sauce, soy sauce, and onions and bell pepper. Simmer for 1 to 1½ hours. Serve over rice.

Makes 6 to 8 servings.

Justin Tubb, singer/songwriter

Troubadour Too—Justin Tubb (pictured here in 1955) continues the musical family tradition pioneered by father Ernest.

LARAMIE GRAPE-FED QUAIL

Robert Fuller relates the tale of how he was out hunting quail with his good friend Red Steagall one day when a covey of quail flew out of a grape vineyard in front of them. Red and Robert nailed a bunch of 'em.

Later they prepared the quail and were surprised to find them the tastiest they had ever eaten. Since then, whenever Robert prepares quail, he goes by this recipe.

Fill the quail with 8 to 10 squeezed, sweet white grapes. Then wrap the quail in strips of bacon and secure with toothpicks. Broil or barbecue. You may also wish to roast the quail over grapevines.

Robert Fuller, actor

Robert Fuller starred in two of TV's most popular western series: as Jess Harper on *Laramie* from 1959 to 1963, and as Cooper Smith on *Wagon Train* from 1963 to 1965. He also starred in the sequel to *The Magnificent Seven, Return of the Seven.*

RUSTY'S VENISON METHOD

My wife Amy's dad, Frank Fitzpatrick, was an avid hunter, and since we had four children it helped our budget a lot that he shared the meat with us. He was expert at dressing out the animals, which is important in keeping down the gamey taste. Even so, whenever I cooked a venison roast, usually in an oven bag with Lawry's Onion Soup Mix and a can of cream of mushroom soup, our kids ate very little of it.

We've been very fortunate to have so many wonderful friends, many of them celebrities. Dinah Shore came to visit several times and even cooked Christmas dinner twice in our old ranch house. Her own home in Beverly Hills was decorated with great taste and filled with beautiful works of art—many of them antiques—Ming Dynasty, etc. Yet whenever she came to visit us she was always a good sport and loved to get down on the floor and play with our kids and their toys. She taught me her mother's recipe for chili, which I usually made the day after we had "eaten" venison roast. I would then dice up the leftover roast and add it to the chili, slow cook it until it was tender, and this time the kids would clean their plates!

Most of the time we ate venison fried, the way Amy's mom, Lucille, taught me and when fixed this way, there was rarely a scrap left. The best cut for this is the back strap or tenderloin, but we also used the haunch or anywhere that we could take lean meat. The trick is to trim away all fat and sinew, making sure you start with only pure red meat. We then pounded it thoroughly on both sides with a spring-loaded hand-held tenderizer until the meat is close to hamburger, but still holding together. Next we dipped each piece of meat into beaten raw egg and then it was immediately dipped into cracker crumbs that had been seasoned with salt and pepper and a little garlic powder, turning each piece over to make sure both sides were well covered.

We fried the crumb coated pieces of meat in a cast-iron skillet until golden brown, making sure the oil never got hot enough to smoke. You can make a great gravy with the leftovers by adding milk and thickening with flour (made smooth with a little cold water). You may need to add more salt and pepper to the gravy, but taste it as you go to get it just right. I hope these tips help you to enjoy venison as much as we have.

Amy and Rusty Richards, Sons of the Pioneers

CODY'S TEX-MEX ROAST CHICKEN

It tastes just like rattlesnake.

- ¼ cup nonfat yogurt
- 1 tablespoon chili powder
- 2 teaspoons cider vinegar
- 1½ teaspoons minced garlic
- 1 teaspoon each: ground cumin, dried oregano, and salt
- 1 whole broiler, fryer chicken (3 to 3½ pounds)

Preheat the oven to 350°. Mix all ingredients except chicken in a small bowl until blended. Rub all over the chicken. Tie the legs together with string. Place chicken breast side up on greased rack in a roasting pan. Roast for 1 hour or until drumsticks move easily and juices run clear when thigh is pierced. Let the chicken stand for at least 5 minutes before carving.

Makes 10 to 12 servings.

Bill Cody, disc jockey

BOY HOWDY HALIBUT STEAKS

- 2 pounds halibut steaks, cut into 6 serving pieces
- 4 tablespoons apricot or peach nectar
- ½ cup low-calorie mayonnaise
- ¼ cup plain low-fat yogurt
- 1 tablespoon ketchup
- 2 teaspoons grated orange peel
- 2 teaspoons curry powder
  Salt and pepper to taste
  Fresh parsley
  Seedless grapes or orange sections (optional)

Arrange the fish in a broiling dish. Combine nectar with mayonnaise, yogurt, ketchup, orange peel, and seasonings. Spread the mixture over the fish and marinate for 30 minutes. Broil for 4 to 5 minutes each side or until fish flakes easily. Before serving, garnish fish with parsley and fruit, if desired.

Makes 8 servings.

Ken Carson, Sons of the Pioneers

Modern troubadour Tracy Byrd keeps lassoing the hits.

TRACY BYRD'S BEER BATTERED BASS

To truly bring out the flavor of this recipe you must catch the bass yourself.

- 1 12-ounce beer
- 2 tablespoons Tabasco sauce
- 4 tablespoons yellow mustard
  Salt and pepper
- 5 pounds fillets (preferably bass, but I guess any fish will do)
- 1 cup yellow cornmeal
- 2 packages Corn-Kits brand corn bread mix
  Vegetable oil or shortening

Mix beer, Tabasco sauce, and mustard in a large bowl. Salt and pepper the fillets and coat them with the beer batter. Put the cornmeal and cornbread mix in a paper sack. Put the battered fillets in sack and shake until fillets are thoroughly coated. Fry in hot oil (360°) until golden brown.

Serve with hushpuppies, French fries, baked beans, coleslaw, and, of course, a cold beer!

Makes 10 to 12 servings.

Michelle and Tracy Byrd, singer

Chuck Connors (right) starred as *The Rifleman,* Lucas McCain. Johnny Crawford played his son, Mark, on the series from 1958 to 1963. Sammy Davis Jr., reputedly one of Hollywood's fastest quick draws, guest starred in a 1962 episode.

RIFLEMAN'S FRIED CATFISH

½   cup cornmeal
½   cup all purpose flour, sifted
1   teaspoon salt
¼   teaspoon pepper
⅛   teaspoon ginger
2   eggs
    Catfish fillets
    Vegetable oil

In a bowl, mix the cornmeal, flour, salt, pepper, and ginger. In a separate bowl, beat the eggs. Dip the fillets into the egg mixture and then coat both sides with the cornmeal mixture. In a skillet, fry the coated fish in very hot oil (360°) until coating turns brown. Do not overcook.

Makes 2 servings per pound of catfish.

Chuck Connors, actor

BRANDED'S BAKED SALMON

¼   cup honey
5   tablespoons soft butter
1   salmon

Preheat the oven to 350°. Mix the honey and butter. Place half of the butter in a dollop in the bottom of a baking dish. Place the salmon on top of the butter and top with the remaining butter. Place the dish in the oven and cook, uncovered, for 19 minutes. Do not overcook.

Makes 4 servings.

Chuck Connors, actor

THE LONER'S GRILLED SWORDFISH

1   pound swordfish fillets, boned and cut into 1-inch pieces
2   tablespoons soy sauce
2   tablespoons orange juice
1   tablespoon oil
1   tablespoon catsup
1   tablespoon chopped fresh parsley
1   small garlic clove, chopped
½   teaspoon fresh lemon juice
¼   teaspoon dried oregano, crumbled
¼   teaspoon freshly ground pepper

Arrange swordfish in a single layer in a shallow baking dish. Combine all remaining ingredients in a small bowl and mix well. Pour over fish, turning to coat well. Let stand at room temperature, turning once, 30 minutes. Preheat broiler or prepare barbecue grill. Broil or grill fish 4 inches from heat source for 8 minutes. Baste with sauce, turn, and continue cooking until fish flakes easily with a fork, about 7 to 10 minutes. Serve over rice.

Makes 2 to 3 servings.

Dorothy and Lloyd Bridges, actor

Lloyd Bridges starred in *High Noon* as the deputy of Marshal Will Kane (Gary Cooper) and also starred as William Colton in the 1965 western TV series *The Loner*, created by Rod Serling.

Foy Willing (top) and the Riders of the Purple Sage—(l-r) Al Sloe, Johnny Paul, and Jimmy Dean, in the Roy Rogers film *Susanna Pass.*

PURPLE SAGE PEPPERS STUFFED WITH SHRIMP

1 cup chopped onions
1 cup chopped celery
1 teaspoon tomato paste
1 stick margarine
  Salt and pepper to taste
1½ pounds shrimp, peeled and cleaned
1½ cups cooked rice
4 green bell peppers, hollowed out and steamed until tender

Preheat the oven to 350°. Cook the onions, celery, and tomato paste in margarine until glazed. Add seasoning. Add the peeled shrimp and cook for 6 minutes. Mix with the rice. Stuff steamed peppers and sprinkle with cracker crumbs. Dot with margarine. Bake for 15 minutes.
  Makes 4 servings.

Foy Willing, Riders of the Purple Sage

MONTANA CREAM CHEESE PATTIES

1 8-ounce package cream cheese, softened to room temperature
6 eggs
1 cup crushed cracker crumbs
1 medium onion, chopped
½ teaspoon each: sage and poultry seasoning
1 teaspoon salt
1 10¾-ounce can cream of mushroom soup

Place the cream cheese in a bowl and add eggs one at a time, alternately with cracker crumbs and continue until well blended. Add the next three ingredients. Mix well. Form into patties by dropping into a skillet by spoonful. Spread out. Fry until browned and patties hold together. Preheat the oven to 350°. Layer in a baking pan, pour slightly diluted cream of mushroom soup over the top, and bake for 45 minutes.
  Makes 4 to 6 servings.

Karen and Jack Hooker, White Tail Ranch Ovando, Montana

Among Steve McQueen's westerns on the silver screen are the classics *The Magnificent Seven* and *Nevada Smith*, and he also starred as Josh Randall in TV's *Wanted: Dead or Alive*.

JOSH RANDALL'S SALMON CROQUETTES

16 ounces salmon
1 egg, whipped
½ cup mashed potatoes (preferably from the night before)
  Flour or bread crumbs
  Butter
  Parsley flakes
  Salt and pepper to taste

Mix salmon (remove bones), potatoes, parsley flakes, and salt and pepper. Make into patties. Dip into whipped egg. Dust with flour or bread crumbs. In a skillet sauté the patties in butter for 2 to 3 minutes and turn the patties over and sauté for another 2 to 3 minutes. Serve immediately.
  Makes 2 to 4 servings.

Steve McQueen, actor

The brothers Maverick, Jack Kelly (left) as Bart and James Garner as Bret, have been known to take a peek at another poker player's hand from time to time. The western comedy series *Maverick* roamed the airwaves from 1957 to 1962.

SUBROSA CHILIES RELLENOS

Support your local appetite.

6	Anaheim chili peppers
6	ounces shredded light Cheddar cheese, divided
	All-purpose flour
4	egg whites
¼	cup Second Nature eggs
2	tablespoons safflower oil
	Medium-hot salsa

Char the chili peppers on gas burners; place in a plastic bag for 5 minutes (no more) and peel off skin. Slit the peppers from stem halfway down and carefully remove the seeds. Insert 1 ounce shredded cheese per pepper. Dredge each filled pepper with flour. Whip the egg whites until stiff. Fold in the eggs. Coat the peppers with beaten egg mixture. Fry in oil. Serve with medium-hot salsa.

Makes 6 servings.

James Garner, actor

Texas-born Audie Murphy was America's most-decorated soldier of World War II. Any good western fan knows he also starred in more than thirty westerns, including *The Unforgiven, No Name on the Bullet,* and *Destry.*

BEEF BANDERA

I remember something that Audie cooked for me during one of our jaunts to Texas. I remember the ingredients but not the amounts. He melted some butter in a frying pan, then browned some onions. He then cut some beef into ¼- to ½-inch by 4-inch strips and browned them in another frying pan. When the onions were browned, he added a can of cream of mushroom soup, some brown sugar, Worcestershire sauce, and let it simmer for about 3 minutes. Then he put the beef strips in the pan with the mushroom mixture and let if cook on low for about 10 minutes. And that was it. He called it "Beef Bandera" only because that's where we were when he made it. I remember that it really tasted great after a day of bad golfing so you might want to give it a try.

Scott Turner, recalling a day with Audie Murphy, actor and songwriter

Like brother Robert, John Mitchum has appeared in many classic movie and TV westerns. Among his credits are *Paint Your Wagon, Chisholm, Breakheart Pass, Bandelero!,* and *Cattle King.* He also played the bartender on TV's *Bonanza.*

BIG JOHN'S BARBECUED SPARE RIBS

This is a simple recipe—although it must be adhered to completely.

8   to 10 pounds ribs
    Hot barbecue sauce
    Plain barbecue sauce

Boil the ribs until tender, about 40 to 45 minutes. Drain. Marinate the ribs overnight in a mixture of barbecue sauces, one hot, one plain. Be sure to mix the two thoroughly. When barbecuing, allow the coals to reduce to a slow, steady heat. Do not put meat on rapidly glowing coals. Cook them evenly on each side for 5 to 7 minutes. Then, munch and enjoy.

John Mitchum, actor

ON THE BORDER CHILIES RELLENOS CASSEROLE

1   27-ounce can Ortega green chilies (rinse and take out seeds)
1   pound each: Monterey Jack cheese and sharp Cheddar cheese, grated and mixed together
6   eggs, separated
1   12-ounce can evaporated milk

Preheat the oven to 325°. In a greased, 9x13-inch baking dish, put one layer of chilies and one layer of cheese. Continue with layers of chilies and cheese. Make about three layers. Beat the egg whites until stiff. Fold in the yolks, then the milk. Pour the mixture over top of layers. Puncture with fork so egg mixture will work down through cheese and chilies. Bake for 50 minutes.

Marilyn and Wesley Tuttle, singer and actor

ENTRÉES

RICHOCHET'S TURKEY ENCHILADAS

A favorite prepared by my cook, Kathy McCaskey.

	Vegetable oil
12	corn tortillas
1	28-ounce can Las Palmas red chili sauce
1	16-ounce carton sour cream
3	cups turkey, cooked and shredded
1	pound Monterey Jack cheese, cut into finger-size strips
1	4-ounce can green chili peppers, cut into strips
¼	pound Cheddar cheese, grated
4	scallions, sliced

In an 8- or 10-inch skillet, pour oil ¼ inch deep and heat over medium-high heat. Soften tortillas, one at a time, by placing in the hot oil for a few seconds on each side, using tongs. Drain tortillas on paper towels. Dip each tortilla, one at a time, in the sauce. Preheat the oven to 325°. Place 1 to 2 teaspoons sour cream down center of each tortilla, ¼ cup turkey, one strip Jack cheese, and 1 or 2 chili strips. Roll tortillas and place seam sides down in a 13x9x2-inch casserole dish. Pour remaining sauce over them, and sprinkle cheese and scallions on top. Bake, uncovered, for about 30 minutes.

Makes 12 servings.

Don Messick, voice actor

Magnum Force—Tom Selleck's westerns have spanned the globe. Among his movie westerns for TV are Louis L'Amour's *The Shadow Riders* and *The Sacketts.* And he fired a shot heard around the world with his classic big-screen western *Quigley Down Under.*

A Real Hare Trigger—Don Messick was the voice of fourteen-carrot cartoon gunslinger Richochet Rabbit.

QUIGLEY'S CHICKEN WITH WINE AND VEGETABLES

The long ranger's best shot.

1	onion, sliced
3	tablespoons butter, divided
4	boned chicken breasts, halved
	Salt and pepper
½	cup all-purpose flour
8	whole mushrooms
1	cup orange juice
1	cup Marsala wine
¼	cup ginger ale
¼	cup lemon juice
1	medium can artichoke hearts
	Hot, cooked brown rice

Brown the onion in 1 tablespoon butter. Set aside. Preheat the oven to 325°. Salt and pepper the chicken. Roll in flour to cover. Brown quickly in remaining butter. Place onion in the bottom of a Dutch oven. Layer with chicken and mushrooms. Mix the liquid ingredients and pour over. Bake, covered, for 1 hour. Add the artichoke hearts and cook for 30 more minutes. Serve with rice.

Tom Selleck, actor

CHUCK WAGON

165

THE BEAR'S PORCUPINE MEATBALLS

Sticks to your ribs.

2   pounds ground meat
½   cup Minute Rice, uncooked
4   10¾-ounce cans Campbell's tomato soup
4   potatoes, skinned and sliced into thirds
6   carrots
    Salt and pepper to taste

Mix the ground meat and uncooked rice. Shape into meatballs. Place all ingredients in a pressure cooker. Set on low to medium heat, and pressurize for 20 minutes. Cool slightly and serve.
    Makes 10 to 12 servings.

John "Bear" Hudkins, stuntman

"If they move, kill 'em"
—William Holden in *The Wild Bunch*

Bearing the Stunt—Stunt legend John "Bear" Hudkins has appeared in a cross-section of best-loved westerns. He worked for director John Ford in *Fort Apache* and *Cheyenne Autumn,* among others. And he worked with John Wayne in *The Alamo, Rio Lobo, McLintock, The Undefeated* (pictured here, with the Duke), and others; and with Clint Eastwood in *Paint Your Wagon, The Outlaw Josie Wales, Bronco Billy,* and more.

BRONZE BUCKAROO'S JUMEBOTIA

Even better than California gold!

- 1   medium eggplant, peeled and diced
- ¾   cup fresh parsley
- 2   medium potatoes, chopped
- 1   large red pepper, chopped
- 4   small zucchini, chopped
- 3   small stalks celery, with leaves
- 1   medium onion, chopped
- 2   large garlic cloves, chopped
- 3   tablespoons olive oil
- 1   teaspoon red pepper flakes
- 3   tablespoons sweet basil
- ½   cup beef stock or bouillon
       Grated Romano cheese
- 1   teaspoon salt with bouillon or 1½ tea-
       spoons salt with stock

Combine all ingredients in a large pot. Cover and bring to a boil for 10 minutes, stirring once or twice, then lower heat and cover for 45 minutes. Remove from heat and let stand for 20 minutes, covered. Serve with hot bread as a main dish or cold as an appetizer with melba toast. Sprinkle with cheese and serve.

Makes 6 to 8 servings.

Herb Jeffries, actor and singer/composer

The Bronze Buckaroo—Herb Jeffries has toured with music legends such as Earl (Fatha) Hines and Duke Ellington and has been cited for excellence by the Department of Defense for his western-influenced entertainment during World War II and the Korean War. Today, he records for Warner Western, a division of Warner Records.

Singer, songwriter, and actor Ed Bruce starred with James Garner as his pal, Tom Guthrie, in *Bret Maverick* from 1981 to 1982. He also co-wrote "Mamas Don't Let Your Babies Grow Up To Be Cowboys" and had hit songs of his own with "The Last Cowboy Song" and "My First Taste of Texas." Living on his Home at Last Ranch in Middle Tennessee, Ed raises horses and is an honorary member of the Pro Rodeo Cowboy Association.

ED'S TATERS AND SAUSAGE AND SUCH

Even doctors and lawyers like it.

My friend, Mario Ferrari, who owns a four-star ristorante in Nashville and is an internationally known expert on fine wines, says, "White is for drinking and red is for eating!"

⅓	to ½ cup olive oil
3	to 5 garlic cloves, finely chopped
6	medium spuds (sliced crossways ⅛- to ¼-inch thick)
4	Italian sausages (approximately 1 pound), skinned and cut into 1-inch lengths
1	cup chopped onion
1	cup chopped green bell peppers
⅓	cup red wine
1	cup chopped fresh mushrooms
1	tablespoon oregano
1	tablespoon sweet leaf basil
1	tablespoon parsley
1	tablespoon rosemary
	Salt and pepper to taste
1	pound spinach (frozen or fresh)
	Parmesan cheese
	Crushed red pepper
1	bottle chilled chenin blanc, for sipping

My wife, Judith, and I cook a lot of one-dish meals, and over years of experimenting, have come up with some strange concoctions. I'm not very good at this, because I'm a pinch of this, a dab of that kind of cook; so feel free to adjust according to your own taste preference. We did make this recipe with these proportions, however, and it wasn't bad! This is a hearty meal well complimented by a dry red.

Pour about half your olive oil into an electric skillet, set at low heat (about 225°). Set aside remainder of oil. Add garlic, and move it around a little with a wooden spoon or spatula. Add potatoes and stir again until lightly coated with oil. Add sausage and mix 'em up again. Add onion and peppers, pour in red wine, and apply wooden spoon again. (All the above is accomplished at a pace of sufficient leisure as to allow one the opportunity for an occasional sip of the chenin blanc.)

Add mushrooms. Add remaining spices and herbs. Add previously washed or thawed and drained spinach and stir gently. Cover and let simmer until taters and sausage are done. You may want to sprinkle a little Parmesan cheese and crushed red pepper at serving.

Makes servings for 4 hearty appetites, or 2 with some great leftovers.

Note: You may use a Dutch-oven type cooker or stove top. The important thing is low heat, so the garlic doesn't burn and the spuds don't stick.

Ed Bruce, singer/songwriter and actor

HOLDIN' HEAVEN SHRIMP BREAD

1	pound shrimp, peeled and deveined
1	stick butter or margarine
1	white onion, chopped
	Salt to taste
	Pepper to taste
	Tony Chasre's Cajun seasoning or red pepper and paprika to taste
1	loaf French bread
1	cup shredded Cheddar cheese

Cut the shrimp into ½-inch pieces. Sauté in butter with onion and seasonings over medium heat for about 5 minutes. Preheat the oven to 350°. Cut French bread loaf in half lengthwise. Take the top half and scrape out the center of it, so it looks like a boat. Take the crumbs and spread them on a cookie sheet. Toast the crumbs and the hollow loaf until brown. Combine crumbs with sautéed shrimp mixture. Mix thoroughly. Stuff mixture into hollowed half of loaf and spread cheese over the top. Bake with bottom half of bread for 3 to 5 minutes or until cheese is melted. Serve open-faced or top with other half of bread and cut into slices, along with a green salad.

Michelle and Tracy Byrd, singer

SUN-UP SPECIALS

RISE 'N' SHINE BREAKFAST BURRITO

  Vegetable oil
8 large eggs
2 tablespoons heavy cream
  Pinch of salt
1 avocado, peeled, pitted, and diced
4 sun-dried tomatoes, rehydrated and chopped
1 scallion, thinly sliced
1 jalapeño pepper, stemmed, seeded, and minced
4 8-inch flour tortillas
4 ounces grated Monterey Jack cheese or sharp Cheddar cheese
1 cup Ranchero Sauce
4 tablespoons sour cream
1 tablespoon chopped cilantro

Heat an iron skillet or griddle and grease with a thin film of oil. Beat the eggs with the cream and salt. Cook scrambled eggs until soft in your favorite egg pan. Fold into eggs the avocado, tomatoes, scallion, and jalapeño. Set bowl aside and keep warm over a water bath. Place a tortilla in the hot skillet, warm thoroughly on one side, and flip over. Spread 1 ounce of cheese over tortilla and allow to melt; add ¼ of the scrambled eggs mixture across the center of tortilla. Roll up and let sit a few seconds. Then place onto warm plate. Ladle 2 ounces of Ranchero Sauce over the center of burrito. Place a dollop of sour cream on top and sprinkle with cilantro. Keep warm and continue with other tortillas. Serve with black beans, re-fried pinto beans, or hash browns.

Ranchero Sauce:
1½ pounds Roma tomatoes
2 serrano chili peppers
½ cup finely chopped white onions
½ teaspoon minced garlic
1 tablespoon peanut oil
2 poblano chili peppers, roasted, peeled, seeded, and cut into julienne strips
¼ bunch cilantro, tied
½ teaspoon salt

Lightly blacken tomatoes and serranos in a skillet, about 4 to 5 minutes. Sauté onions and garlic in oil over low heat until soft. Combine all ingredients in a saucepan, reserving a few strips of poblano for garnish. Cook, partially covered, over low heat for 20 to 30 minutes; add water if necessary. Remove cilantro. Garnish with reserved poblanos.
  Makes 4 servings.

The Home Ranch
Clark, Colorado

Although many film historians consider "The Great Train Robbery" to be the first western film ever made, ironically the entire movie was shot in New Jersey.

Film giant Gregory Peck has made many great films, including a number of westerns, such as *Duel in the Sun, The Gunfighter* (pictured here), *The Bravados, The Big Country, Mackenna's Gold, The Stalking Moon,* and *Billy Two Hats.*

SUNDAY MORNING HAPPY PAPPY EGGS

8	eggs
4	slices baked ham
⅓	cup chopped chives
⅓	cup cream or whole milk
2	to 3 pats of butter

Soft scramble the eggs in butter after mixing them with the milk or cream. Toss in the chives and ham, which has been cut into nickel-size pieces. Do not let the eggs get hard. Keep the flame just below medium and stir gently with a long-handled fork the whole time. Do not overcook.

When ready to eat, heap on the salsa and Tabasco sauce as hot as you can stand it. Children may not favor the chives or hot stuff. This is really a grown-up recipe. It will serve 4 adults with or without hangovers. Add a generous helping of home-fried potatoes, black-eyed peas, or chili and beans.

Start the whole procedure with a good bloody mary made with vodka and served in a large, chilled glass. Don't do this more than once a month or your cholesterol count will go through the roof.

Makes 4 servings.

Gregory Peck, actor

From 1968 to 1970, Jimmy Dean co-starred as backwoodsman Josh Clements on *Daniel Boone.* Here he jaws with Cincinnatus (Dal McKennon, left).

COUNTRY BREAKFAST PIE

Turns Big Bad John into a good little boy.

- 1 16-ounce package Jimmy Dean roll sausage
- 1 9-inch pie shell, ready-made or from scratch
- 4 eggs, lightly beaten
- 1½ cups grated Swiss cheese
- ¼ cup chopped green bell pepper
- ¼ cup chopped red bell pepper
- 2 tablespoons chopped onions
- 1 cup light cream

Preheat the oven to 375°. Cook sausage until done. Crumble, then drain. Prepare pie shell. Mix cheese and sausage. Sprinkle in shell. Lightly beat eggs in bowl. Combine remaining ingredients and add to egg mixture. Pour into shell. Bake for 40 to 45 minutes. Cool on a rack for 10 minutes.

Makes 6 to 8 servings.

Jimmy Dean, singer/songwriter and actor

Paul Fix played Marshal Micah Torrance in *The Rifleman* from 1958 to 1963, and also performed in numerous western films with legends like his friend John Wayne.

MICAH'S COUNTRY EGGS

Here's the only recipe that I remember my father really liking when I was growing up. He was a big breakfast lover, and my mother used to fix these eggs often for him. When John "Duke" Wayne was staying at our house in the early 1940s, he really enjoyed them too.
—Marilyn Carey

1   tablespoon butter
¾   to 1 cup light cream or half and half
4   eggs
2   tablespoons crushed cornflakes (optional)
4   slices hot, buttered sourdough toast
    Salt and pepper to taste
    Paprika

Melt butter in a skillet. Add cream and heat until just bubbling. Break eggs carefully into a small dish and then slip them into the hot milk. Cook over low heat until the whites are firm around the edges. Sprinkle with cornflakes. Cover and cook to desired doneness. Arrange eggs on the toast with the cream, which should have thickened somewhat. Sprinkle with salt, pepper, and paprika. This is great served with sausage.
    Makes 4 servings.

Paul Fix, actor

"A gun is a tool, Marion. No better, no worse than any other tool—an ax, a shovel, or anything. A gun is as good or as bad as the man using it. Remember that."—Alan Ladd to Jean Arthur (as Marion, Jody's mother) in *Shane*

"We'd all be much better off if there wasn't a single gun left in this valley—including yours."
—Jean Arthur's response

And in the end:

"A man has to be what he is, Jody. You can't break the mold. . . . Now, you run on home to your mother and tell her—tell her everything's all right and there aren't any more guns in this valley."—Alan Ladd

The cast of the radio version of *Gunsmoke:* Howard McNear as Doc, William Conrad as Matt Dillon, Georgia Ellis as Kitty, and Parley Baer as Chester. (Courtesy of Kit McNear)

DOC'S BEAT-UP EGGS

6   slices lean bacon
3   slices white bread
6   eggs (brown preferred)
    Salt, pepper, and paprika to taste

Fry bacon until crisp. Drain and crumble into small pieces. Toast the bread and break into small pieces. In a frying pan, scramble the eggs until almost done; add in the toast pieces and bacon. Add salt, pepper, and paprika to taste while the eggs are still in the pan. Serve immediately.

Makes about 3 servings.

Howard McNear, actor

HIDDEN CREEK MACARONI PIE

For hungry cowboys—tastes great hot or cold! To serve cold, chill overnight. Cut into pie slices and take it to go on the trail!

1   16-ounce box macaroni
1   cup milk
2   eggs, lightly beaten
3   garlic cloves
¼   teaspoon pepper
¼   teaspoon salt
    Dash of Pistol-Packin' Pepper Sauce
    (p. 190)
    Pinch of thyme
    Pinch of oregano
½   teaspoon sweet basil
1   teaspoon Knorr all-purpose seasoning
1   teaspoon Kraft beef extract
2   drops Worcestershire sauce
2   tablespoons soy sauce
4   cups grated Gouda cheese, divided
2   cups diced cooked ham
1   bunch parsley, diced

Cook macaroni in salted water according to package directions (not too soft!). Preheat the oven to 350°. Mix milk with eggs, and add garlic, pepper, salt, pepper sauce, thyme, oregano, sweet basil, all-purpose seasoning, beef extract, Worcestershire sauce, and soy sauce. Season generously to taste. Add Gouda cheese (keep about 1 cup aside), cooked ham, and diced parsley. Mix with macaroni. Place in a baking dish. Sprinkle remaining 1 cup Gouda cheese on top and bake for about 1½ hours. When pie starts to brown, cover with foil. Serve hot or cold.

Makes 4 to 6 servings.

*Iris Behr, Hidden Creek Ranch
Harrison, Idaho*

Real people's real names—Billy the Kid, William Bonney; Black Bart, Charles E. Boles; Calamity Jane, Martha Jane Canary; Kit Carson, Christopher Houston Carson; Butch Cassidy, Robert Leroy Parker; Buffalo Bill Cody, William Frederick Cody; Wild Bill Hickok, James Butler Hickok; Doc Holliday, John Henry Holliday; Annie Oakley, Phoebe Ann Moses; and Belle Starr, Myra Belle Shirley.

EASY OVERNIGHT BREAKFAST

1   pound bulk pork sausage
1   cup chopped onions
1   cup sliced mushrooms
½   cup chopped green bell peppers
1   4-ounce can green chili peppers
1   cup milk or cheese
1   10¾-ounce can cream of mushroom soup
¾   teaspoon dry mustard
1   16-ounce package frozen shredded hash
    brown potatoes
12 eggs, beaten, and seasoned to taste
    Shredded cheese

Brown the sausage and drain. Then add any or all of the following: onion, mushrooms, bell peppers, and chilies. Mix together the milk or cheese, soup, and mustard. In a well-greased 9x13-inch pan, layer the hash browns (straight from the freezer), sausage mixture, soup mixture, and the eggs. Cover with cheese as desired. Do not stir. Refrigerate for 10 or more hours, covered with plastic wrap. The next morning, pull it out, remove cover, and bake at 350° for 50 to 60 minutes. Serve with fresh fruit for an easy meal for company.

Makes 12 or more servings.

Red Steagall, singer

DANCE HALL EGGS

A western star.

Bread
Butter
Eggs

Dance Hall Eggs are a little tough to cook around a campfire, unless you have a loaf of bread and a pound of butter. Here's what ya do, and it's simple. Tear the center out of a slice of bread. Brown lightly in butter on both sides. Crack one egg into the hole in the bread and let 'er cook to taste. Be sure to keep fire low or butter will burn badly. I suggest you add butter with each different slice of bread. I usually have about three for me, and swill it down with a pot of coffee.

Rory Calhoun, actor

DON'T TOUCH THAT DIAL, PARDNER!

Westerns from the Nielsen Top Twenty, October 1958 through April 1959

1. *Gunsmoke*
2. *Wagon Train*
3. *Have Gun, Will Travel*
4. *The Rifleman*
6. *Maverick*
7. *Tales of Wells Fargo*
10. *The Life and Legend of Wyatt Earp*
15. *The Texan*
16. *Wanted: Dead or Alive*
18. *Cheyenne*

Rory Calhoun starred as Bill Longley in TV's *The Texan,* from 1958 to 1961. He also made a number of feature film westerns, including 1954's *River of No Return* with Marilyn Monroe as his girlfriend.

HORSE WRANGLERS SCRAMBLED BREAKFAST

I like this recipe because most of the ingredients can be precooked. It's also quick to make and can be made in batches if ya' got hands comin' in to eat at different times. Served with sourdough biscuits and hot coffee this will shore stick to 'yer ribs. This recipe is for one person. If you're feedin' ten hands, use 20 eggs and 10 spuds.

- 1 boiled spud
- ⅛ cup chopped onions
   Butter
- 3 to 4 strips bacon
   Milk
- 2 eggs
   Mild chunky salsa

Grate boiled spuds (hash browns); brown with onions in a skillet with some butter. Cut bacon into pieces 1 to 2 inches wide; cook in separate skillet. Drain on paper towel. When onions are cooked, add a little milk and the eggs. Scramble everything. As eggs begin to cook, add bacon and a little of the salsa. (I like my scrambled eggs to taste creamy so the salsa is just for color. If you want more flavor then use more, but experiment before adding too much).
   Makes 1 serving.

Jack Bradt, Triple R Dude Ranch
Keystone, South Dakota

OUTCASTS CHEESE AND VEGETABLE OMELET

The bus stops here.

   Diced mushrooms
   Diced green onions
   Diced tomatoes
   Butter or olive oil
- 4 egg whites and 2 yolks
- ¼ cup milk
- ⅛ cup water
   Leiden cheese (with seeds)

Sauté mushrooms, onions, and tomatoes in butter or olive oil in a frying pan. Beat egg whites and yolks with milk and water. Pour over sautéed veggies. Slice a very thin layer of Leiden cheese and place on top. Cook over low heat. When eggs begin to harden, cover pan to create a semi-soufflé.
   Makes 1 to 2 servings.

Don Murray, actor

SERGEANT O'ROURKE'S CREAMED EGGS ON ENGLISH MUFFINS

Fortifies you with courage.

- 4 tablespoons vegetable oil
- 4 tablespoons all-purpose flour
- 2 cups milk
- 1 10¾-ounce can cream of mushroom soup
- 6 to 8 hard-boiled eggs, sliced
- 4 English muffins, halved

Heat oil in a skillet; add flour and stir to blend. Add milk slowly, stirring until thickened. Add soup; stir to blend. Add sliced eggs and mix. Serve over toasted English muffins.
   Makes 4 servings.

Forrest Tucker, actor

BACK IN THE SADDLE AGAIN

Part Two

Match the movie cowboys to their horses.

1. Sunset Carson	A. Brownie and Boy
2. Fred Scott	B. Lightning
3. Bob Steele	C. Duke and Dollar
4. John Wayne	D. Sonny and Thunder
5. Rex Allen	E. Black Jack
6. Charles Starrett	F. Tony and Old Blue
7. Buck Jones	G. Cactus and Silver
8. Tom Tyler	H. Starlight and
9. Ken Maynard	Midnight
10. Bill Elliott	I. King, Silver, White
11. Monte Hale	Eagle
12. Col. Tim McCoy	J. White Dust
13. Tom Mix	K. Ace and Baron
14. Tim Holt	L. Ko-Ko
15. Allan Rocky Lane	M. Pardner
	N. Tarzan
	O. Raider

Solution: 1. G; 2. J; 3. A; 4. C; 5. L; 6. O; 7. I; 8. K; 9. N; 10. D; 11. M; 12. H; 13. F; 14. B; 15. E

DUKE'S SOUFFLÉ

We first had the pleasure of trying this most delicious dish at the home of Dr. and Mrs. Thomas Doan. The occasion was a brunch in honor of President Miguel Aleman of Mexico. Duke had one bite of this south-of-the-border dish and flipped. Rue (a beautiful blonde, my son Ethan's first "crush," and a great cook) graciously gave me the recipe. Rue is now Mrs. Robert Byars. From that day, this became Duke's favorite dish, and he would carry the recipe with him wherever he went. Sometimes he would call me from Africa or Europe and ask me questions like "How much cheese?" or "What temperature?" I always got a kick out of this.

This became one of his "two most favorite recipes." The other one being Duke's Hominy Grits Soufflé (p. 179).

1 pound Cheddar cheese, grated
1 pound Jack cheese, grated
2 cans diced chilies (size of can depends on how hot you like it!)
4 eggs, separated
1 medium-size can stewed tomatoes, drained

Preheat the oven to 325°. Butter a deep casserole dish. Make layers of cheeses and chilies. Beat egg whites until stiff. Beat egg yolks and fold into egg whites. Gently pour the egg mixture over all, covering the cheeses and chilies. Bake for 30 minutes. Add drained tomatoes, pushing them down with a fork. Bake for 30 more minutes.

Pilar and John Wayne, actor
Courtesy of *Pilar Wayne's Favorite and Fabulous Recipes*

"I mean to kill you in one minute, Ned, or see you hanged in Fort Smith at Judge Parker's convenience. Which'll it be?"—John Wayne to Robert Duvall in *True Grit*

"I call that bold talk for a one-eyed fat man."—Robert Duvall in response

John Wayne's young cowboys enjoy grub during *The Cowboys.* (Courtesy of Steve Cox Collection)

DUKE'S HOMINY GRITS SOUFFLÉ

True grits.

- 6 cups water
- 1½ cups quick grits
- 1½ sticks butter
- 1 pound mild Cheddar cheese, grated
- 2 teaspoons salt
- 3 eggs, beaten

In a saucepan bring the water to a boil. Add the grits and continue to boil for 10 minutes, uncovered. Remove from heat and add the butter, cheese, salt, and eggs. Place in an 8x10-inch baking dish and bake at 350° for 1½ hours. Serve hot.

Pilar and John Wayne, actor
Courtesy of Pilar Wayne's Favorite and Fabulous Recipes

OTTO EITEL'S HOLIDAY ONION CAKE

Holidays bring new memories and renew old ones. One of my favorite reminiscences is centered around onions.

When Fess and I moved to Santa Barbara more than 30 years ago, one of the first friends we met was our neighbor Otto Eitel from Stuttgart, Germany. He was quite dapper with pure white hair, a ruddy complexion, and a very small, curled, and impeccably cared for mustache. Formerly a well-known restaurateur from Chicago, Otto knew how to entertain royally and did so frequently on an international basis. Yet, our greatest pleasure was when Fess and I were invited to dine in his kitchen. It was always a joy. Many a fine evening was spent around the kitchen table with his housekeeper and Dr. Gates, a renowned radiologist. Otto would prepare sensational dishes. Of particular note was his Holiday Onion Cake—absolutely wonderful. It took quite a bit of coaxing but he finally relented and gave me the recipe with the agreement that I would never part with it until he was gone. For us, this cake has become a Christmas standard that is made in quantity. It has been about fifteen years since Otto has left this world and in his memory (and hopefully with his blessing) I give you Otto Eitel's Holiday Onion Cake. (Though called a "cake," this is more like a quiche. This can be served as an appetizer, a first course, or as a main entrée with a simple green salad.)

- 8   ounces all-purpose flour
- 2   sticks sweet butter, softened
- ½   pound Farmer's country-style cottage cheese
-     About 2 tablespoons caraway seed
- 8   slices smoked bacon, finely chopped
- 3½ pounds white onions, chopped
- 4   whole eggs
- 2   egg yolks
- 2   cups sour cream
-     Salt
-     Fresh ground black pepper,
-     Lawry's seasoned salt

Mix flour and butter until very finely crumbled. Add cottage cheese a little at a time. Shape into a ball, cover with plastic wrap, and refrigerate overnight. Roll out dough on a lightly floured board and transfer to a glass casserole dish with a 1½-inch edge or a 9-inch pie pan. Sprinkle bottom of pastry with about 2 tablespoons caraway seed (save some for topping) and half the bacon.

Hand cut onions. Food processing makes them too mushy. In a covered earthenware (not stainless steel) container over an asbestos pad, sauté onions over very low heat. Stir from time to time (takes about 45 minutes). Cool completely. Preheat the oven to 375°. Beat eggs and egg yolks lightly and blend with sour cream. Add to onions. Season with salt and pepper to taste and pour into crust. Top with a sprinkling of caraway seed and remaining bacon. Bake for 1 hour or until bubbly and brown.

Makes 4 to 6 servings.

Marcy and Fess Parker, actor

ELI'S EGGS BIRMINGHAM

Join the hole in the wall gang.

- 4   strips bacon
- 2   slices wheat bread
-     Vegetable cooking spray
- 2   eggs

Fry bacon until crisp. Drain on a paper towel. Cut a hole in the center of each slice of bread. Grease frying pan with vegetable cooking spray. Place bread in pan and drop an egg in each hole. Cover pan and cook until eggs are done. Place bacon strips on top and serve.

Makes 2 servings.

Eli Wallach, actor

Things get ugly:

"There are two kinds of spurs, my friend—those that come in by the door, those that come in by the window."—Eli Wallach to Clint Eastwood in *The Good, the Bad, and the Ugly*

But good prevails a little later:

"You see, in this world, there are two kinds of people, my friend—those with loaded guns and those who dig. You dig."—Clint Eastwood to Eli Wallach

TROY'S BREAKFAST PIZZA

Scores early in the game.

- 1   can refrigerated Crescent dinner rolls
- 1   pound bulk pork sausage
- 1   cup frozen hash browns, thawed
- 1   cup grated sharp Cheddar cheese
- 5   eggs
- ¼   cup milk
- ½   teaspoon salt
- ¼   teaspoon pepper
- ¼   cup Parmesan cheese

Preheat the oven to 375°. Separate and place crescent rolls flat on an ungreased pizza pan; press together as if making a pizza crust. Crumble and brown sausage; drain. Spread sausage over crust. Sprinkle with thawed hash browns; then top with Cheddar cheese. Beat eggs with milk, salt, and pepper; pour over top of pizza. Top with Parmesan cheese. Bake for 30 minutes.

Makes 6 to 8 servings.

Troy Aikman, Dallas Cowboy

Troy Aikman—Dallas Cowboy fast on the draw

Eli Wallach and Clint Eastwood are the Ugly and the Good in *The Good, The Bad, and The Ugly.*

Side Arms

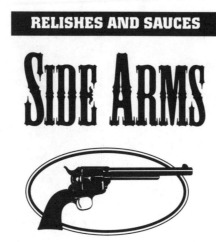

YIPPEE . . . . . FIERY PICANTE

- 10 fresh jalapeño peppers
- 10 fresh habanero peppers
- 2 fresh red chilie peppers
- 3 cups distilled vinegar
- 1 cup sugar
- ½ tablespoon cayenne pepper
- ¼ tablespoon white pepper
- ⅛ tablespoon black pepper
- 10 red tomatoes
- 10 tomatillos
- 2 green bell peppers
- 10 ripe Vidalia onions (or any sweet onion)
- 20 green onions
- 1 bunch parsley
- 3 bunches cilantro/coriander
  Juice of 1 lemon
  Mexican oregano

Puree the jalapeños, habaneros, and red chilie peppers and place in a big bowl. Add vinegar and sugar. Jump up and down three times fast while tossing in the cayenne, white, and black pepper. Do a three-minute raindance . . . then dice the red tomatoes, tomatillos, green peppers, and Vidalia and green onions. Do five somersaults before chopping the parsley and cilantro. Throw into the big bowl along with the lemon juice. Turn around three times and shout "Olé!" Add coriander and Mexican oregano, along with any other spices you might like, so the picante won't be so bland. Mix all ingredients together and seal very tightly. Dig a hole in the yard by the light of the full moon. Cover bowl with dirt. . . let sit for 6 hours, 5 minutes, and 47 seconds. Then douse yourself with holy water, dig up the bowl, grab a bag of taco chips and a gallon of sour cream. Say a quick prayer and dig in! (For fullest flavor, recipe must be made at the third hour of the full moon. A fire extinguisher is optional.)

Makes about 1 gallon.

Sheb Wooley, actor and singer/songwriter

LAND OF ENCHANTMENT SALSA

Wild fire!

- 2 onions, chopped
- 5 large garlic cloves, minced
- 2 tablespoons vegetable oil
- 2 16-ounce cans crushed tomatoes
- 1 10-ounce can chopped hot green chilies or 10 large fresh chilies, roasted, peeled, and chopped
- 3 teaspoons ground cumin
- 1 teaspoon salt

Sauté onions and garlic in oil until soft. Add tomatoes and chilies and simmer until thick. Add cumin and salt to taste. Cool and serve. Freezes well.

Makes approximately 6 cups.

Michael Martin Murphey, singer/songwriter

MICKEY'S PICO DE GALLO

- 2 fresh tomatoes
- 1 medium white onion
- 3 jalapeño peppers, seeds removed
- ½ bunch cilantro

Chop all ingredients and mix well. Store in a jar in the refrigerator.
Makes 2 cups.

Mickey Gilley, singer

HIDDEN VALLEY RANCH SALSA CRUDA

- 9 cups chopped ripe Roma tomatoes
- 3 cups puréed Roma tomatoes
- 1 cup fresh cilantro
- 3 cups chopped white or yellow onions
  Juice and pulp of 2 limes
- 1 cup chopped green onions
- 4 to 6 medium jalapeño peppers
- ¾ cup red wine vinegar
- 2 tablespoons chimayo powder or red pepper flakes
- 1 tablespoon oregano
- 2 tablespoons cumin
- 1 tablespoon salt
- 3 tablespoons chopped garlic

In a food processor or by hand, chop the fresh ingredients and purée the tomatoes. The cilantro and jalapeños can be chopped with a little red wine vinegar to keep them from sticking to the sides of the processor. Include the seeds from the jalapeños along with the spices. This should sit for 24 hours to let the ingredients mellow and fuse.
Makes 1 gallon.

Bruce Coe, Hidden Valley Ranch
Cle Elum, Washington

TANYA'S CON QUESO DIP

- 1 pound Velveeta cheese, cubed
- ¼ cup milk
- 1½ cups strained Tanya Tucker's Salsa

Blend cheese and milk in a saucepan over medium heat, until creamy and hot. Stir in salsa.
Makes approximately 4 cups.

Tanya Tucker, singer

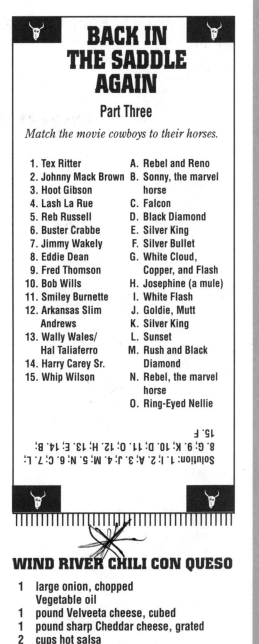

BACK IN THE SADDLE AGAIN

Part Three

Match the movie cowboys to their horses.

1. Tex Ritter	A. Rebel and Reno
2. Johnny Mack Brown	B. Sonny, the marvel horse
3. Hoot Gibson	
4. Lash La Rue	C. Falcon
5. Reb Russell	D. Black Diamond
6. Buster Crabbe	E. Silver King
7. Jimmy Wakely	F. Silver Bullet
8. Eddie Dean	G. White Cloud, Copper, and Flash
9. Fred Thomson	
10. Bob Wills	H. Josephine (a mule)
11. Smiley Burnette	I. White Flash
12. Arkansas Slim Andrews	J. Goldie, Mutt
	K. Silver King
13. Wally Wales/ Hal Taliaferro	L. Sunset
	M. Rush and Black Diamond
14. Harry Carey Sr.	
15. Whip Wilson	N. Rebel, the marvel horse
	O. Ring-Eyed Nellie

Solution: 1. I; 2. A; 3. J; 4. M; 5. N; 6. C; 7. L; 8. G; 9. K; 10. D; 11. O; 12. H; 13. E; 14. B; 15. F.

WIND RIVER CHILI CON QUESO

- 1 large onion, chopped
  Vegetable oil
- 1 pound Velveeta cheese, cubed
- 1 pound sharp Cheddar cheese, grated
- 2 cups hot salsa
- 1 tablespoon ground cumin
- 1 4-ounce can chopped green chilies

Sauté onion in oil until transparent. Add remaining ingredients. Stir until the cheeses are well blended and completely melted. Serve in a fondue pot with candle to keep warm. Serve with large corn chips or tortilla chips. This freezes well.
Makes about 6½ cups.

Garey and Ken Neal, T Cross Ranch
Dubois, Wyoming

ALLEN RANCH BARBECUE SAUCE

1   quart tomato sauce
1   cup vinegar
1   pound brown sugar
1   teaspoon dry mustard
1   teaspoon chili powder
2   teaspoons paprika
1   teaspoon red pepper
1   to 2 teaspoons liquid smoke (to taste)
2   13-ounce bottles ketchup
3   teaspoons cinnamon
3   teaspoons salt
1   teaspoon allspice
1   teaspoon mace
1   teaspoon celery salt
3   teaspoons garlic juice
2   tablespoons Worcestershire sauce

Combine all ingredients. Simmer, uncovered, for several hours until desired thickness is reached.
Makes about 1 gallon.

Allen Ranch
Bixby, Oklahoma

BEST OF THE WEST BARBECUE SAUCE

Put it to the test.

1¼   cups ketchup
1   tablespoon Worcestershire sauce
2   tablespoons brown sugar
1   tablespoon dry mustard
1   medium yellow onion, chopped
2   tablespoons vinegar
2½   cups water
½   large garlic clove, minced
4   tablespoons lemon juice
½   tablespoon ground black pepper
    Salt to taste

Combine ingredients in a 2-quart saucepan. Place on medium heat and slowly bring to a boil (stirring frequently). Turn down heat and simmer for about 3 hours until the sauce becomes like a thick soup.
Serve hot in small, individual bowls for dipping country-style pork ribs.
Makes 4 to 6 servings.

Dick Jones, actor

HIDDEN VALLEY RANCH BARBECUE SAUCE

1   gallon Cattleman's BBQ sauce
5½   cups pepper purée or 1½ cups mild chili powder
1   tablespoon cumin
½   teaspoon anise seed
1¾   cups puréed onion
1¾   cups molasses
2¼   cups packed brown sugar
1   tablespoon nutmeg
¾   cup cocoa powder
5   tablespoons granulated garlic
4   jalapeño peppers
1½   tablespoons sweet basil
3   tablespoons chimayo powder

Combine all ingredients in a large pot. Simmer for 30 minutes. Pour into bottles; store in the refrigerator. This sauce needs a few days to settle in and mellow.
Makes 1 gallon.

Bruce Coe, Hidden Valley Ranch
Cle Elum, Washington

JESTS OF THE WEST

Match the comedians with their westerns.

1. Marx Brothers
2. Three Stooges
3. Abbott and Costello
4. Laurel and Hardy
5. Bob Hope
6. Jack Benny
7. Lucille Ball
8. Don Knotts
9. Martin and Lewis
10. Cleavon Little

A. *Shakiest Gun in the West*
B. *Pardners*
C. *Fancy Pants*
D. *The Wistful Widow of Wagon Gap*
E. *Buck Benny Rides Again*
F. *Blazing Saddles*
G. *Way Out West*
H. *Go West*
I. *The Outlaws Is Coming*
J. *The Paleface*

Solution: 1. H; 2. I; 3. D; 4. G; 5. J; 6. E; 7. C; 8. A; 9. B; 10. F

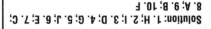

N.Y.P.D. Dude—As Sam McCloud, Dennis Weaver was a New Mexico deputy marshal who took on the criminals of New York City.

McCLOUD'S NEW YORK CITY PESTO SAUCE

New York City?!

We are vegetarians who try to grow as much of our own food as possible without the use of pesticides. The fresh basil we use year-round is from our indoor greenhouse boxes. Although Colorado's outdoor growing season is short, because we live in a solar home we are able to grow lettuce, tomatoes, and herbs all year long. We watch the fat we eat, so a sprinkle of Parmesan is the only cheese we use. Real cowboys do eat pesto!

2½	cups firmly packed fresh basil leaves, chopped
2	large garlic cloves, pressed
½	cup chopped walnuts, almonds, or pine nuts
½	cup fresh, grated Parmesan cheese (1 ounce)
½	cup olive oil
	Salt to taste (use sparingly)
	Angel hair pasta

Mix basil, garlic, nuts, and Parmesan in a blender or food processor until well blended. Then add the olive oil in a slow, steady stream until a smooth paste is formed. Go easy on the oil.

Mix in with a serving of angel hair pasta. You might want to add a small amount of canola margarine to make the mixture a bit more wet. Mix to your own specifications. If you like, add additional fresh Parmesan.

Pesto may be refrigerated for several weeks in an airtight jar. Cover sauce with a thin layer of olive oil to prevent discoloration.

Gerry and Dennis Weaver, actor

Jim Rogers, son of Will, is an accomplished cowboy himself. He appeared in several Hal Roach westerns starring Hopalong Cassidy.

ROGERS ROPIN' MEAT SAUCE

This sauce never met a meat it didn't like!

I've spent most of my life around cowboys and ranches. I've eaten in cow camps, off chuck wagons, and in a lot of ranch houses and I can tell you the best meals came from the ranches where the women did the cooking—to date I've yet to run into a gourmet chef wearing boots and spurs.

I do have one foolproof recipe for a cowboy fellow. It's one I followed and is real simple: Marry a good cook!

Because we were in the cattle business the one thing we had plenty of was beef and we ate a lot of it. Somehow I usually got the job of barbecue cook. There weren't a lot of these fancy barbecue sauces back in the late thirties and I got to fooling around and came up with this one.

½   cup ketchup
1   tablespoon A-1 steak sauce
1   teaspoon Worcestershire sauce
1   tablespoon brown sugar
     Pinch of chili powder

Combine all ingredients well. It goes with most cuts of beef, from hamburgers to T-bones.

Makes ½ cup.

Jim and Will Rogers, cowboy actor and cowboy humorist/actor

RANGO-LOBO MARINARA SAUCE

1   28-ounce can Italian plum tomatoes
½   medium onion, chopped
1½   tablespoons extra virgin olive oil
¼   pound mushrooms, thinly sliced
2   tablespoons tomato paste
⅓   cup dry white wine
2   teaspoons sugar
4   scrapes whole nutmeg
2   sprigs basil, chopped
    Sea salt
    Black pepper

Pass tomatoes through food mill to remove seeds; scrape any pulp into bowl. Sauté onion in oil until clear, not brown. Add mushrooms and sauté on high, stirring to keep from burning. Dissolve tomato paste in white wine and stir into onion-mushroom mixture. Cook until alcohol has evaporated, then add remainder of ingredients and simmer on low for 20 minutes. Stir frequently; do not allow to boil. Serve over gnocchi (or other pasta of choice), topped with grated Pecorino, Parmesan, or Romano cheese.
    Makes 4 cups.

Frankie Laine, singer

OLD COUNTRY MUSTARD

This mustard is designed to clear sinuses and repel mosquitoes!

    Sugar
    Dry mustard
    Water
    Vinegar
    Honey

Mix in a double boiler or bowl over hot water, equal parts sugar, dry mustard, and a mixture of water and vinegar (vinegar to taste, but not too much). When sugar is dissolved and the mixture is creamy, add honey to taste. Keep tasting tiny bits of the mixture until you like the results. Age overnight. Warm slightly to serve, as mustard will thicken. Will keep indefinitely in the refrigerator. Thin with hot water as needed. Serve with ham, pork chops, or any meat deserving a good mustard. Use sparingly, as it can bite.

Uncle Hank, Circle Bar Guest Ranch
Utica, Montana

Will Rogers—Cowboy, actor, writer, humorist, and one of the world's greatest trick ropers

ACADEMY AWARD-WINNING WESTERNS

1928–29 Best Actor—Warner Baxter (in *Old Arizona*)
1930–31 Best Picture—*Cimarron*
    Best Writing—*Cimarron*
    Best Interior Decorating—*Cimarron*
1934 Assistant Director—John Waters *(Viva Villa)*
1938 Sound Recording—*The Cowboy and the Lady*
1939 Best Supporting Actor—Thomas Mitchell *(Stagecoach)*
    Best Score—*Stagecoach*
1940 Best Supporting Actor—Walter Brennan *(The Westerner)*
    Film Editing—*Northwest Mounted Police*
1948 Supporting Actor—Walter Huston *(The Treasure of the Sierra Madre)*
    Director—John Huston *(The Treasure of the Sierra Madre)*
    Writing/Screenplay—*The Treasure of the Sierra Madre*
    Music (Song)—"Buttons and Bows" from *The Paleface*
1949 Color Cinematography—*She Wore a Yellow Ribbon*
1950 Music (Scoring of a Musical Picture)—*Annie Get Your Gun*
1952 Best Actor—Gary Cooper *(High Noon)*
    Music: (Song)—"High Noon (Do Not Forsake Me, Oh My Darlin')" *(High Noon)*
    Scoring of a Dramatic or Comedy Picture—*High Noon*
    Film Editing—*High Noon*
1953 Cinematography (Color)—*Shane*
    Music (Song)—"Secret Love" *(Calamity Jane)*
1954 Writing (Motion Picture Story)—*Broken Lance*

1958 Best Supporting Actor—Burl Ives *(The Big Country)*
1960 Sound—*The Alamo*
1963 Writing (Story and Screenplay written directly for the Screen)—*How the West Was Won*
    Sound—*How the West Was Won*
    Film Editing—*How the West Was Won*
1965 Best Actor—Lee Marvin *(Cat Ballou)*
1969 Best Actor—John Wayne *(True Grit)*
    Writing (Screenplay based on material not previously published or produced)—*Butch Cassidy and the Sundance Kid*
    Cinematography—*Butch Cassidy and the Sundance Kid*
    Music (Song)—"Raindrops Keep Fallin' on My Head" *(Butch Cassidy and the Sundance Kid)*
    Music (Original Score)—*Butch Cassidy and the Sundance Kid*
1973 Documentary (Features)—*The Great American Cowboy*
1990 Best Picture—*Dances with Wolves*
    Best Director—Kevin Costner *(Dances with Wolves)*
    Best Screenplay—*Dances with Wolves*
    Original Score—*Dances with Wolves*
    Cinematography—*Dances with Wolves*
    Editing—*Dances with Wolves*
    Sound Recording—*Dances with Wolves*
1992 Best Picture—*Unforgiven*
    Best Director—Clint Eastwood *(Unforgiven)*
    Best Supporting Actor—Gene Hackman *(Unforgiven)*
    Best Editing—*Unforgiven*

WILD BILL HICKOK SALSA

1 can stewed tomatoes, Mexican style
1 small can whole chilis (the kind with the carrots and onions on the label)
2 peppers (or more if you're a real man!)
2 or 3 tablespoons (or ¼ cup) onions
⅓ bunch of fresh cilantro

Mix in a blender, using the pulse. Don't overblend.

Guy Madison, actor

PERFECTLY HOT SWEET MUSTARD

1   cup packed dry mustard
1   cup white vinegar
3   eggs
1   cup sugar

Combine mustard and vinegar and let stand for 12 hours. Beat eggs and sugar, and combine with mustard mixture. Cook in a double boiler until thickened.
    Makes approximately 3 cups.

Tommy Doss, Sons of the Pioneers

GOOD 'N' SPICEY APPLE CIDER SAUCE

1   cup sugar
3   tablespoons biscuit mix
¼   teaspoon cinnamon
¼   teaspoon nutmeg
2   cups apple cider
2   tablespoons lemon juice
½   stick margarine

Mix sugar, biscuit mix, cinnamon, and nutmeg in a saucepan. Stir in cider and lemon juice. Cook, stirring constantly, until mixture thickens and boils. Boil for 1 minute. Remove from heat and stir in margarine.
    Makes approximately 2½ cups.

Elk Mountain Ranch
Buena Vista, Colorado

CIBOLO SALSA

12   plum tomatoes
6   jalapeño peppers
1   medium onion, cut into quarters
3   garlic cloves
1   bunch cilantro
2   limes, juiced
    Salt and pepper to taste
    Tortilla chips

Place tomatoes, peppers, onion, and garlic in a pot. Cover with water and poach for 15 minutes or until peppers are just soft. Drain and pour into a food processor. When cool, add cilantro and pulse to chop. Add lime juice, salt, and pepper to taste. Serve with tortilla chips.
    Makes 2 cups.

Mike Pawlick, Cibolo Creek Ranch
Shafter, Texas

Bob Hoy was a stuntman in TV and film westerns for twenty-five years, going back to the late 1940s. He made a number of films with Alan Ladd and Audie Murphy, was a double for Tony Curtis and David Janssen, and crossed over from stunt work into acting during the 1960s while appearing on *Bonanza*. His film credits include *Bite the Bullet*, *The Legend of the Lone Ranger*, and *The Outlaw Josey Wales*. Hoy was a regular cast member of *The High Chaparral* from 1967 to 1971, and in the early 1990s was the second unit director for the Family Channel's *Zorro*.

COWBOY VANILLA EXTRACT

Use this to bake cakes that will get the bull riders ready!

6   vanilla beans (split lengthwise)
½   pint brandy

Soak the beans in the brandy for a month. Use instead of regular vanilla.
    Makes ½ pint.

Bob Hoy, stuntman/actor

Gold Guards—Randolph Scott (left) and Joel McCrea star as former lawmen hired to protect a gold mine in Sam Peckinpah's *Ride the High Country.*

PISTOL-PACKIN' PEPPER SAUCE

1 8-ounce jar hot peppers
4 ounces garlic
½ cup sugar
¼ cup parsley flakes
   Soy sauce to taste
   Knorr All-Purpose Seasoning to taste

Strain hot peppers and reserve juice. Remove stalks and mince peppers. Mince the garlic and mix with peppers. Add sugar, parsley flakes, and as much of the reserved pepper juice as needed to obtain a pulpy consistency for your sauce. Season with soy sauce and all-purpose seasoning. The easiest way to taste the hot sauce is on a piece of buttered bread.

Be warned: This sauce is hot, hot, hot! Use it to season your favorite meals and add that little "zip" wherever you like. If you really like it hot, it even tastes good on bread with butter!

Makes about 14 ounces.

Iris Behr, Hidden Creek Ranch
Harrison, Idaho

"'Texas is a woman,' she used to say, "big, wild, beautiful woman. Get a kid raised up to where he's got some size, there's Texas whispering in his ears—smiling, saying come out with me and have some fun. It's hard enough to raise children any place. If you gotta fight Texas, a mother hasn't a chance.'"
—*The Sons of Katie Elder*

BREADS

DOUGH-SI-DOUGHS

CODY SWEET CORNBREAD

Makes enough to feed a stampede of hungry cow hands!

- 3 sticks butter
- 1½ cups sugar
- 6 large eggs
- 3 cups coarse yellow cornmeal
- 4 cups milk
- 4 cups all-purpose flour
- 2 tablespoons baking powder
- 1 teaspoon salt
  Whipped honey butter

Preheat the oven to 375°. Cream the butter and sugar until fluffy. Mix in the eggs and cornmeal. Add alternately with milk the flour, baking powder, and salt. Pour into a greased 11x17-inch pan. Bake for 25 to 30 minutes. Serve large, warm squares with whipped honey butter.
  Makes 24 servings.

  Bobbie Brown, 7 D Ranch
  Cody, Wyoming

SKY BLUE CORNBREAD

- 1 cup blue cornmeal
- ½ cup all-purpose flour
- 3 teaspoons baking powder
- 1 tablespoon sugar
- 2 eggs
- ½ cup buttermilk
- 2 tablespoons melted shortening or vegetable oil

Preheat the oven to 425°. Combine all ingredients just enough to moisten. Place in a greased 8x8-inch pan or muffin tins. Bake for 23 to 25 minutes for bread, 12 to 15 minutes for muffins.
  Note: Blue cornmeal used to be difficult to find, but now it is available in most grocery stores and health food stores.
  Makes 6 servings.

  Allen Ranch
  Bixby, Oklahoma

BIG SKY CORNBREAD

- 1 cup cornmeal
- 1 cup all-purpose flour
- 1 tablespoon baking powder
- 1 tablespoon sugar
- ½ teaspoon salt
- ¼ cup nonfat dry milk
- 1 egg, beaten
- 1 stick margarine, melted
- 1 cup water
- ½ cup grated Cheddar cheese
- 1 tablespoon chopped jalapeño peppers

Preheat the oven to 350°. Mix together the cornmeal, flour, baking powder, sugar, salt, and milk. Add the egg, margarine, water, cheese, and peppers. Stir well. Pour into a 9x9 baking pan, skillet, or 8-inch Dutch oven. Bake for 20 to 25 minutes or until a toothpick inserted in the center comes out clean.
  Makes 6 to 8 servings.

  Karen and Jack Hooker, White Tail Ranch
  Ovando, Montana

GLORIOUSLY GRITTY CORNBREAD

1   cup cornmeal
¼   cup corn germ (found in health food stores)
¼   cup oat bran
½   cup protein powder
2   tablespoons raw sugar
1   teaspoon baking powder
¼   teaspoon salt
¼   teaspoon baking soda
¾   cup sour milk
1   egg
2   tablespoons vegetable oil or melted butter
    Vegetable cooking spray

Preheat the oven to 350°. Sift together first eight ingredients. Stir in milk, egg, and oil. If mixture is too thick, add a little sour milk. If too thin, add some cornmeal. Spray a 6x10-inch glass dish or a stainless steel loaf pan with cooking spray. Pour in the mixture. Bake for 30 minutes or until a toothpick inserted in the center comes out clean and cornbread shrinks slightly from the sides. Serve with honey and butter.
   Makes 8 to 10 servings.

Coleen Gray, actress

LEAVIN' CHEYENNE CHEESE ROLLS

Goin' to Montana.

1   cup warm water
2   tablespoons sugar
2   teaspoons active dry yeast
3   to 4 cups all-purpose flour
1   egg
⅓   cup nonfat dry milk
1   teaspoon salt
1   stick margarine, melted
¾   teaspoon garlic powder
½   cup cheese sauce

Combine the first three ingredients. Set aside for 5 minutes. After the yeast has proofed, add all remaining ingredients except flour. Mix well. Stir in enough flour so that the batter barely sticks to the palms of your hands. Put in a warm place and let rise until doubled in bulk. Turn out onto a clean surface and knead for 2 minutes or so. Add more flour if needed. Dough should feel like velvet. Roll out and cut into biscuits or squeeze into rolls. Place in a greased baking pan. Put in a warm place to rise until almost doubled. Preheat oven to 350°. Bake for 30 minutes.
   Makes 16 servings.

*Karen and Jack Hooker, White Tail Ranch
Ovando, Montana*

Coleen Gray was a leading lady of the forties and fifties, but she is best remembered as the girl John Wayne left behind in the classic Howard Hawks western *Red River*.

Bob Wills and his Texas Playboys take a break from the road in this picture from the early 1940s.

SAN ANTONIO ROSE CORNBREAD

Great dough for light crusts, boys!

My father had simple tastes in foods: red beans and corn bread, chicken and dumplings, country fried steak, etc. He would often make a midnight snack of cornbread crumbled in milk, a reminder of his childhood treats. The following is my mother, Betty Wills's, recipe for cornbread (her Mother's Lemon Pie is on p. 223) that Daddy and I loved.

1	cup all-purpose flour
¾	teaspoon baking soda
1	teaspoon salt
1	teaspoon baking powder
1	cup cornmeal
¼	cup melted shortening
2	tablespoons brown sugar
2	eggs, well beaten
1½	cups sour milk

Preheat the oven to 425°. Sift flour and measure. Sift again with baking soda, salt, and baking powder. Mix with cornmeal. Combine shortening, sugar, and eggs. Add sour milk and combine with dry ingredients. Bake for 25 to 30 minutes (works best in a greased cast-iron skillet).

Note: To make 1 cup sour milk, mix 1 tablespoon lemon juice plus milk to equal 1 cup. Let it stand for 5 minutes.

Makes 8 servings.

Diane Wills Malone and the family of Bob Wills, singer

OKLAHOMA CORNBREAD

This stuff is Okie-doughkie.

1   cup sifted all-purpose flour
1   cup cornmeal
¾   cup wheat germ
⅓   cup sugar
5   teaspoons baking powder
1   teaspoon salt
2   eggs, beaten
1½   cups milk
1   medium onion, chopped
⅓   cup shortening, melted
1   15-ounce can cream-style corn
¾   cup shredded Cheddar cheese

Preheat the oven to 425°. Mix dry ingredients in bowl. Combine eggs, milk, onion, and shortening in a separate bowl. Add to flour mixture. Stir until moist. Stir in corn. Pour half the mixture into a greased 9x9x2-inch baking pan. (I put pan with grease in the oven to heat before adding mixture for a crispy crust.) Sprinkle cheese on top of batter. Pour remaining mixture on top. Bake for 25 to 30 minutes.

Susie Luchsinger, singer

World champion rodeo cowboy Casey Tibbs said of all the actors he saw ride a horse, "Ben Johnson is the best, I'd have to rate Joel McCrea second, followed by Audie Murphy, Dale Robertson, and James Caan."

Positive country singer Susie Luchsinger grew up on an Oklahoma ranch, and her father was a world champion rodeo cowboy.

Airborne Cowboy—Chuck Yeager definitely has the right stuff. As a test pilot, he was the first man to break the sound barrier.

BIG BREWERY BEER BREAD

This is from my days as a Miller Lite All-Star.

3½   cups self-rising flour
1   12-ounce bottle Miller or Miller Lite beer,
      at room temperature
      Butter

Preheat the oven to 375°. Combine flour and beer; mix well. Place in a well-greased loaf pan. Bake for 40 minutes. Butter top well while bread is hot. Biscuits may also be made this way, but you must work fast and avoid excessive kneading.
    Makes 6 servings.

Jim Shoulders, rodeo champion

GRANDMOTHER'S 1880 CORNBREAD

Happy contrails to you!

1   cup white cornmeal
3   tablespoons all-purpose flour
½   teaspoon salt
½   teaspoon baking soda
1   tablespoon bacon grease or vegetable oil
      Buttermilk (lots for crispy, less for not crispy)

Preheat the oven to 450°. Combine all ingredients well, adding enough buttermilk to make a smooth batter. Bake in a greased cast-iron skillet for 45 minutes or until brown.
    Makes 6 servings.

Gen. Chuck Yeager, aviation maverick

My latest Capitol record...
"You Can Give Me Back My Heart"
and "Weeping Willow"
Thompson

Hank Thompson started his music career with a group he called the Brazos Valley Boys. Today, he's known as the "Crown Prince of Western Swing." (Courtesy of Fred Goodwin Collection)

HUMPTY-DUMPTY HEART MEXICAN CORNBREAD

⅔ cup buttermilk
⅓ cup vegetable oil
1 8-ounce can cream-style corn
1 4-ounce jar chopped pimientos
1 cup grated Cheddar cheese
2 eggs
1 or 2 jalapeño peppers, chopped
1 cup yellow cornmeal
1 teaspoon salt
1 teaspoon baking soda

Blend together the first seven ingredients. (These may be doubled or quadrupled and frozen in convenient portions. Then thaw and add remaining ingredients.) Preheat the oven to 350°. Preheat a cast-iron skillet with a little oil. When hot, pour in cornbread mixture and brown slightly on bottom. Place in the oven for 30 to 40 minutes. Switch to broiler and brown the top.

Makes 6 to 8 servings.

Hank Thompson, singer

SURE IS MONDAY MEXICAN CORNBREAD

1 cup cornmeal
1 cup all-purpose flour
¼ cup sugar (optional)
4 teaspoons baking powder
½ teaspoon salt
1 egg
1 cup milk
¼ cup shortening, melted
1 8-ounce can cream-style corn
½ cup chopped onions
½ cup grated Cheddar cheese
Chopped jalapeño peppers to taste

Preheat the oven to 425°. Combine all ingredients well. Pour into a greased ovenproof dish or skillet. Bake for about 25 minutes or until done.

Makes 6 to 8 servings.

Mark Chesnutt, singer

Tanya

Some Like It Hot—Country music star Tanya Tucker sizzles with her own line of salsa and Tex-Mex food products.

PECOS PROMENADE CORNBREAD DRESSING

- 1 recipe Cornbread
- 1 medium onion, diced
- ¾ cup butter
- ¼ cup chopped parsley
- 1¼ cups diced celery
- ¾ teaspoon salt
- ½ teaspoon paprika
- ⅛ teaspoon nutmeg
  Mushrooms, diced (to taste)
- 2 tablespoons white wine
- 2 large eggs, beaten
- 1½ cups chopped pecans

Sauté the onion in butter until soft. Add parsley, celery, salt, paprika, nutmeg, mushrooms, and wine. Let simmer for 2 to 3 minutes. Preheat the oven to 350°. Crumble prepared cornbread in a food processor. Transfer cornbread to a large mixing bowl and add sautéed mix, eggs, and pecans. Mix well. Place in a well-greased baking dish. Cover and bake for 30 minutes.

Makes 8 to 10 servings.

Cornbread:
- 1½ cups cornmeal
- ⅓ cup whole-wheat flour
- 1 teaspoon salt
- 1 teaspoon baking soda
- 1 egg, beaten
- 2 cups buttermilk
- 2 tablespoons honey

Preheat the oven to 350°. Mix dry ingredients together. In a separate bowl, stir together egg, buttermilk, and honey. Stir dry ingredients into wet ingredients until well mixed, but not smooth. Bake in a greased cast-iron skillet for 20 minutes.

Tanya Tucker, singer

"Nobody gets to be a cowboy forever."
—Jack Palance to Lee Marvin in *Monte Walsh*

BANDIT BEER BUNS

They'll steal your taste buds!

2   cups Bisquick
2   tablespoons sugar
⅔ cup beer

Mix together the Bisquick and sugar. Stir in the beer just until moist. Spoon into 12 greased muffin pans. Let stand for 15 minutes. Preheat the oven to 400°. Bake for 18 minutes.
   Makes 12 servings.

   Clarence Swensen, actor

The diminutive gang of cowboys from 1938's all little-people western, *The Terror of Tiny Town*. That's Clarence Swenson in the middle of the back row with his cowboy hat tilted backward. Many of the buckaroos went on to become Munchkins in *The Wizard of Oz* a year later.

ELK MOUNTAIN CHEESE AND BACON IN BREAD BOAT

1   pound bacon, diced
1   loaf round bread, hollowed out, bread pieces reserved
1   8-ounce package cream cheese, softened to room temperature
1   cup sour cream
½ cup chopped green peppers
½ cup thinly sliced green onions

Preheat the oven to 350°. Heat bread bowl and pieces for 20 to 30 minutes. Fry bacon until crisp. Drain. Combine bacon with remaining ingredients. Stuff the loaf with filling. Bake for 15 to 20 more minutes (filling can also be baked separately).
   Makes 10 to 12 servings.

   Elk Mountain Ranch
   Buena Vista, Colorado

The Original Cast of TV's *Gunsmoke*—(l-r) Milburn Stone, Dennis Weaver, Amanda Blake, and James Arness

CHESTER'S CHEESE NUT LOAF

It's Goode!

1 cup dry bread crumbs
2 cups finely chopped walnuts
6 tablespoons minced onion
4 stalks celery, finely chopped
   Chopped olives to taste
4 eggs
2 cups half and half
½ teaspoon salt
2 teaspoons dry mustard
1 teaspoon paprika
⅛ teaspoon pepper
½ teaspoon marjoram
1 pound grated Cheddar cheese (low-fat or nonfat okay)
5 cups fresh whole-wheat bread crumbs

Preheat the oven to 350°. Mix the dry bread crumbs, walnuts, onion, celery, and olives in a bowl. Stir in eggs and half and half. Add salt and spices to mixture. In another bowl, mix cheese and fresh bread crumbs. Combine with the first mixture. Place in a greased shallow loaf pan. Bake for about 40 minutes.

Note: Nuts and vegetables can be chopped in a food processor.

Makes 1 loaf.

Gerry and Dennis Weaver, actor and singer

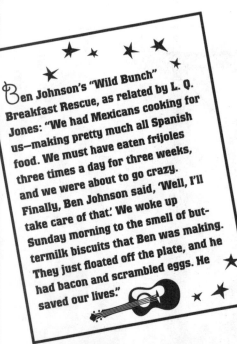

Ben Johnson's "Wild Bunch" Breakfast Rescue, as related by L. Q. Jones: "We had Mexicans cooking for us—making pretty much all Spanish food. We must have eaten frijoles three times a day for three weeks, and we were about to go crazy. Finally, Ben Johnson said, 'Well, I'll take care of that.' We woke up Sunday morning to the smell of buttermilk biscuits that Ben was making. They just floated off the plate, and he had bacon and scrambled eggs. He saved our lives."

BEN JOHNSON'S BUTTERMILK BISCUITS

2   cups all-purpose flour
2   heaping teaspoons baking powder
1   tablespoon sugar
¼   teaspoon baking soda
¼   teaspoon salt
2   cups buttermilk
¼   cup shortening, melted in a biscuit pan

Preheat the oven to 400°. Mix together all dry ingredients. Add buttermilk and blend in well. Roll out on a floured board. Cut with a biscuit cutter, then turn in melted shortening in a pan. Bake until lightly browned.
    Makes about 16 to 20 2-inch biscuits.

Ben Johnson, actor and rodeo champion

When it comes to cowboying, Ben Johnson is the real thing. An Oklahoma cowboy, he went west to California to deliver some horses for a Howard Hughes western, *The Outlaw,* and ended up staying. He has since appeared in some of Hollywood's greatest westerns including *Shane, Wagonmaster, She Wore a Yellow Ribbon, Rio Grande, One-Eyed Jacks, Will Penny, Junior Bonner,* and *The Wild Bunch.* A great horseman, the Cowboy Hall of Fame member is the only person ever to win a World Champion Cowboy title (team roping, 1953) and an Academy Award (*The Last Picture Show,* 1971). He continues to host pro-celebrity rodeos to raise funds for underprivileged and disabled children.

Cowboy troubadour Don Edwards has been making western music for thirty years. A great western yodeler, he put together the book *Classic Cowboy Songs from the Minstrel of the Range* (Gibbs Smith Publisher) in 1994. (Photo by Jim McBride)

SHEEPHERDER'S BREAD

You'll be hooked!

3   cups very hot tap water
½   cup sugar
1   stick butter
2½ teaspoons salt
2   packages active dry yeast
8½ to 9 cups all-purpose flour, divided

In a large bowl, combine water, sugar, butter, and salt. Stir until butter melts. Let cool to warm (110–115°). Stir in yeast. Cover and set in a warm place until bubbly (about 15 minutes). Add 5 cups flour, and beat to form a thick batter. With a spoon, add enough flour (3½ to 4 cups) to form a stiff dough. Knead until smooth (about 10 minutes). Let rise until dough doubles in bulk. Punch down, and let rise again. Preheat the oven to 400°. Form into a round loaf. Bake for 20 minutes.

Makes 1 huge loaf.

Shirley Mikita, Laughing Water Ranch
Fortine, Montana

RANCH BISCUITS

Next to beef and chilies, bread and biscuits are my favorite eating. Here is a recipe I think you will enjoy.

½   cup water
½   cup sugar
2   cups buttermilk
½   teaspoon baking soda
1   teaspoon salt
1   package active dry yeast
½   cup vegetable oil
5   cups sifted, all-purpose flour
4   teaspoons baking powder

Preheat the oven to 450°. Combine the ingredients thoroughly. Roll dough out on a floured surface to a ¾-inch thickness. Cut out biscuits with a baking powder lid or biscuit cutter. Bake for 15 to 20 minutes.

Makes 3 to 4 dozen 2-inch biscuits.

Don Edwards, singer/songwriter

BUTTERMILK YEAST BUNS

Trigger your taste buds!

2 tablespoons yeast
¼ cup warm water
3 cups buttermilk
½ cup sugar
1 stick butter, melted
2 eggs, beaten
1 teaspoon baking soda
1 teaspoon salt
Approximately 8 cups flour, divided

Place the yeast into warm water in a large mixing bowl. Stir to dissolve. Add buttermilk and sugar. Let the mixture stand for 15 minutes. Add warm butter and eggs. Mix well. Sift baking soda and salt with 4 cups flour. Add to the liquid mixture. Beat until a smooth batter forms. Add remaining sifted flour, stirring with spoon until thick enough to handle with your hands. Knead on a floured board. Cover. Let rise until doubled in bulk, about 1 hour. Punch down dough; form into buns. Place on a greased baking sheet; flatten slightly with hand. Let rise until doubled, about 30 minutes. Preheat the oven to 400°. Bake for 15 to 20 minutes. Remove from oven and brush tops with butter.

Makes approximately 2 dozen rolls.

CIMARRON CINNAMON ROLLS

After first rising, roll out dough into ½-inch-thick rectangles. Brush with melted butter and sprinkle with mixture of ½ cup sugar, ½ cup packed brown sugar, and 1 tablespoon cinnamon. Add nuts and raisins if desired. Roll up the dough jelly-roll style. Slice into 1-inch pieces. Place on a baking sheet 1 inch apart. Let rise for 20 minutes. Preheat the oven to 375°. Bake until golden brown.

Don K Ranch
Pueblo, Colorado

SCONE, SCONE ON THE RANGE

2 cups all-purpose flour
2 cups whole-wheat flour
½ cup sugar
2 teaspoons baking powder
1 teaspoon baking soda
1 teaspoon salt
2 sticks chilled butter
2 cups rolled oats
1 cup raisins
1½ to 2 cups buttermilk

Preheat the oven to 400°. Mix together flours, sugar, baking powder, baking soda, and salt. Cut in butter with two knives or pastry cutter until butter pieces are very small. Add oats and raisins and mix thoroughly. Mix in 1½ cups buttermilk all at once (if too dry, add some more buttermilk). Flour your hands and knead the dough several times. Divide the dough in half, and press each half into a greased cast-iron skillet. Score tops into pie-shaped pieces. If desired, brush tops with melted butter and sprinkle with a little sugar.

Bake until firm to the touch and lightly browned, about 20 to 25 minutes.

Makes 12 to 16 servings.

Chase Reynolds Ewald, Breteche Creek Ranch
Cody, Wyoming

COWBOY BISCUITS

4 cups sifted all-purpose flour
8 teaspoons baking powder
2 tablespoons sugar
1½ teaspoons salt
6 tablespoons butter, softened to room temperature
6 tablespoons Crisco
1½ cups milk

Preheat the oven to 450°. Sift flour, baking powder, sugar, and salt into a bowl. Cut in butter and Crisco until the mixture resembles coarse meal. Stir in milk with a fork to form a soft dough. Turn onto a floured board and knead for 30 seconds. Roll out to ½-inch thickness. Cut out biscuits and place on an ungreased cookie sheet. Bake for 10 to 15 minutes or until lightly browned. Great with honey butter.

Makes 20 servings.

Kay Galyon, Sky Corral Ranch
Bellvue, Colorado

Cowboy singer Eddie Dean starred in a number of western films from the 1930s through the 1950s, and was one of the top cowboy stars of the 1940s. He also wrote several country music hits, such as "I Dreamed of a Hillbilly Heaven."

Can you name the seven actors who made up the Magnificent Seven? How 'bout Yul Brynner, Steve McQueen, Charles Bronson, James Coburn, Robert Vaughn, Brad Dexter, and Horst Buchholz?

SILVER SCREEN SOURDOUGH ENGLISH MUFFINS

English muffins
Butter or margarine
Chunky-style peanut butter
Jelly

Take sharp knife and split each muffin. Put butter or margarine on one side and chunky peanut butter over the butter or margarine. Then put your favorite jelly on the other half. Place in the toaster oven and toast.

Eddie Dean, singer and actor

The Sons of the Pioneers of the Nineties—(back row, l-r) Luther Nallie, Dale Warren, Sunny Spencer; (front row, l-r) Johnny Nallie, Gary LeMaster, Roy Warhurst

HAPPY ROVIN' COWBOY LEMON COCONUT LOAF

- 2 sticks butter or margarine, softened to room temperature
- 2 cups sugar
- 3 tablespoons lemon juice
- 4 eggs
- 3 cups all-purpose flour
- 2 teaspoons baking powder
- ¾ teaspoon salt
- ½ cup evaporated milk
- ½ cup milk
   Grated peel of 2 lemons
- ½ cup flake coconut

Glaze:
- ½ cup lemon juice
- 1 cup sugar

Preheat oven to 350°. Grease and flour two 8x4-inch loaf pans and set aside. In a large mixing bowl, beat butter, sugar, and lemon juice until fluffy. Add eggs, one at a time, beating well after each addition. Sift flour, baking powder, and salt together. Combine evaporated milk and milk. Add dry ingredients and milk alternately to butter mixture in three additions. Do not overbeat. Fold in lemon peel and coconut. Pour into prepared pans. Bake for 1 hour and 20 minutes or until a toothpick inserted in the center comes out clean. Remove from the oven. Combine lemon juice and sugar. Brush on tops of loaves to glaze. Cool for 20 minutes. Remove from pans and cool completely.
   Makes 2 loaves.

Linda and Sunny Spencer, Sons of the Pioneers

Maureen O'Hara was an equal match to John Wayne in three western films: *Rio Grande*, *McLintock!*, and *Big Jake*. She also starred in *Buffalo Bill* and *The Rare Breed*.

RIO GRANDE PUMPKIN NUT BREAD

3½   cups of unsifted flour
2   teaspoons of baking soda
1½   teaspoons of cinnamon (ground)
½   teaspoon of baking powder
2   cups of white sugar
⅔   cup shortening
4   eggs
½   cup of water
1   9-ounce package of condensed mincemeat (crumbled) (Nonsuch brand best)
1   16-ounce can of pumpkin (2 cups)

Preheat the oven to 350°. Stir the following in bowl: flour, baking soda, cinnamon, and baking powder. Set aside.

In another large bowl, beat the sugar and shortening until fluffy. Add the eggs, pumpkin, and water. Mix well. Stir in contents of first bowl. Add the mincemeat and nuts. Turn out into two greased 9x5 loaf pans. Bake for 55 to 60 minutes or until inserted toothpick comes out clean. Cool for 10 to 12 minutes. Remove from pans. Cool again. Can be stored in aluminum foil or frozen.

Makes 2 loaves.

Maureen O'Hara, special thanks to Ray Nielsen

SOUTH DAKOTA SOURDOUGH FRY-BREAD

2½   teaspoons active dry yeast
2   tablespoons warm water
1   cup scalding milk
⅓   cup vegetable oil
⅓   cup sugar
1½   cups sourdough starter
5   cups all-purpose flour, divided
1   teaspoon salt
   Whipped honey

Mix yeast and water in a large mixing bowl until dissolved. Heat milk, and add oil and sugar to cool milk. Combine with yeast mixture in a large mixing bowl. Add sourdough starter, 2 cups flour, and salt. Beat with a mixer for 5 minutes. Place dough hooks on the mixer. Add 3 cups flour. Knead for 8 minutes or until mixed. Place in a greased bowl, turning to grease top. Cover and let rise for 1½ hours or until doubled in bulk. Form into small balls. Let rise a little. Fry in deep fat until brown. Serve with whipped honey.

Note: To make the sourdough starter, combine 1 cup flour, 1 package active dry yeast, and 1 cup water. Let stand in a warm place overnight. Keep refrigerated. Always add equal amounts of flour and water.

Dorothy and Lavon Shearer, Western Dakota Ranch Vacations Wall, South Dakota

SAGEBRUSH SWISS CHEESE BREAD

1   12-ounce can warm beer or 1½ cups milk
½   cup warm water
2   tablespoons sugar
1   tablespoon salt
2   tablespoons butter
1   8-ounce package pasteurized processed Swiss cheese (not natural)
5   cups all-purpose flour, divided
2   ¼-ounce packages active dry yeast

In a large saucepan over low heat, place warm beer, water, sugar, salt, butter, and cheese. Stir to blend; cheese does not need to melt completely. Cool to lukewarm. In a large mixing bowl, combine 2 cups flour with yeast. Add warm, not hot, cheese mixture, and, using an electric mixer, beat for 3 minutes at medium speed. By hand, gradually stir in remaining 3 cups flour to make a fairly stiff dough. Knead on a lightly floured surface until smooth and elastic, about 5

Clint Eastwood splits a grin with Paul Brinegar, who played camp cook Wishbone on *Rawhide.*

minutes. Place in a greased bowl, turning to grease top. Cover and let rise in a warm place until light and doubled in bulk, about 45 to 60 minutes. Punch down and divide in half. Place in greased and floured bread pans or form into rolls. Cover, and let rise in a warm place until light and doubled, about 45 to 60 minutes. Preheat the oven to 350°. Bake for 45 minutes. Remove from pans immediately and eat.

Makes 2 loaves.

Mabel Boehm, Peaceful Valley Lodge
Lyons, Colorado

Austin-based singer Don Walser is Pure Texas.

JAILHOUSE ROLLS

1½	cups warm water
2	packages active dry yeast
1	cup leftover mashed potatoes
2	sticks soft margarine
3	eggs
7	cups all-purpose flour
1½	teaspoons salt
1	cup sugar

Mix yeast with water. Stir and set aside. Combine potatoes, margarine, and eggs. Mix dry ingredients and add to yeast. Blend in potato mixture. This can be left in covered bowl in refrigerator for 4 or 5 days. Preheat the oven to 350°. As needed, drop by spoonsful onto greased cookie sheet. Bake for 15 minutes or until lightly browned.

Makes approximately 4 dozen rolls.

Don Walser, singer

LAZY HILLS FAMOUS PANCAKES

1   cup non-fat dry milk
1   tablespoon salt
2   tablespoons sugar
2   heaping tablespoons baking powder
1   cup vegetable oil
4   eggs
4   cups all-purpose flour
1   cup whole-wheat flour

Preheat the griddle to 375°. Combine all ingredients and mix together well. Cook on hot griddle until puffed and dry around the edges. Turn and cook other side until golden brown. This batter will keep well a couple of days in the refrigerator.

Makes enough for a large group.

Carol and Bob Steinruck, Lazy Hills Ranch Ingram, Texas

EARL COREY'S APPLE-BANANA PANCAKES

    Diced, peeled apples and bananas
    Butter or vegetable oil
½   cup white all-purpose flour
½   cup wheat, rye, or buckwheat flour
½   cup milk
2   egg whites
1   egg yolk
½   teaspoon baking soda

Sauté apples in a small amount of butter. Mix flours, milk, egg whites and yolk, and baking soda. Add enough water to make desired batter consistency. Mix in sautéed apples and sliced bananas. Cook on a preheated griddle or skillet until done on one side, then flip to cook other side.

Makes 10 to 12 pancakes.

Don Murray, actor

In 1969, Don Murray starred in one of TV's most interesting westerns, *The Outcasts,* about a gunman, Earl Corey, who teamed with a bounty hunter (Otis Young) to track down criminals. Murray made his film debut in the 1956 *Bus Stop* as an innocent cowboy who falls in love with Marilyn Monroe's saloon singer character.

ROLLIN', ROLLIN', ROLLIN' ROLLS

Rowdy yeasts!

½ stick butter or margarine, melted
½ teaspoon parsley flakes
½ teaspoons dill seed
¼ teaspoon onion flakes
1 package refrigerated buttermilk biscuits

Try this in a ring mold or bundt pan. It's great for a buffet. Preheat the oven to 425°. Place first four ingredients in a 9-inch pie pan and melt in oven. Blend well. Cut biscuits in quarters. Swish each one in melted mixture. Arrange pieces so that they touch in the pan. Bake for 12 minutes or until golden brown. Let stand a moment to absorb butter/herbs.

Makes 6 servings.

(*Alternative:* Use 4 cans of biscuits: Then use 1 cup of melted butter. After dipping, pour ½ cup of the butter over biscuits in the pan.) Bake at 350° for 30 to 35 minutes. After inverting ring onto the plate, pour remaining butter over the bread. Enjoy!

Don K Ranch
Pueblo, Colorado

The Pony Express began business on April 3, 1860, and closed down on October 24, 1861.

DAW'S QUICK DRAW FLUFFY PANCAKES

Here is a recipe from Mike Roy that Daws would make. When he made the pancakes, he would make our sons' initials—two "D"s, a "P," and a "C" for David, Donald, Paul, and Charles.

1 cup all-purpose flour
   Dash of baking soda
1½ teaspoons baking powder
   Pinch of salt
1 teaspoon sugar
1 egg yolk
3 teaspoons melted butter
1¼ cups milk
1 egg white, stiffly beaten

Sift flour, baking soda, baking powder, salt, and sugar. Add egg yolk, butter, and milk. Mix but don't beat. Fold in egg white. Cook on a hot, well-greased griddle.

Makes 8 to 10 pancakes.

Daws Butler, voice actor

PONY EXPRESS POPPY SEED BREAD

3 eggs
1½ cups milk
1¼ cups vegetable or canola oil
2¼ cups sugar
3 cups all-purpose flour
1½ teaspoons salt
1½ teaspoons baking powder
1½ tablespoons poppy seeds
1½ teaspoons vanilla or almond extract

Preheat the oven to 350°. Combine the first four ingredients. Add flour, salt, and baking powder. Mix thoroughly. Add the remaining ingredients and mix well. Important: Prepare bread pans by spraying or greasing them, then dusting with flour. Pour batter into pans. Bake for 1 hour or until a toothpick inserted in the center comes out clean.

Makes 2 loaves.

Eli Elfland, Cherokee Park Ranch
Livermore, Colorado

HAPPY TRAILS

TREASURE STATE APPLE CAKE WITH CARAMEL SAUCE

- 1 cup sugar
- 1 egg
- ½ stick butter, melted
- 1 cup all-purpose flour
- 1 teaspoon baking soda
- ½ teaspoon salt
- ½ teaspoon nutmeg
- ½ teaspoon cinnamon
- 2 cups peeled apple slices

Preheat the oven to 350°. Combine all ingredients and mix well. Pour into a greased 9x9-inch baking pan. Bake for about 40 minutes or until a toothpick inserted in the center comes out clean.

Caramel Sauce:
- ½ cup packed brown sugar
- ½ cup sugar
- 1 teaspoon vanilla extract
- 1 tablespoon butter
- ½ cup half and half

Bring sauce ingredients to a boil. Serve hot over slices of cake.
    Makes 9 servings.

Conni Kaufman, Circle Bar Guest Ranch Utica, Montana

APPALOOSA APPLESAUCE CAKE

- 3 eggs
- 1½ sticks margarine, softened to room temperature
- 2 cups sugar
- 3 cups sifted flour
- 2 cups cold applesauce, divided
- 1 large teaspoon baking soda (add to 1 cup applesauce and set aside)
- 1 teaspoon cinnamon
- 1 teaspoon cloves
- 1 teaspoon allspice
- 2 cups raisins
- 1 cup black walnuts
- 1 cup crushed pineapple
- ½ cup flake coconut

Preheat the oven to 325°. Mix eggs, margarine, and sugar. Add applesauce and soda mixture. Mix together. Add remaining applesauce and dry ingredients and mix. Fold in raisins, walnuts, pineapple, and coconut. Grease and flour a tube cake pan. Bake for 1½ hours.

Wilma and Phil Balsley, the Statler Brothers

Emmylou Harris, a modern-day "Cowboy's Sweetheart," released an album in 1994 titled *Cowgirl's Prayer.*

COWGIRL'S LEMON POPPY SEED POUND CAKE

An Emmy winner.

3   cups all-purpose flour
2   cups sugar
¼   cup poppy seeds
2   sticks sweet cream butter, softened to room temperature
1   cup buttermilk
4   eggs
½   teaspoon baking soda
½   teaspoon baking powder
½   teaspoon salt
4   teaspoons grated fresh lemon rind
½   teaspoon vanilla extract

Glaze:
1   cup confectioners' sugar
1   to 2 tablespoons lemon juice (fresh)

Preheat the oven to 325°. In a large mixing bowl, combine all cake ingredients. Beat on low speed, scraping bowl often, until all ingredients are moistened. Beat on high speed, scraping bowl often, until smooth, about 1 to 2 minutes. Pour into greased and floured 12-cup bundt pan or 10-inch tube pan. Bake for 55 to 65 minutes or until a toothpick inserted in the center comes out clean. Cool for 10 minutes and remove from pan. Cool completely. In a small bowl, stir sugar and lemon juice until smooth. Drizzle over cake.

Makes 8 to 10 servings.

Emmylou Harris, singer/songwriter

Richard Petty—King of Horsepower

KING RICHARD'S ANGEL FOOD CAKE

From good stock.

- 1½ cups egg whites
- 1 teaspoon cream of tartar
- 1½ cups sugar
- ¼ teaspoon salt
- 1 teaspoon vanilla extract
- 1 cup all-purpose flour, sifted, then sift 4 times

Preheat the oven to 325°. Beat egg whites until foamy. Add cream of tartar and beat until stiff, but not dry. Gradually beat in sugar. Add vanilla, then gently fold in flour. Pour into a tube pan. Bake for 1 hour and 15 minutes or until top is nicely browned.

Makes 8 to 10 servings.

Lynda and Richard Petty, stock car champion

Rodeo films—"The Cowboy and the Lady," "Bronco Buster," "The Lusty Men," "Junior Bonner," "JW Coop," "The Honkers," "When the Legends Die," "My Heroes Have Always Been Cowboys," and "8 Seconds."

PECOS RIVER CHOCOLATE CAKE

1¾ cups all-purpose flour
1½ cups sugar
1 teaspoon salt
1¼ teaspoons baking soda
⅓ cup cocoa
½ cup vegetable oil or soft margarine
1 cup milk
2 eggs
1 teaspoon vanilla extract

Frosting:
2⅔ cups confectioners' sugar
⅓ cup cocoa
⅓ cup solid shortening
3 tablespoons butter, softened
3 to 4 tablespoons strong coffee

Grease and flour 2 layer pans (preferably glass). Preheat the oven to 375°. Mix flour, sugar, salt, baking soda, and cocoa. Add oil, milk, eggs, and vanilla. Beat well and pour into pans. Bake for 40 to 45 minutes or until a toothpick inserted in the center comes out clean. Combine remaining ingredients until well blended. Frost cake as desired.
Makes 8 to 10 servings.

Alice McSweeney, Los Pinos Ranch
Cowles, New Mexico

CHARLIE'S GREAT CHOCOLATE CAKE

Better than a fiddle made of gold!

2 sticks butter or margarine, softened to room temperature
2 cups sugar
2 eggs
1 teaspoon vanilla
3 cups sifted all-purpose flour
½ cup cocoa
2 teaspoons baking soda
1 teaspoon salt
2 cups buttermilk

Chocolate Butter Frosting:
1 1-pound box confectioners' sugar
½ cup cocoa
⅛ teaspoon salt
1 stick butter or margarine, softened to room temperature
1 teaspoon vanilla extract
5 to 7 tablespoons milk

Preheat the oven to 350°. Grease and flour two 9-inch layer cake pans or one large sheet cake pan. Cream butter, gradually beating in sugar until fluffy. Add eggs one at a time. Beat well, for about 2 minutes. Add vanilla. Sift dry ingredients together. Add, alternately with buttermilk, using low speed of mixer. Pour into pans. Bake for 35 to 40 minutes. Remove from pans after a few minutes. Cool on rack. Mix together frosting ingredients and beat on low speed until smooth. Spread on cool cake. (Icing tastes better after it sets on cake for about 1 hour.)
Makes 8 to 10 servings.

Charlie Daniels, singer/songwriter

CHAMPION'S CHOCOLATE BROWNIE CAKE

2 cups all-purpose flour
2 cups sugar
½ cup Crisco
1 stick margarine
4 tablespoons cocoa
1 cup water
2 eggs
1 teaspoon cinnamon
½ teaspoon salt
1 teaspoon vanilla extract
1 teaspoon soda, dissolved in ½ cup buttermilk

Icing:
1 stick margarine
4 tablespoons cocoa
6 tablespoons milk
1 1-pound box confectioners' sugar
1 teaspoon vanilla extract
1 cup pecans, chopped

Preheat the oven to 400°. Sift flour and sugar in a large bowl. In a saucepan, bring Crisco, margarine, and cocoa to a boil. Pour over flour mixture. Add eggs, cinnamon, salt, vanilla, and soda-buttermilk mixture. Mix well and pour into a greased and floured 15½x10½x1-inch pan. Bake for 20 to 25 minutes. Remove from oven and frost. While cake is baking, combine margarine, cocoa, and milk in a saucepan. Bring to a boil. Add confectioners' sugar. Remove from heat and add vanilla and pecans. Spread carefully on hot cake.
Makes 10 to 12 servings.

Jim Shoulders, rodeo champion

The Barkleys of *The Big Valley*—Barbara Stanwyck, Peter Breck, Lee Majors,
Linda Evans, Charles Briles, and Richard Long

DESSERTS

NICK BARKLEY'S TOMATO SOUP CAKE

Flour
1 18½-ounce box spice cake mix
2 eggs
1 10¾-ounce can tomato soup
⅔ cup water
⅓ cup vegetable oil
1 8-ounce package cream cheese, softened to room temperature

Preheat the oven to 350°. Grease sides and bottoms of 2 loaf pans. Flour lightly. Blend all ingredients, except cream cheese, until moistened. Beat on medium speed for 2 minutes. Pour into loaf pans. Bake for 50 minutes. Cool, in pans, for 15 minutes on a wire rack. Remove from pans and let cool completely. Then spread with cream cheese.

Makes 20 servings.

Peter Breck, actor

PALOMINO POTATO-CHOCOLATE PEPPER CAKE

½ teaspoon salt
3 cups raw potatoes, grated
¾ cup cocoa
1 3-pound box devil's food cake mix
1 cup sugar
1 teaspoon ground pepper
2 cups milk
2 eggs
1 cup sour cream or yogurt

Preheat the oven to 350°. Mix salt with the potatoes to prevent them from turning brown. In a mixing bowl, combine all dry ingredients well. Mix milk, eggs, and sour cream together in a separate bowl. Add half the sour cream mixture to the dry ingredients and mix until the lumps have disappeared. Add the rest of the mixture slowly, then add the potatoes. Pour into a greased and floured 12x21-inch pan. Bake for 40 minutes or until a toothpick inserted in the center comes out clean. (You can also add nuts, mini-marshmallows, and chocolate chips to make a rocky road cake.) Serve with whipped topping and a drizzle of raspberry or grenadine syrup over the top.

Makes 24 3x3-inch servings.

Bruce Coe, Hidden Valley Ranch
Cle Elum, Washington

COCK-EYED CAKE

Dutch oven

It's a Butte!

We use this recipe on pack trips, mixing the dry ingredients at the ranch and then adding the wet ingredients in the mountains. (We use a Dutch oven for baking. Using the top of the wood stove for bottom heat and briquettes or coals from the fire for top heat works great.)

1½ cups all-purpose flour
3 tablespoons cocoa
1 teaspoon baking soda
1 cup sugar
½ teaspoon salt
5 tablespoons vegetable oil
1 tablespoon vinegar
1 teaspoon vanilla extract
1 cup water

Preheat the oven to 350°. Mix flour, cocoa, baking soda, sugar, and salt in a bowl. Make three wells in the dry ingredients. In each well, put oil, vinegar, and vanilla. Pour 1 cup water over top. Stir until nearly smooth and you can't see the flour. Pour into a 9x9-inch baking pan or an 8-inch Dutch oven. Bake for 30 minutes.

Makes 9 servings.

Karen and Jack Hooker, White Tail Ranch
Ovando, Montana

SHOOT 'EM UP 7-UP CAKE

Bang-up dessert!

3 sticks butter
3 cups sugar
5 eggs
3 cups all-purpose flour
¾ cup 7-Up

Beat butter and sugar for 20 minutes at medium speed. Add eggs, one at a time, and beat well. Fold in flour, alternating with 7-Up. Preheat the oven to 375°. Pour into a bundt pan. Bake for 1¼ hours. Remove from pan and glaze with your favorite confectioners' sugar frosting.

Makes 8 to 10 servings.

Shirley Mikita, Laughing Water Ranch
Fortine, Montana

Lane Frost was posthumously inducted into the Pro Rodeo Cowboy Hall of Fame in 1990. He is the youngest cowboy ever to be awarded that honor. His life story was the subject of the 1994 feature film *8 Seconds*.

LANE'S FAVORITE CHOCOLATE CAKE

I got this recipe from my sister-in-law, Audrey Benson. I always made this chocolate cake when I knew Lane was coming home. No matter what time of night he came in, he always ate some of this cake and drank milk with it.

2 cups sugar
½ cup cocoa
1 cup liquid shortening
2 eggs
Pinch of salt
2 cups all-purpose flour
1 cup sour or buttermilk
1 cup hot water
2 teaspoons baking soda
1 teaspoon vanilla extract

Icing:
About ½ stick margarine, melted
About 2½ cups confectioners' sugar
About 3 tablespoons cocoa
Milk

Preheat the oven to 375°. Mix sugar, cocoa, shortening, eggs, salt, flour, and buttermilk. Add water, soda, and vanilla. Batter will be thin. Pour into a 9x13-inch pan. Bake for about 30 minutes or until a toothpick inserted in the center comes out clean.

To make icing, mix margarine, confectioners' sugar, and cocoa with enough milk to be creamy.

Makes 10 to 12 servings.

Elsie Frost, mother of Lane Frost, rodeo champion

"Rodeo's not just about winning and making money. It's about being your best and helping others to be their best too."—Luke Perry as Lane Frost in *8 Seconds*

DESSERTS

PAMELA'S PLANTATION PRUNE CAKE

Really draws a crowd.

1   jar (1 pound) cooked prunes (can substitute canned plums)
2½ cups sifted all-purpose flour
1   teaspoon baking soda
1   teaspoon salt
1   teaspoon each: allspice, cinnamon, and nutmeg
1   cup finely chopped pecans
3   eggs
1¼ cups sugar
1   cup vegetable oil
½   cup buttermilk
    Vanilla Glaze

Grease a 12-cup tube pan or 10-inch angel-food cake pan. Flour lightly, tapping out any excess. Drain liquid from prunes into a cup. Pit prunes, then cut each into 3 or 4 pieces. Place in a 1-cup measure. Add enough prune juice to make 1 cup. Sift flour, soda, salt, allspice, cinnamon, and nutmeg into a medium bowl. Stir in pecans. Beat eggs well in a large bowl. Slowly beat in sugar until mixture is fluffy (about 8 minutes). Beat in vegetable oil, then buttermilk. Stir in prunes. Beat in flour mixture, a third at a time, until well blended. Pour into prepared pan, spreading evenly. Bake in a moderate oven for 1 hour and 5 minutes, or until top springs back when lightly pressed with fingertips. Cool for 10 minutes in pan on a wire rack. Loosen cake around the edges and tube with a knife. Turn out onto the rack and spoon hot Vanilla Glaze over the cake immediately. (If cake is to be frozen, cool completely.)

Vanilla Glaze:
1   cup sugar
½   teaspoon baking soda
½   cup buttermilk
1   tablespoon light corn syrup
1   stick butter
1   teaspoon vanilla

Combine all ingredients except the vanilla in a medium saucepan. Heat slowly, stirring constantly. Bring to a boil, then cook, stirring constantly, for 2 minutes. Remove from the heat and stir in vanilla.

Ben Cooper, actor

Ben Cooper starred in many films of the 1950s and 1960s, but was always at his best in westerns. One of the fastest draws among the Hollywood cowboys, his films include *Johnny Guitar, The Fastest Gun Alive, The Last Command, Duel at Apache Wells, Waco, Support Your Local Gunfighter, Gunfight at Apache Creek,* and *Arizona Raiders.*

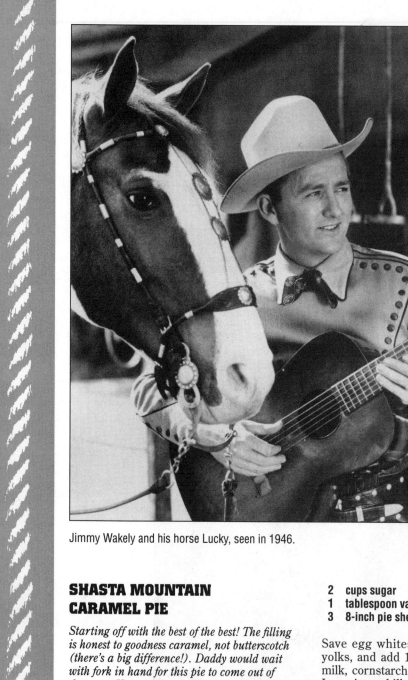

Jimmy Wakely and his horse Lucky, seen in 1946.

SHASTA MOUNTAIN CARAMEL PIE

Starting off with the best of the best! The filling is honest to goodness caramel, not butterscotch (there's a big difference!). Daddy would wait with fork in hand for this pie to come out of the oven. He would eat half of it in one sitting. It is outrageously fattening and outrageously wonderful! It takes a while to prepare, so be forewarned.

—Lindalee Wakely

5   eggs, separated
1   cup flour
5   tablespoons cornstarch
3   cups milk
3   tablespoons butter
2   cups sugar
1   tablespoon vanilla
3   8-inch pie shells, baked

Save egg whites for meringue. Beat egg yolks, and add 1 cup sugar and flour. Add milk, cornstarch, and vanilla and set aside. In an iron skillet over medium heat, melt butter and caramelize 1 cup sugar. Keep stirring until it becomes liquid. Add milk mixture. The sugar will crackle and pop and look like plastic! That's fine. Stir constantly until it all melts into a thick creamy caramel. Pour into baked pie shells, top with a stiff meringue, and brown.

Jimmy Wakely, singer and actor
From The Wakely Family Cookbook

218   DESSERTS

GRANDMOTHER'S APPLE PIE

Serve with ice cream for apple pie Alamo.

1   pastry for double crust, 9-inch pie
6   medium apples, peeled, cored, and thinly sliced
1½ tablespoons lemon juice
⅓   cup packed brown sugar
⅓   cup sugar
½   tablespoon cornstarch or 3 tablespoons all-purpose flour
⅛   teaspoon salt
¾   teaspoon ground cinnamon
¼   teaspoon nutmeg
1½ tablespoons butter or margarine

Preheat the oven to 450°. Line a 9-inch pie plate with half of rolled-out pastry. Arrange apple slices in pie crust. Sprinkle lemon juice over apples. In a small mixing bowl, combine sugars, cornstarch, salt, cinnamon, and nutmeg. Mix in apples. Pour into crust. Dot with butter. Place remaining pastry over top. Seal edges. Prick crust, or cut slits or design to allow steam to escape during cooking. Bake for 10 minutes. Reduce temperature to 350° and bake for 35 to 40 more minutes, or until apples are tender.

Makes 6 to 8 servings.

Michael Martin Murphey, singer/songwriter

MOM'S NO-MESS PIE CRUST

½   cup plus 2 tablespoons vegetable oil
½   cup milk
1   teaspoon vinegar
2   cups all-purpose flour

Combine all ingredients at once. Stir with fork. Roll out between sheets of waxed paper.

Makes two 9-inch crusts.

Ben Johnson, actor and rodeo champion

Michael Martin Murphey has had numerous country hits but also is one of the most renowned troubadours of cowboy songs today. Among his cowboy collections of tunes are *Cowboy Songs, Volume 1,* and *Cowboy Songs, Volume 2: Rhymes of the Renegades.* (Photo by Mary Murphey)

AUNT BABE'S MINCEMEAT PIE

For hungry cowboys!

2 pounds lean beef
1 pound raisins
1 pound currants
5 pounds sour apples, peeled, cored, and cut
   up
2 cups packed brown sugar
1 tablespoon cinnamon
½ tablespoon allspice
½ teaspoon salt
1 cup molasses
½ pound citron, finely cut
1 cup apple cider (or grape or apple juice)
3 pastries for double-crust pies

Boil beef until it's nice and tender. Let it get cold. Preheat the oven to 400°. Grind beef, raisins, currants, and apples. Combine all ingredients except cider and crust. Stir in cider. Place mixture in a big saucepan with a loose lid and simmer for 30 minutes. Spread about 4 cups of mincemeat mix into a pastry-lined 9-inch pie tin. Cut slits or patterns of your own design into top crust and place on top of filling. Pinch the top crust and bottom crust together to seal. Bake for 15 minutes, then decrease heat to 350° and bake for 30 more minutes. Remove from oven and let cool. Mincemeat pie may be served warm or cold.
    Makes 3 big pies.

Rance Howard, actor

Oklahoma native and versatile actor Rance Howard is right at home on the range and in western films. He is the father of director Ron Howard and Mayberry's cowboy, actor Clint Howard.

STAGECOACH CINNAMON PIE PASTRY

Great stage for your favorite fillings!

3 cups all-purpose flour
1 teaspoon salt
½ teaspoon cinnamon
¼ teaspoon baking powder
3 tablespoons sugar
1 cup very cold, unsalted butter, cut into ¼-inch pieces
2 large egg yolks
½ cup ice water

Sift together flour, salt, cinnamon, baking powder, and sugar into a mixing bowl. Cut in butter with pastry blender or paddle attachment on mixer until mixture resembles coarse meal. Add egg yolks, one at a time, along with ice water. Do not overwork the dough if using a mixer. Use on/off switch to incorporate ingredients. Wrap in plastic wrap and refrigerate for at least 30 minutes.
    After dough is chilled, it can be rolled out to about ⅛-inch thickness on a lightly floured surface. Shape and cut to desired size. Be sure to grease the pie pan.
    To prebake the pie shell, preheat the oven to 400°. Line pastry with parchment paper and fill with dried beans. Bake until the edges begin to turn golden, for about 12 to 15 minutes. Remove the beans and continue baking until the bottom is golden, for another 10 minutes.
    Note: Brushing the crust edges with 1 egg beaten with 2 tablespoons water adds a nicer browning color.
    Makes enough pastry for 1 double-crust pie.

Joe Cobb, Skyline Guest Ranch
Telluride, Colorado

Cake for Pie—Jimmy Stewart shares some carrot cake with his favorite horse, Pie, whom Stewart rode in many a western, beginning with *Winchester '73* in 1950. (Courtesy of Steve Cox Collection)

More riders and horses—Don Red Barry and Cyclone, Bob Livingston and Shamrock, Rod Cameron and Knight, William S. Hart and Fritz, Kermit Maynard and Baron, Little Beaver and Papoose, Jack Holt and Robin Hood, Jack Hoxie and Scout, and Dick Foran and Smoky.

AWESOME AUSTIN PECAN PIE

¼   cup sugar
1   cup white Karo syrup
2   teaspoons butter
2   eggs, beaten
     Dash of salt
1   cup pecans (or more)
1   teaspoon vanilla extract
1   9-inch pie crust, unbaked

Preheat the oven to 375°. Combine all ingredients except crust. Pour into an unbaked pie crust. Bake for 45 minutes to 1 hour or until filling doesn't shake.

Makes 6 to 8 servings.

Don Walser, singer

WAPITI WALNUT RUM PIE

¾   cup sugar
1   stick butter, melted
½   cup all-purpose flour
2   eggs, beaten
1   cup chocolate chips
1   cup chopped walnuts
2   tablespoons dark rum
1   partly baked 9-inch pie crust

Preheat the oven to 350°. Combine sugar, butter, flour, and eggs. Beat until smooth. Stir in chips, nuts, and rum. Pour into crust. Bake for 30 to 35 minutes.

Makes 6 to 8 servings.

*Diana Haynes, Wapiti Meadow Ranch
Cascade, Idaho*

COLORADO CRANBERRY PECAN-PUMPKIN CUSTARD PIE

Marmalade:
½   bag frozen cranberries
½   cup brown sugar
½   teaspoon allspice
½   cup water
2   teaspoons orange zest

Filling:
¾   cup pumpkin purée
3   eggs, separated
½   cup packed brown sugar
⅔   cup sugar
1   cup milk
     Pinch of salt
1   teaspoon vanilla extract
1   tablespoon unsalted butter, melted
3   tablespoons all-purpose flour
1½ cups pecans, toasted and chopped
1   prebaked Stagecoach Cinnamon Pie Pastry (p. 220)
¼   teaspoon cinnamon

To make the marmalade, combine all ingredients and bring to a boil. Lower heat and simmer for 15 minutes, stirring occasionally. Cranberries may pop like popcorn. Transfer to a blender or food processor and purée. Set aside to cool.

To make the filling, whisk together in a medium-sized bowl, pumpkin purée and egg yolks until combined. Add both sugars, then milk, salt, vanilla, and butter. Add flour and mix until smooth.

In another bowl, whisk egg whites until they become foamy but not completely stiff. Fold into pumpkin mixture. Preheat the oven to 350°.

To assemble pie, spread marmalade using a rubber spatula on bottom and sides of the prebaked pastry, but not on the edges. Sprinkle toasted pecans around all marmalade-covered areas, and then pour in pumpkin custard filling.

Sprinkle cinnamon over the top and bake on lowest rack for about 35 minutes or until pie is set and moves only slightly in center. If pie becomes too brown, cover with foil. Whipped cream or vanilla ice cream goes great with this pie.

Note: Bake pecans on a cookie sheet at 350° for 10 minutes.

*Joe Cobb, Skyline Guest Ranch
Telluride, Colorado*

MOTHER'S LEMON PIE

Wills power!

3   eggs, separated
2   tablespoons water
¾   cup sugar, divided
    Juice of 1 lemon
¼   teaspoon cream of tartar
1   baked 9-inch pie crust

Cook egg yolks, water, ½ cup sugar, and lemon juice over medium heat. Stir until thick, and set aside to cool. Beat egg whites, ¼ cup sugar, and cream of tartar until stiff peaks form, then fold into the first mixture. Pour into a baked pie shell and brown slightly under broiler.
Makes 6 servings.

Diane Wills Malone and the family of Bob Wills, singer

T CROSS MILE HIGH PIE

    Oreo or Chocolate Hydrox Cookies, finely crumbled
½   stick butter or margarine
1   quart coffee ice cream
1   quart chocolate ice cream
4   Heath Bars, chopped into small pieces
1   cup pecans, chopped

Preheat the oven to 350°. Mix the cookie crumbs and butter and pat into a greased 9-inch pie plate. Bake for 20 minutes. Remove from the oven and allow to cool before filling. Allow ice cream to soften a little before mixing both flavors. Add candy and pecans and mix well. Spread into a pie crust. Freeze for at least 4 hours before serving. You can top with whipped cream or chocolate sauce before serving and sprinkle each piece with more pecans.
Makes 6 to 8 servings.

Garey and Ken Neal, T Cross Ranch Dubois, Wyoming

BUNKHOUSE BUTTERMILK PIE

1½   cups sugar
¼   cup all-purpose flour
1   stick margarine or butter, melted
1   cup buttermilk
3   eggs, beaten
1   teaspoon vanilla extract
1   teaspoon lemon extract or lemon juice
1   10-inch pie crust, unbaked

Preheat the oven to 450°. Mix together flour and sugar. Melt margarine and add to first mixture. Add remaining ingredients. Beat well. Pour into a pie crust. Bake for 10 minutes. Decrease heat to 350° and bake for 30 to 35 minutes.
Makes 6 to 8 servings.

Carol and Bob Steinruck, Lazy Hills Ranch Ingram, Texas

FLUFFY PEANUT BUTTER PIE

Will stick to your ribs.

Chocolate Crunch Crust:
- 6 tablespoons margarine
- 1 6-ounce package semi-sweet chocolate chips
- 2½ cups rice cereal

Filling:
- 1 8-ounce package cream cheese, softened to room temperature
- 1 14-ounce can Eagle Brand sweetened condensed milk
- ¾ cup peanut butter (with or without nuts)
- 3 tablespoons lemon juice concentrate
- 1 teaspoon vanilla extract
- 1 cup whipping cream, whipped, or 1 4-ounce container frozen nondairy whipped topping, thawed
- 1 to 2 teaspoons chocolate-flavored syrup

To make crust: In a heavy saucepan over low heat, melt margarine and chocolate chips. Remove from heat, gently stirring in cereal until completely coated. Press into bottom and up sides of a greased 9-inch pie plate. Chill for 30 minutes.

To make filling: In a large bowl, beat cheese until fluffy. Beat in condensed milk and peanut butter until smooth. Stir in lemon juice and vanilla. Fold in whipped cream. Pour into crust. Drizzle syrup over top of pie; gently swirl with spoon. Chill for 4 hours or until set. Refrigerate any leftovers.

Gail Lander, Kedesh Ranch
Shell, Wyoming

Elvis Presley made four western films: "Love Me Tender," "Frankie and Johnny," "Stay Away Joe," and "Charro!"

GENE AUTRY'S PEANUT BUTTER PIE

A real Champion dessert.

This recipe, which has been served on many special occasions, is from the chef of the Gene Autry Dining Room.

- 1 cup peanut butter
- 1 8-ounce package cream cheese, softened to room temperature
- 1 cup sugar
- 2 tablespoons melted butter
- 1 cup whipping cream, whipped
- 1 tablespoon vanilla extract
- 1 graham-cracker pie crust
  Hot fudge sauce

Cream together peanut butter, cream cheese, and sugar. Stir in butter, whipped cream, and vanilla. Mix well and pour into graham-cracker crust. Chill for 4 to 5 hours or until very well set. Top with melted, thinned hot fudge sauce. Chill again for 30 minutes.

Makes 6 to 8 servings.

Gene Autry, singer and actor

Jerry Scoggins (right) and the other members of the Cass County Boys help Gene Autry celebrate his twelfth anniversary on CBS Radio.

GRANDMA'S FUDGE PIE

2   cups sugar
3   tablespoons all-purpose flour or cornstarch
3   tablespoons cocoa
    Dash of salt
2   cups milk
5   egg yolks, beaten
½   stick butter
1   teaspoon vanilla extract
2   baked pie crusts
1   teaspoon cream of tartar
2   teaspoons sugar

Meringue:
5   egg whites
1   teaspoon cream of tartar
2   teaspoons sugar

Preheat the oven to 350°. Mix the first four ingredients in a saucepan. Gradually stir in milk. Cook over moderate heat until mixture thickens and boils. Boil for 1 minute. Stir half of the mixture into egg yolks, then blend egg mixture into the hot mixture in the saucepan. Add butter and vanilla and boil until very thick. Pour into baked pie crusts. Beat egg whites until stiff. Fold in sugar and cream of tartar. Place half of the meringue on each pie and bake until brown.
  Makes 2 pies.

Kay Galyon, Sky Corral Ranch
Bellvue, Colorado

CATTLE CALL COCONUT CREAM PIE

Filling:

⅔ cup sugar
½ teaspoon salt
2½ tablespoons cornstarch
1 tablespoon all-purpose flour
3 cups milk
3 egg yolks, beaten
1 tablespoon butter
1½ teaspoons vanilla extract
¾ cup shredded coconut, moist
1 9-inch baked, fluted pastry crust

Meringue:

3 egg whites
¼ teaspoon cream of tartar
6 tablespoons sugar
1 teaspoon vanilla extract
  Coconut

Mix sugar, salt, cornstarch, and flour in a saucepan. Gradually stir in milk; cook over moderate heat, stirring constantly until mixture thickens and boils. Boil for 1 minute. Remove from heat. Slowly blend in beaten egg yolks. Cook for 1 more minute. Remove from heat. Blend in butter, vanilla, and coconut. Pour into pastry crust. Preheat the oven to 400°.

Beat egg whites with cream of tartar until frothy. Gradually beat in sugar, a little at a time. Continue beating until stiff and glossy. Pile onto pie filling; sprinkle with extra coconut. Bake for 8 to 10 minutes or until brown.

Makes 6 to 8 servings.

Eddy Arnold, singer

Eddy Arnold—The "Tennessee Cowboy" in 1947

226

SOUTHWEST BUTTERMILK BROWNIES

1 stick margarine
1 cup boiling water
¼ cup cocoa
1 cup vegetable oil
2 cups sugar
2 eggs, beaten
1 teaspoon vanilla extract
½ cup buttermilk
2 cups all-purpose flour
½ teaspoon salt
1 teaspoon baking soda

Frosting:
1 stick margarine
¼ cup cocoa
⅓ cup buttermilk
3 cups confectioners' sugar
1 teaspoon vanilla extract

Preheat the oven to 350°. In a saucepan, combine margarine, boiling water, cocoa, and oil. Bring to a boil. Set aside. Beat together sugar, eggs, vanilla, buttermilk, flour, salt, and soda. Combine with hot mixture. Pour into a greased jellyroll pan. Bake for 25 minutes.

To make the frosting, combine margarine, cocoa, and buttermilk in a saucepan and bring to a boil. Remove from heat and add sugar and vanilla. Spread over brownies. Sprinkle nuts on top. Can be frozen.
Makes 10 to 12 servings.

Carol and Bob Steinruck, Lazy Hills Ranch Ingram, Texas

BILLY THE KID'S BROWNIES

2 sticks butter
2 squares semi-sweet chocolate
3 eggs, well beaten
2 cups sugar
1¼ cups all-purpose flour
1 cup chopped nuts
1 teaspoon vanilla extract

Preheat the oven to 300°. In a double boiler, over low heat, melt butter and chocolate. When melted, remove from heat. Add remaining ingredients and mix together. Pour into a greased pan. Bake for 45 minutes. Do not overcook. Slice after cooled.
Makes 8 to 10 servings.

Billy Dean, singer/songwriter

Billy Dean scored a No. 1 hit with his self-composed tune "Billy the Kid."

Country music's Randy Travis loves the cowboys and has a palomino that is related to Roy Rogers' Trigger. Here Travis plays a cowboy in the TV movie *Deadman's Revenge*.

WIND IN THE WIRE OATMEAL COOKIES

1	cup raisins
1	cup water
¾	cup shortening
1½	cups sugar
2	eggs
1	teaspoon vanilla extract
2½	cups flour
1	teaspoon baking soda
1	teaspoon salt
1	teaspoon cinnamon
½	teaspoon baking powder
½	teaspoon cloves
2	cups oats
½	cup chopped nuts

Simmer raisins and water over medium heat until raisins are plump, about 15 minutes. Drain raisins, reserving the liquid. Add enough water to reserved liquid to measure ½ cup. Preheat the oven to 400°. Thoroughly mix the shortening, sugar, eggs, and vanilla. Stir in reserved liquid. Blend in remaining ingredients. (If using self-rising flour, omit soda, salt, and baking powder.)

Drop dough by rounded teaspoonfuls about 2 inches apart onto ungreased baking sheets. Bake for 8 to 10 minutes or until lightly browned.

Makes about 6½ dozen cookies.

Randy Travis, singer/songwriter

COWBOY SPURS

2　sticks margarine
1　cup packed brown sugar
1　cup white sugar
2　eggs
½　teaspoon baking powder
1　teaspoon baking soda
½　teaspoon salt
1　cup rolled oats
1　cup coconut
2　cups chocolate chips
2⅔　cups all-purpose flour

Preheat the oven to 350°. Cream margarine and add sugars. Add eggs, one at a time, beating well after each addition. Add remaining ingredients in order. Shape into balls and place on cookie sheets. Bake for 12 minutes.

Note: I usually bake one tester cookie to make sure I have added enough flour. You may need to adjust your recipe for flour depending on elevation: more for higher and less for lower.

Makes 4 to 6 dozen cookies.

Jeana Leavell, Idaho Rocky Mountain Ranch
Stanley, Idaho

Jay Novacek—All-Pro Dallas Cowboy end

LUCKY PEAK PEANUT BUTTER OATIES

1½　cups peanut butter
1½　cups packed brown sugar
¾　cup sugar
3　eggs
1　tablespoon vanilla extract
3¾　cups oats
1½　cups all-purpose flour
1　tablespoon baking soda
1½　cups chocolate chips

Preheat the oven to 350°. Cream together peanut butter and sugars. Then add eggs and vanilla. Blend well. Mix in oats, flour, and soda until well mixed. Stir in chips. Drop by the teaspoonful onto greased cookie sheets. Bake for 10 to 15 minutes.

Makes 5 to 6 dozen cookies.

Shepp Ranch
Boise, Idaho

GREAT CATCH INDOOR S'MORES

No one passes on these!

8　cups Golden Grahams cereal
6　cups miniature marshmallows, divided
⅓　cup light corn syrup
6　tablespoons margarine or butter
1½　cups milk chocolate chips
1　teaspoon vanilla extract

Measure cereal into a large bowl. Butter a 13x9x2-inch rectangular pan. Put 5 cups of marshmallows, corn syrup, margarine, and chocolate chips in a 3-quart saucepan over low heat, stirring constantly. Remove from heat. Stir in vanilla. Pour over cereal. Mix quickly, until cereal is completely coated with chocolate. Stir in 1 cup marshmallows. Form squares by pressing mixture evenly into prepared pan with the back of a buttered spoon. Let stand for at least 1 hour, or refrigerate if a firmer bar is desired. Cut into 2-inch squares.

Makes 24 squares.

Yvette and Jay Novacek, Dallas Cowboy

BRONZE BUCKAROO'S CHOCOLATE CHIP COOKIES

- ¼ cup shortening
- ¾ cup packed brown sugar
- 1 large egg, well beaten
- ½ teaspoon vanilla extract
- 1¼ cups all-purpose flour
- ½ teaspoon baking powder
- ¼ teaspoon salt
- ¼ teaspoon cinnamon
- ⅛ teaspoon nutmeg
- ½ cup sour cream
- ⅔ cup chopped milk chocolate or chocolate chips

All ingredients must be at room temperature. Preheat the oven to 400°. Cream together shortening and sugar. In a separate bowl, add egg and extract. Blend into sugar mixture. Sift together dry ingredients. Add to shortening mixture, alternately with sour cream. Stir in chocolate chips. Drop by tablespoonful onto a cookie sheet. Bake for 10 minutes.

Makes 3 dozen cookies.

Herb Jeffries, actor and singer/composer

Double-Barrelled Talent—In addition to his musical talents, Herb Jeffries was the pioneer black cowboy star of westerns that featured all-black casts during the 1930s. Among his films were *Harlem on the Prairie, California Gold,* and *Bronze Buckaroo,* which is also Jeffries' nickname. This scene is from *Harlem Rides the Range.*

PATTY'S CARAMEL CRUNCH COOKIES

32 caramels
½ cup heavy cream
1 cup all-purpose flour
½ teaspoon baking soda
¼ teaspoon salt
1½ cups rolled oats
⅔ cup packed light brown sugar
¾ cup unsalted butter, softened to room temperature
1 cup chopped pecans
1 12-ounce package chocolate chips

Preheat the oven to 350°. Melt caramels in heavy cream in a small saucepan over low heat. Allow to cool slightly. Sift together flour, soda, and salt. Stir in oats and brown sugar. Mix in butter with pastry cutter or mixer. Press mixture evenly into a greased 9 x13-inch pan. Cover bottom. Sprinkle with pecans. Pour melted caramels over pecans to cover entire surface. Bake for 20 minutes. Place on a rack. Immediately sprinkle surface with chocolate chips. Allow chips to melt, about 2 to 3 minutes. Swirl slightly to cover entire surface as frosting and to create a marbled effect. Allow to cool completely before cutting into squares. These freeze well.

Makes 10 to 12 servings.

Garey and Ken Neal, T Cross Ranch
Dubois, Wyoming

GRAPEVINE CANYON BREAD PUDDING

Remember: You herd it here!

¾ loaf of bread, dried and broken into pieces
¾ cup sugar
⅓ teaspoon salt
¾ teaspoon nutmeg
3 whole eggs
3 cups milk
3 cups light or whipping cream (do not substitute milk)
6 tablespoons raisins

Sauce:
6 tablespoons sugar
2¼ teaspoons all-purpose flour
1½ tablespoon vinegar
¾ cup water
1½ tablespoons butter

Preheat the oven to 350°. Break bread into bite-size pieces. Put in buttered pan. Mix the sugar, salt, and nutmeg with slightly beaten eggs. Add milk, cream, and raisins. Pour over the bread. Bake for 90 minutes.

To make the sauce, combine the ingredients until thickened slightly. Serve warm.

Makes 16 servings.

Eve and Gerry Searle, Grapevine Canyon Ranch
Pearce, Arizona

OLD-TIME BREAD PUDDING

For grown-up cowboys only!

4 slices buttered toast
¼ to ½ cup dried cherries
2 eggs, slightly beaten
¼ cup sugar
⅛ teaspoon salt
1 cup sweetened condensed milk
1 teaspoon vanilla extract
1 cup boiling water
2 tablespoons DeKuyper wilderberry schnapps liqueur
4 teaspoons cinnamon sugar
1 jar sour cherry compote

Preheat the oven to 350°. Cut buttered toast into quarters, and place in a greased 1½-quart baking dish. Sprinkle dried cherries over toast. Mix eggs with sugar, salt, condensed milk, vanilla, boiling water, and 2 tablespoons liqueur. Sprinkle mixture over toast, and let stand for 10 minutes. Sprinkle with cinnamon sugar. Bake for 30 minutes or until a knife inserted in the center comes out clean.

Take sour cherry compote out of jar, and fill jar with ¾ water and ¼ schnapps. Mix with sour cherry compote and pour over bread pudding immediately before serving.

Makes 4 servings.

Iris Behr, Hidden Creek Ranch
Harrison, Idaho

Wild Bill Hickok (Guy Madison, right) and his sidekick Jingles (Andy Devine) are tempted by Howdy Doody to try a "rip-snortin' treat" of Howdy Doody's Marshmallow Crispy Squares.

BULL'S-EYE CREAMY BANANA PUDDING

Right on the Mark.

- 1   14-ounce can Eagle Brand sweetened condensed milk
- 1½ cups cold water
- 1   3½ ounce-package instant vanilla pudding and pie filling mix
- 2   cups (1 pint) Borden or Meadow Gold whipping cream, whipped
- 36 vanilla wafers
- 3   medium bananas, sliced and dipped in lemon juice

In a large mixing bowl, combine sweetened condensed milk and water. Add pudding mix and blend well. Chill for 5 minutes. Fold in whipped cream. Spoon 1 cup pudding mixture into 2½-quart round, glass serving bowl. Top with ⅓ each of vanilla wafers, bananas, and pudding. Repeat layering twice, ending with pudding mixture. Chill thoroughly. Garnish as desired. Refrigerate leftovers.
    Makes 8 to 10 servings.

Mark Chesnutt, singer

SLOW POKE BLUEBERRY COBBLER

- ½ cup sugar or 6 packets artificial sweetener
- 1   tablespoon cornstarch
- 4   cups fresh or frozen (thawed) blueberries
- 2   tablespoons water
- 1   cup reduced-fat baking mix
- 1   tablespoon sugar or 1 packet artificial sweetener
- ¼ cup skim milk
- ¼ cup fat-free sour cream

Preheat the oven to 425°. Grease a 1½-quart casserole dish. Mix ½ cup sugar and cornstarch in a 2-quart pan and stir in blueberries and water. Heat to boiling, stirring constantly. Boil and stir for 1 minute. Pour into a casserole dish. Mix remaining ingredients until soft dough forms. Drop by the spoonful onto hot fruit mixture. Bake for about 25 minutes or until brown.

Pee Wee King, singer/songwriter

Clyde Frost qualified for the pro rodeo national finals in five out of the first six years they were held (1959–65). He is the father of Lane Frost.

FROST'S BEST HOMEMADE ICE CREAM

Frosty good!

    I got this recipe for raw ice cream from Edith Brown, wife of 1962 World Champion Bull Rider, Freckles Brown.

- 9   eggs, separated
- 2¾ cups sugar
- 2   teaspoons vanilla extract
- 2   cans Milnet or other canned milk or cow's cream
- 2   or 3 bananas, mashed
- 1   16-ounce can pineapple or other fruit

Separate the eggs and beat yolks until foamy. Add sugar and beat well. Add vanilla, milk, bananas, and pineapple. Beat egg whites until stiff. Fold into first mixture. Put into a 1-gallon ice cream freezer. Add milk to fill can. Freeze according to manufacturer's directions and eat immediately.
    Makes 1 gallon.

Elsie and Clyde Frost, rodeo cowboy

FORT COURAGE LEMON ICE CREAM

2⅔ cups half and half
1 cup sugar
⅓ cup lemon juice
⅓ cup chopped, toasted almonds
2 tablespoons lemon peel mix
1 teaspoon vanilla extract
1 teaspoon almond extract

Combine all ingredients well. Chill and put into an ice cream freezer. Freeze according to manufacturer's directions.

To make lemon peel mix, take 2 lemons, wash well, slice into thin slices, take out seeds, and put into a food processor. (Makes a wonderful mix to add to all baked goods when lemon peel is needed.)

Makes 1 quart.

Larry Storch, actor

Larry Storch was Corporal Randolph Agarn on *F Troop* from 1965 to 1967.

Cindy Walker reigns as the greatest female composer of country music, not to mention cowboy songs. Besides such classics as "You Don't Know Me," "Dream Baby," and "Distant Drums," thirty-seven of Cindy's songs were featured in Bob Wills and his Texas Playboys' films.

CHOCOLATE DELIGHT

We got this recipe from Carolyn Palmer, wife of V.A. Palmer, PRCA saddle bronc rider and bull rider. He qualified for the NFR in bronc riding in Los Angeles in 1962.

Crust:
1   stick butter or margarine, softened to room temperature
1   cup all-purpose flour
1   cup finely chopped nuts
½   cup sugar (optional)

First Layer:
1   8-ounce package cream cheese, softened to room temperature
1   cup Cool Whip
1   cup confectioners' sugar

Second Layer:
1   3-ounce package instant vanilla pudding
1   3-ounce package instant chocolate pudding
3   cups milk

Preheat the oven to 350°. Mix crust ingredients well and smooth over bottom of a cake pan. Bake for about 20 minutes. Mix cream cheese, Cool Whip, and sugar. Pour over mixture in the cake pan and chill. Mix instant puddings, chocolate, and milk. Pour over first mixture and chill. Top with additional Cool Whip.

Makes 8 to 10 servings.

Elsie and Clyde Frost, rodeo cowboy

CINDY'S SUNDOWN SUNDAE

3   large scoops vanilla ice cream
    Medium amount of chocolate syrup
    Big dollop of Cool Whip
    Stemmed maraschino cherry

Combine ice cream and syrup in a large iced tea glass or goblet. Top with Cool Whip and cherry.

Makes 1 serving.

Cindy Walker, songwriter

THE MAGNIFICENT SEVENTY-SEVEN WESTERNS THAT NO COWBOY FAN SHOULD MISS

(available on video)

The Alamo
Along Came Jones
Angel and the Bad Man
The Ballad of Cable Hogue
Bend of the River
The Big Country
Big Jake
Blazing Saddles
The Bravados
Broken Arrow
Butch Cassidy and the Sundance Kid
Cheyenne Autumn
The Cowboys
Dances with Wolves
Destry Rides Again
Dodge City
Duel at Diablo
Duel in the Sun
El Dorado
Fort Apache
The Good, the Bad, and the Ugly
The Great Train Robbery
The Grey Fox
Gunfight at the O.K. Corral
The Gunfighter
Hang 'Em High
The Hanging Tree
High Noon
Hombre
How the West Was Won
Jeremiah Johnson
Johnny Guitar
Little Big Man
Lonely Are the Brave
Lonesome Dove
The Magnificent Seven
A Man Called Horse
The Man from Laramie
The Man Who Shot Liberty Valance

Maverick
Monte Walsh
My Darling Clementine
The Naked Spur
Nevada Smith
Once Upon a Time in the West
One-Eyed Jacks
The Outlaw Josey Wales
The Ox-Bow Incident
Pat Garrett and Billy the Kid
Quigley Down Under
Red River
Ride the High Country
Ride Lonesome
Rio Bravo
Rio Grande
River of No Return
The Searchers
Shane
She Wore a Yellow Ribbon
The Shootist
Silverado
The Sons of Katie Elder
Stagecoach
Support Your Local Sheriff
There Was a Crooked Man
3:10 to Yuma
Three Godfathers
The Treasure of Sierra Madre
True Grit
Ulzana's Raid
The Unforgiven
Unforgiven
The Virginian
The Westerner
The Wild Bunch
Will Penny
Winchester '73

HOSS CARTWRIGHT'S STRAWBERRY GLAZED CREAM CHEESECAKE

A true Bonanza for your taste buds!

Crust:
- ¾ cup coarsely ground walnuts
- ¾ cup finely crushed graham crackers
- 3 tablespoons melted, unsalted butter

Filling:
- 4 8-ounce packages cream cheese, softened to room temperature
- 4 eggs
- 1¼ cups sugar
- 1 tablespoon fresh lemon juice
- 2 teaspoons vanilla extract

Topping:
- 2 cups sour cream
- ¼ cup sugar
- 1 teaspoon vanilla extract

Strawberry Glaze:
- 1 quart medium strawberries
- 1 12-ounce jar red raspberry jelly
- 1 tablespoon cornstarch
- ¼ cup Cointreau liqueur
- ¼ cup water

Position rack in center of the oven. Preheat the oven to 350°. Lightly butter a 9- or 10-inch springform pan. For crust, combine walnuts, graham crackers, and butter. Press into bottom of pan. Beat cream cheese in a large bowl with electric mixer until smooth. Add eggs, sugar, lemon juice, and vanilla and beat thoroughly. Spoon over crust. Set the pan on a baking sheet. Bake for 40 to 45 minutes for a 10-inch pan, or 50 to 55 minutes for a 9-inch pan. Cake may rise and crack. It will settle and topping will cover cracks. Let stand at room temperature for 15 minutes. Retain 350° oven temperature.

While cake is baking, combine sour cream, sugar, and vanilla and blend well. Cover and refrigerate. When cake finishes baking and stands for 15 minutes, spoon topping from center to within ½ inch of edge. Return to oven and bake for 5 minutes. Allow to cool, then chill for at least 24 hours (even better, chill for 2 to 3 days).

Several hours before serving, wash and hull berries and dry on paper towels. Combine a small amount of jelly with cornstarch in a saucepan and mix well. Add rest of jelly, Cointreau, and water. Cook over medium heat, stirring frequently until thick and clear, for about 5 minutes. Cool to lukewarm, stirring occasionally.

Use a knife to loosen cake from pan. Remove springform. Arrange berries (pointed end up) over top of cake. Spoon glaze over berries, allowing some to drip down sides of cake. Chill until glaze sets.

Makes 8 to 10 servings.

Dan Blocker, actor

PLAINS AND SIMPLE CHERRY CHEESECAKE

- ½ pound graham crackers, crushed
- 2 tablespoons sugar
- 1 stick margarine
- 2 8-ounce packages cream cheese, softened to room temperature
- 1 14-ounce can Eagle Brand condensed milk
- 4 tablespoons lemon juice
- 2 1-pound cans cherry pie filling

Preheat the oven to 350°. Mix graham crackers, sugar, and margarine in a 10x13-inch pan. Pat into place. Bake for 10 to 15 minutes. Use a blender to combine cream cheese, milk, and lemon juice. Pour over crust. Top with cherry pie filling and chill.

Makes 10 to 12 servings.

Dorothy and Lavon Shearer, Western Dakota Ranch Vacations Wall, South Dakota

MISS RODEO USA'S CHOCOLATE AMARETTO CHEESECAKE

A real winner!

Crust:
- ½   stick butter, melted
- 1¼   cups vanilla wafer crumbs

Filling:
- 3   ounces semi-sweet chocolate
- 2   8-ounce packages cream cheese, softened to room temperature
- 3   large eggs
- 1⅓   cups sugar
- 1   cup sour cream
- ½   teaspoon cinnamon
- ½   teaspoon almond extract
- 2   teaspoons Amaretto liqueur
    Whipped cream
    Toasted, sliced almonds

Preheat the oven to 350°. To make crust, mix melted butter with crumbs. Press into the bottom of a 8- or 9-inch springform pan. Bake for 8 minutes. Let cool.

For filling, melt chocolate over hot water in a double boiler or melt in the microwave. Add softened cream cheese and heat until soft. Process mixture in a food processor until smooth, adding eggs and sugar while motor is running. Add sour cream, cinnamon, almond extract, and amaretto; process until smooth. Preheat oven to 350°. Pour into crust and bake for 50 to 60 minutes. Center should jiggle slightly. Remove from the oven. Run a knife around edge to release cake from sides. Chill for 2 hours.

Makes 8 to 10 servings.

Lucynda Hendricks, Miss Rodeo USA, 1994

Lucynda Hendricks—Miss Rodeo USA, 1994

Bandy Around—Besides having more than thirty top-ten singles, including hits like "It's a Cheatin' Situation," "Barstool Mountain," and "Bandy the Rodeo Clown," singer Moe Bandy also has been a real working cowboy on a ranch and has competed in bull riding and bareback bronc riding in rodeos. His brother Mike has competed in the PRCA National Finals Rodeo more than half a dozen times in bull riding.

BANDY THE RODEO CLOWN'S WONDERFUL CHOCOLATE CAKE

Just good ole cake.

- 2 cups flour
- 2 cups sugar
- 1 teaspoon baking soda
- 2 sticks butter
- 4 tablespoons cocoa
- 1 cup water
- 2 eggs
- ½ cup buttermilk
- 1 teaspoon vanilla

Icing:
- 1 stick butter
- 6 tablespoons buttermilk
- 4 tablespoons cocoa
- 1 box confectioners' sugar

- 1 cup chopped nuts
- 1 teaspoon vanilla

Preheat the oven to 350°. Sift together flour, sugar, and baking soda. Set aside. In a medium saucepan over medium heat, combine butter, cocoa, and water. Bring to a boil, stirring constantly. Pour liquid ingredients over dry ingredients. Add eggs, buttermilk, and vanilla. Mix well. Pour into a jelly-roll pan and bake for 15 to 20 minutes.

To make the icing, combine butter, buttermilk, and cocoa in a saucepan. Bring to a boil, stirring constantly. Remove from heat and add confectioners' sugar, chopped nuts, and vanilla. Mix well and pour over hot cake. Cool before serving.

Makes 8 to 10 servings.

Moe Bandy, singer

CORRAL CARAMEL DUMPLINGS

1   lump of butter
2   tablespoons butter
½   cup milk
2   cups packed brown sugar
2   cups water
1   cup sugar
2   teaspoons vanilla extract
2   cups all-purpose flour
4   teaspoons baking powder

Preheat the oven to 350°. Boil butter, brown sugar, and water together. Combine remaining ingredients and drop by spoonsful into boiling syrup. Place on baking sheet. Bake until brown.
    Makes 8 to 10 servings.

Bar H Bar Ranch
Soda Springs, Idaho

DOBE'S CHOCOLATE MOUSSE

A godfather's favorite.

1   12-ounce package chocolate bits
1½ cups milk, heated
2   eggs, beaten

Put the chocolate bits in a blender. Heat milk until hot but not boiling. Pour hot milk over whirring bits, and blend in eggs. Pour into small custard cups.
    Note: Add some instant coffee and a small amount of sugar for a mocha flavor.
    Makes 6 servings.

Marilyn and Harry Carey Jr., actor

F Troop's Ken Berry helps Wrangler Jane (Melody Patterson) celebrate her eighteenth birthday.

Ranch Round-Up

If you enjoy cooking and eating the recipes contributed from some of the West's top ranches, then you'll likely enjoy visiting the ranches in person and sampling more of their favorite dishes, plus their other offerings and genuine cowboy hospitality. Here's how you can contact each of the participating ranches, most of which welcome overnight guests.

Allen Ranch
19600 South Memorial
Bixby, OK 74008
918-366-3010

Allen's Diamond Four Ranch
P.O. Box 243
Lander, WY 82520
307-332-2995

Bar H Bar Ranch
1501 Eight Mile Creek Road
Soda Springs, ID 83276
208-547-3082

Breteche Creek Ranch
P.O. Box 596
Cody, WY 82414
307-587-3844

Cherokee Park Ranch
P.O. Box 97
Livermore, CO 80536
303-493-6522

Cibolo Creek Ranch
P.O. Box 44
Shafter, TX 79850
915-229-3507

Circle Bar Guest Ranch
Utica, MT 59452
406-423-5454

Don K Ranch
2677 South Siloam Road
Pueblo, CO 81005
719-784-6600

Elk Mountain Ranch
P.O. Box 910
Buena Vista, CO 81211
719-395-6313

Grapevine Canyon Ranch
P.O. Box 302
Pearce, AZ 85625
602-826-3185

Hargrave Cattle & Guest Ranch
300 Thompson River
Marion, MT 59925
406-858-2284

Hidden Creek Ranch
7600 East Blue Lake Road
Harrison, ID 83833
208-689-3209

Hidden Valley Guest Ranch
3942 Hidden Valley Road
Cle Elum, WA 98922
509-857-2322

The Home Ranch
Box 822
Clark, CO 80428
303-879-1780

Idaho Rocky Mountain Ranch
HC 64, Box 9934
Stanley, ID 83278
208-774-3544

Kedesh Guest Ranch
1940 Highway 14
Shell, WY 82441
307-765-2791

Laughing Water Ranch
P.O. Box 157
Deep Creek Road
Fortine, MT 59918
406-882-4680

Lazy Hills Guest Ranch
P.O. Box G
Henderson Branch Road
Ingram, TX 78025
210-367-5600

Los Pinos Ranch
Box 8, Route 3
Tererro, NM 87573
505-757-6213

North Fork Guest Ranch
P.O. Box B
Shawnee, CO 80475
303-838-9873

Peaceful Valley Lodge and Ranch Resort
Star Route
Lyons, CO 80540
303-747-2881

7 D Ranch
Sunlight Basin
P.O. Box 100
Cody, WY 82414
307-587-9885

Shepp Ranch
P.O. Box 5446
Boise, ID 83705
208-343-7729

Sky Corral Ranch
8233 Old Flowers Road
Bellvue, CO 80512
303-484-1362

Skyline Guest Ranch
Box 67
Telluride, CO 81435
303-728-3757

Sweet Grass Ranch
Melville Route, Box 161
Big Timber, MT 59011
406-537-4477

T Cross Ranch
Box 638
Dubois, WY 82513
307-455-2206

Triple R Ranch
Box 124
Keystone, SD 57751
605-666-4605

Wapiti Meadow Ranch
HC 72
Cascade, ID 83611
208-382-4336

Western Dakota Ranch Vacations
HCR 1
Wall, SD 57790
605-279 2198

White Tail Ranch
82 White Tail Ranch Road
Ovando, MT 59854
406-793-5666

Additional information about dude and guest ranches is also available through

The Dude Ranchers' Association
P.O. Box 471
LaPorte, CO 80535
303-223-8440

(Ask about the *Dude Ranch Cookbook,* compiled by Wapiti Meadow Ranch owner Diana Haynes.)

And probably the definitive printed guide to guest and resort ranches is *Ranch Vacations* by Gene Kilgore (John Muir Publications, Santa Fe), which is available for around $20 in the travel section of most bookstores.

Dallas Cowboys recipes used in this cookbook are courtesy of *The Dallas Cowboys Wives' Family Cookbook and Photo Album,* published by Happy Hill Farm Academy/Home, Star Route, Box 56, Granbury, TX 76048.

Recipes from John Wayne are courtesy of *Pilar Wayne's Favorite and Fabulous Recipes.* For more information, send a self-addressed stamped envelope to "Pilar Wayne Cookbook," 30801 South Coast Highway #9, Laguna Beach, CA 92651.

Ernest Tubb and His Texas Troubadours in 1960

The Cartwrights of the Ponderosa—(clockwise from top right) Lorne Greene as Ben, Dan Blocker as Hoss, Pernell Roberts as Adam, and Michael Landon as Little Joe

WESTERN MUSEUM CORRAL

WESTERN MUSEUM CORRAL

Some of the best places to learn about cowboy history and culture and the American West are the nation's historical and art museums. Among the museums with an emphasis on western exhibits are:

National Cowboy Hall of Fame
1700 Northeast 63rd St.
Oklahoma City, OK 73111
405-478-2250

Buffalo Bill Historical Center
P.O. Box 1000
Cody, WY 82414
307-587-4771

    Includes:
        Buffalo Bill Museum
        Cody Firearms Museum
        Plains Indian Museum
        Whitney Gallery of Western Art

Gene Autry Western Heritage Museum
Griffith Park
4700 Western Heritage Way
Los Angeles, CA 90027
213-667-2000

Amon Carter Museum
3501 Camp Bowie Blvd.
Fort Worth, TX 76107
817-738-1933

Cowboy Artists of America Museum Foundation
1550 Bandera Highway
Box 1716
Kerrville, TX 78028
210-896-2553

Cowboy Hall of Fame and Western Heritage Center
Campus of New Mexico Junior College
5317 Lovington Highway
Hobbs, NM 88240
505-392-4510, ext. 371

Eiteljorg Museum
500 West Washington St.
White River State Park
Indianapolis, IN 46204
317-636-9378

Gilcrease Museum
1400 Gilcrease Museum Rd.
Tulsa, OK 74127
918-596-2700

Heard Museum
22 East Monte Vista Rd.
Phoenix, AZ 85004
602-252-8840

Joslyn Art Museum
2200 Dodge St.
Omaha, NE 68102
402-342-3300

Montana Historical Society
225 North Roberts
Box 201
Helena, MT 59620
406-444-2694

Museum of Fine Arts
107 West Palace
Santa Fe, NM 87503
505-827-4455

Museum of Indian Arts and Culture
710 Camino Lejo
Santa Fe, NM 87503
505-827-8320

Museum of International Folk Art
706 Camino Lejo
Santa Fe, NM 87503
505-827-8350

Museum of Western Art
1727 Tremont Place
Denver, CO 80202
303-296-1880

National Cowgirl Hall of Fame
515 Ave. B
P.O. Box 1742
Hereford, TX 79045
806-364-5252

The R.W. Norton Art Gallery
4747 Creswell Ave.
Shreveport, LA 71106
318-865-4201

Palace of the Governors
On the Plaza, West Place
P.O. Box 2087
Santa Fe, NM 87504
505-827-6483

Phoenix Art Museum
1625 North Central Ave.
Phoenix, AZ 85004
602-257-1222

Pro Rodeo Hall of Fame and Museum of the American Cowboy
101 Pro Rodeo Dr.
Colorado Springs, CO 80919
719-593-8840

Frederic Remington Art Museum
303 Washington St.
Ogdensburg, NY 13669
315-393-2425

Sid Richardson Collection of Western Art
309 Main St.
Fort Worth, TX 76102
817-332-6554

The Rockwell Museum
111 Cedar St.
Corning, NY 14830
607-937-5386

The Roy Rogers-Dale Evans Museum
15650 Seneca Rd.
Victorville, CA 92392
619-243-4547

C.M. Russell Museum
400 13th St. North
Great Falls, MT 59401
406-727-8787

Stark Museum
P.O. Box 1897
Orange, TX 77630
409-883-6661

Tex Ritter Museum
300 West Panola
Carthage, TX 75633
903-693-6634

Wildlife of Western American Art
110 N. Center St.
P.O. Box 6825
Jackson, WY 83001
307-733-5771

Will Rogers Memorial
P.O. Box 151
Claremore, OK 74018
918-341-0719

Woolaroc Museum
Route 3, Box 2100
Bartlesville, OK 74003
918-336-0307

INDEX

Cowboy Corral—Nearly fifty famous TV and film cowboy actors got together for the TV special *How the West Was Fun* in 1979. The group included (1) Dewey Martin, (2) Johnny Crawford, (3) Chuck Connors, (4) Glenn Ford, (5) Alan Hale Jr., (6) Henry Darrow, (7) Larry Storch, (8) Neville Brand, (9) Denver Pyle, (10) Iron Eyes Cody, (11) Harry Lauter, (12) Jeanette Nolan, (13) John Ireland, (14) Darby Hinton, (15) Joe Bowman, (16) Fred Putnam, (17) Pat Buttram, (18) Milburn Stone, (19) Dan Haggerty, (20) Guy Madison, (21) Rex Allen, (22) John Bromfield, (23) Keenan Wynn, (24) Jackie Coogan, (25) George Montgomery, (26) X Brands, (27) Bill Williams, (28) Michael Ansara, (29) Slim Pickins, (30) Dick Young, (31) Don Diamond, (32) Ken Curtis, (33) John Russell, (34) Peter Brown, (35) James Drury, (36) Rod Cameron, (37) Jock Mahoney, (38) Jack Kelly, (39) Tony Young, (40) John McIntire, (41) Ty Hardin, (42) Mark Slade, (43) Lee Van Cleef, (44) Will Hutchins, (45) Terry Wilson, (46) Clayton Moore, (47) Doug McClure, and (48) Linda Cristal.

BROCK TRUCKING
Rt. 1 Box 35
Littlefield, TX 79339

BROCK TRUCKING
Rt. 1 Box 35
Littlefield, TX 79339